PHENOMENOLOGY AND
DECONSTRUCTION

Phenomenology and Deconstruction

VOLUME ONE · *The Dream is Over*

Robert Denoon Cumming

CHICAGO & LONDON · *The University of Chicago Press*

Robert Denoon Cumming is professor emeritus
of philosophy at Columbia University. He is the
author of numerous books including *Starting-
Point* and the two-volume *Human Nature and
History,* both published by the University of Chicago Press.

The University of Chicago Press, Chicago 60637
The University of Chicago Press, Ltd., London

© 1991 by The University of Chicago
All rights reserved. Published 1991
Printed in the United States of America
00 99 98 97 96 95 94 93 92 91   5 4 3 2 1

Library of Congress Cataloging-in-Publication
Data

Cumming, Robert Denoon, 1916–
    Phenomenology and deconstruction / Robert
Denoon Cumming.
        p.   cm.
    Includes bibliographical references and in-
dex.
        Contents: v., 1. The dream is over.
        ISBN 0–226–12366–9 (v. 1). —
ISBN 0–226–12367–7 (pbk. : v. 1)
        1. Phenomenology—History. I. Title.
    B829.2.C85   1991
    142′.7′09—dc20   91–12696
                                                  CIP

⊗ The paper used in this publication meets the
minimum requirements of the American National Standard for Information Sciences—Per-
manence of Paper for Printed Library Materials,
ANSI Z39.48–1984.

In Memory of
C H A R L I E
1951–1982

CONTENTS

*We must immerse ourselves in historical
considerations, if we are to be able to understand
ourselves as philosophers, and understand what
philosophy is to become through us.*
—*Edmund Husserl*

NOTE ON TRANSLATIONS AND CITATIONS

Works are cited in English translation, except when no translation, or no reliable or easily obtainable translation, is available. The translations themselves, however, are usually my own. Citations from Heidegger's *Being and Time* are to the German pagination, which is found in the margin of the English translations.

The End of Philosophy

*What does it mean that philosophy at the
present time has entered into its end?*
—Heidegger

Perspectives

Once upon a time the owl of Minerva took
flight in the dusk. It was a leisurely flight,
with no attempt to make up for the late de-
parture. Nowadays most philosophy has
been rescheduled. While fairly steady work
continues in certain specialized areas such as
logic, much of the excitement occurs where
there is temporary congregating around
some formulation, line of argument, article,
or book—until the party breaks up. The
morning after, one may not quite remember
what was at stake. The issues may not have
quite shaped up as a decisive triumph or
defeat. The retrospect is as uncertain as
Fabrice's "Have I really been present at a
battle?" Even though one had tried to partic-
ipate by eagerly heading toward some "puff
of smoke" or (as he did) cherished the fan-
tasy of having been "some sort of ambassador to Napoleon."

I could pile up further analogies in order
to suggest the variety of perspectives that we
can be aware of, when we find it worthwhile
to pause and reflect on what has been going
on in philosophy, before going on ourselves.
But let the analogies so far suffice: more or
less congenial partying, the hazy sobriety of
the morning after, hectic engagement in some
skirmish, some sense of mission in relation to
a commanding authority. All these analogies
remain too episodic to yield a sense of having
really been present at a decisive triumph or
defeat.

Today, however, there is a certain impulse in some philosophical circles to push beyond the episodic and to try to tell an all-embracing story—or at least to adopt a perspective that implies that such a story can be told. From the vantage point of this perspective, what is going on in philosophy is that it is coming to an end. If so large-scale and final a change is taking place in our thinking, in our culture, it would seem to deserve the attention it has been receiving.

In my assessment I do not intend to head toward every puff of smoke that might be construed as philosophy's Waterloo. Admittedly, much end-of-philosophy talk is merely fireworks. Some of it belongs with other self-images of our time—"postmodernism," "poststructualism," "after virtue"—which suggest our future shock is such that we haven't been able to figure out where we are at except by reference to what we seem to be leaving behind.

In one respect the problem is comparable to Fabrice's as he rushed around—to locate the battle. But he at least had *terra firma* under his feet. It is difficult for us to determine what is to count as the end of philosophy. Even if something final is transpiring, there are so many competing versions as to what it is that, if the protagonists—Marxist, positivist, Wittgensteinian, Heideggerian, Derridian, Rortyan, and so on—were to try to clarify their differences, they might be saddled with a revival of philosophy.

I shall not pursue so reactionary an argument. Anyway, there seems little risk of a revival taking this guise. Many who are most entranced by the end-of-philosophy perspective are less enticed by the revelation that philosophy has been an instrument of the class struggle, or of obscurantist resistance to scientific enlightenment, or bewitchment by language, or that it has been onto-theological, or phallocentric. Rather, they get their apocalypse out of the blurring together of some assortment of these revelations. They would no longer feel so illuminated if they were deprived of the medley by having the differences pinned down.

The History of Philosophy

There is another difficulty. The end-of-philosophy perspective is often adopted mainly in the course of justifying going on to other subjects besides philosophy. Take the famous Marxist brushing of philosophy to one side: "Philosophers have only interpreted the world in various fashions; the point, however, is to change it." [1] If so, there is relatively little point in examining the various philosophical interpretations themselves. The discovery that the point is to change the world is of course not limited to some Marxists, but it can be overwhelming to many whose orientation is generally practical. There is also the discovery—usually positivist, sometimes Wittgensteinian—that the emperor has no clothes. This conviction about philosophy is pretty well established at the back of the minds of some scientists.

To the extent that these proponents of an end-of-philosophy perspective still provide some account of how philosophy has come, or is coming, to an end, this end becomes largely a *fait accompli*. For they employ a largely nonphilosophical terminology drawn from the successor subject they favor—from the history of class warfare, or of technology, or from a science, say, linguistics or cognitive science. To this extent, their conceptions of the end of philosophy depend on what is to come after philosophy. The merits of such accounts do not concern me here. I am claiming only that if it is in fact philosophy which has come or is coming to an end, it should be feasible to trace the history by which the end is reached, up until the end (or almost), as something happening to philosophy itself.

However, even if we sift the history of philosophy for evidence as to whether or not it is coming to an end, we still come up against a difficulty: how we conceive the end of philosophy depends on how we conceive philosophy—and on the account, in justifying this conception, we give of its history. There is no simple elucidation of the end of philosophy, since there is no simple elucidation of the multifarious evidence of what has gone on during the history of philosophy. There are different conceptions of the end, as there are different histories.

So cowardly a conclusion may condemn philosophy to a thousand deaths. But so far I have been beating around the bush. Some sweeping gestures seemed initially appropriate to the stupendousness of the perspective. At last I am zeroing in on a bush—that is, the cluster of more manageable questions which yet bear on the virtually unmanagable question of the end of philosophy.

There are three thinkers who are prominently committed both to an end-of-philosophy perspective and to reliance on the evidence of the history of philosophy in upholding this perspective: Martin Heidegger, Jacques Derrida, and Richard Rorty. Heidegger was originally the most influential proponent of this perspective. Derrida acknowledges debts to Heidegger; and Rorty, to Heidegger and Derrida. I shall defer examining Heidegger's perspective on the history of philosophy until the third volume of the present work. My canvassing of both Heidegger and Derrida in this first volume is merely preliminary. Unlike Heidegger and Derrida, Rorty is a native speaker, and I shall use (and abuse) him as my foil in this Introduction.[2]

The History of Phenomenology

In one obvious respect I shall marshal historical evidence differently than these three thinkers do. They determine what philosophy has been by reference to the history of philosophy as a whole, even though they usually take individual philosophies as illustrations. The history of philosophy as a whole is more than I care to embrace. Instead, I focus on episodes during a specific stretch of this history—the history of phenomenology and of its aftermath, deconstruction.

I am focusing on episodes, rather than sweeping along through the entire history of phenomenology, because I would single out certain issues that have emerged during the course of this history. My selection of this history itself is in a considerable measure dictated by Heidegger, Derrida, and Rorty. Heidegger identifies his mentor and predecessor, Edmund Husserl, whom he credits with being the founder of phenomenology, as a representative of philosophy as a tradition going back in the first instance to Descartes but ultimately to Plato. Heidegger's break with Husserl and phenomenology is a considerable step toward the emergence of his end-of-philosophy perspective. One route Derrida takes in arriving at his own end-of-philosophy perspective is by a deconstruction of Husserl, in which he admits he obtains "support at decisive junctures from themes of Heidegger's,"[3] though he has gone on to the deconstruction of Heidegger as well. Rorty finds a significant illustration of arrival at the end-of-philosophy perspective in Heidegger's break with Husserl.

Of course the history of philosophy is the history of differences at issue between philosophers, and frequently the differences have eventuated in a successor's breaking away from a previous philosophy (or philosophies) and arriving at his own. Thus one question I face, in deciding what is to count as the end of philosophy, is to determine if Heidegger's break with Husserl and phenomenology differs from the breaks which have taken place traditionally between philosophies.

A similar question will come up with Derrida's deconstruction of Husserl and phenomenology. It was once feasible for Emmanuel Levinas to begin his appraisal of Derrida with the question, "Does Derrida's work cut across the development of western thought with a line of demarcation, similar to Kantianism, which separated criticism from dogmatic philosophy? Are we again at the end . . . of an unsuspected dogmatism which slumbered underneath what we took for the critical spirit?"[4] Here Levinas regards Derrida's break with traditional philosophy as "similar to" Kant's, not as a final break that brings the history of philosophy to an end.

Philosophers have frequently been convinced (in William James's phrase) that philosophy is "on the eve of a considerable rearrangement."[5] I would go further: notable philosophy is usually commitment to the considerable rearrangement of philosophy. The only trouble is that the philosopher (or philosophers) involved often overestimates its finality.

Hence, my question—What distinguishes from past rearrangements the drastic disruption with which philosophy is supposed now to be coming to its end?

Deconstruction

There is an inadequate one word answer to this question: what Heidegger is undertaking vis-à-vis the history of philosophy is its *Destruktion*. Derrida has allowed his undertaking to be characterized in a similar fashion as "deconstruction." This has become the better-known term. In both the cases of Heidegger and of Derrida the procedure has emerged as the history of philosophy reaches its end, though it is also in some sense the procedure by which this history is being brought to its end.[6]

The procedure itself will eventually require detailed elucidation. In the first place, Derrida denies that deconstruction is a "procedure."[7] Though the *Destruktion* may seem to be a distinct procedure in Heidegger's earlier accounts of it, we are warned by Thomas Buchheim that it cannot be readily isolated, for "Heidegger has applied the *Destruktion* throughout his thinking in all its guises."[8] If so, the relation between these different applications will have to be examined. But the particular guise that concerns me is the application of the *Destruktion* to the history of philosophy. And since it is the entire history that is in question, this application cannot be assessed without determining how the history of philosophy is envisaged as a whole—that is, as a homogeneous tradition—from the vantage point of its end. As I have already indicated, I am for the present shrinking from such scope; Heidegger's concept of "tradition" I am deferring until Volume 3.

A difficulty with Derrida's deconstruction is that he is convinced it has been misconceived and misapplied, particularly in the United States.[9] Heidegger had comparable misgivings over misinterpretations of the *Destruktion*, but it did not become in his time as fashionable as Derrida's deconstruction has since. Indeed, if I referred to the "one word" as a way of characterizing Heidegger's or Derrida's undertaking, a reason was that "deconstruction" has become a buzzword, as "alienation" and "authenticity" did earlier in our century. If Heidegger were around it would become an illustration of how language "has become worn out"—a "means of *Verständigung* ["understanding" or "communication"], which may be employed as anyone pleases, as indifferent [*gleichgültig*] as a means of public transportation as a streetcar which everyone climbs on and climbs off."[10] The term has even lost the intimate association it has for both of them with the history of philosophy coming to an end. Its most omnivorous application is perhaps by those feminists who would "deconstruct" the cultural tradition as phallocratic. The evidence they would display of its sway is much more often taken from the history of literature or art than that of philosophy.

Again, as I did with the many versions of the end of philosophy, I am encountering broader considerations than I am able to encompass and, consequently, face the problem of extricating myself and delimiting my own undertaking. At least many feminists are ready to acknowledge their indebtedness to Derrida, not merely for the term "deconstruction" but also for some of its implications. At the same time, Derrida himself acknowledges the relation between his deconstruction and Heidegger's *Destruktion*. In fact, Heidegger himself characterizes the *Destruktion* as a "deconstruction" (*Abbau*), and sometimes I shall use this term to cover both their undertakings.[11] But there are differences which pose problems, and I am postponing any detailed consideration of Derrida's deconstruction until I have expounded Heidegger's *Destruktion*. If I retain the German, it is as a warning that the implications of the term have not yet been tracked down.

The Change in Subject

With this postponement I return to the original formulation of my question: What distinguishes the change with which the end of philosophy is reached from the way in which philosophers have traditionally proceeded from previous philosophies? I begin with the distinction which is probably the most familiar. The last of the essays which Heidegger published (and which he himself singled out as the final, climactic essay for an anthology of English translations of his works) is "The End of Philosophy and the Task of Thinking." Here he indicates that a task at the end of philosophy is asking, "What does it mean that philosophy at the present time has entered into its end [*ist . . . in Ende eingegangen*]?"[12] One thing it means to Heidegger is the "development [*Ausfaltung*] of philosophy into the sciences," which have in some fashion displaced it. This development is probably the least controversial sense in which the end of philosophy can be said to have been reached, and I shall not be concerned with it except indirectly.

What will concern me is Rorty's designation of the displacement of philosophy by the sciences as "a changing of the subject" of philosophy. According to Rorty, philosophy, which traditionally has been "philosophy-as-science," should be replaced (and, indeed, is to an extent being replaced) by "philosophy-as-literature."

Heidegger's break with Husserl will provide a preliminary, more definite illustration of this sort of replacement. In a fragment (summer 1935) associated with Husserl's last work, *The Crisis of the European Sciences,* Husserl made a famous announcement, which has sometimes been construed as his contemplating the end of philosophy: "Philosophy as rigorous science, . . . the dream is over." In English this may come through as a pale romantic sigh. Husserl's bitterness is more effectively conveyed by the German: "Der Traum ist . . . ausgeträumt," [13] and I hope my readers from now on will hear the German resonate behind my English title. It may help remind them that many of the misunderstandings with which a history of phenomenology has to cope are due to misleading English or French translations from the German. Thus I could already be faulted for having translated *Wissenschaft* as "science."

At least there is no dearth of historical evidence as to what Husserl meant by "philosophy as rigorous science." This phrase had been the title of a programmatic work he had published a quarter of a century before, and it had been followed up by other works. But he was less specific as to what exactly was taking place in philosophy that prompted his announcement, "the dream is over." He merely alludes to "a powerful and constantly increasing torrent of philosophy which renounces its scientific character." The metaphor of an innundating torrent implies that what is taking place in philosophy is not discriminating and itself deserves no discrimination.

Can we be more discriminating? In Volume 3 I shall consider one matter Husserl obviously seems to have been bitter about when he made his announcement—the increasing vogue enjoyed by Heidegger. Husserl regarded Heidegger as a defector from phenomenology. He had counted on Heidegger's collaboration. Indeed, Heidegger had presented his *Being and Time* (1927) as phenomenology and had dedicated it to Husserl. In turn, Heidegger had been sponsored by Husserl as the successor to his chair at Freiburg in 1928. But the leisure of retirement enabled Husserl to reread Heidegger with more care, and he was dismayed. By 1931 their relation was broken off.

All this may sound as if what soured was to a considerable extent their personal relationship. But I shall later argue that how the distinction is to be drawn between the personal and the philosophical can itself become a philosophical issue.

In any case, I believe we can be more discriminating than Husserl was when he denounced the innundating torrent. On the one hand, almost any philosopher who is committed to "philosophy-as-science," including Husserl, patiently discriminates the sense in which he takes philosophy to be scientific and makes some attempt to determine its relation to other sciences. Thus the issues covered by Rorty's broad umbrella term "philosophy-as-science" have been formulated and reformulated with some scrupulousness over the centuries. On the other hand, almost any philosopher who is committed to "philosophy-as-science" is, like Husserl, too impatient to discriminate alternative conceptions of philosophy. All that matters to him is that the conception of a philosophy as a scientific subject is being swept aside.

The Shift in Affiliation

My first effort to be more discriminating is to single out the change in subject, and other comparable changes I shall acknowledge later, and dignify them as "shifts," in order to distinguish them from the multifarious changes (but, for my philosophical purposes, less drastic changes) that have shaped the history of philosophy. My next effort is to distinguish another shift from the shift in *subject*. I don't know if word reached Husserl in the 1930s that Heidegger was refusing in his lectures to regard philosophy any longer as a science. It was only after Husserl's death that Heidegger explicitly criticized in a published work phenomenology's "inappropriate aspiration to science." [14]

During the summer of 1935, when Husserl wrote in the privacy of his study that the dream of philosophy as rigorous science was over, Heidegger declared in his lectures that philosophy and science were incommensurable:

> Philosophy never emerges [*entsteht*] from science or through science, and it can never be coordinated [*gleichordnet*] with the sciences. . . . It belongs [*steht*] to an entirely different realm. . . . Only poetry belongs with it in the same order [*Ordnung*] as philosophy and its *thinking*.[15]

What I mean by a shift in *affiliation* is illustrated by Heidegger's declaration that philosophy is no longer "coordinated" with the sciences but "belongs . . . in the same order" with poetry. This shift in *affiliation* brings us up against a certain incommensurability. Heidegger has spoken of phenomenology's "inappropriate [*ungemäss*] aspiration to science." The root of *ungemäss* is *Mass* ("measure"). Heidegger is allowing for the incommensurability when he admits we are *befremdt* ("put off" or—to be more formidable—"alienated") by Hölderlin's thinking of poetry as a "measuring": we think of measurement as a quantitative, scientific procedure, whereas Hölderlin is transferring it (at least in Heidegger's interpretation of such lines as "Is there a measure on earth?") from the realm of science to that of poetry. And, presumably, transferred along with it is the concept of "order" which is implicit in "measuring." [16] In the setting of this "dialogue between poet and thinker," the concepts transferred undergo transformation, so that they are no longer concepts in the strict "philosophy-as-science" sense.[17]

Translation

Even a concept so standard, so indispensable to the historian as "transformation," on which I have just relied, would be suspect to Heidegger as a translation for his *Wandlung*. I bring up this problem of reliability to indicate how difficult it is to do justice to the shift in philosophy from a scientific subject without succumbing to an inherited terminology that is itself more or less scientific. To us the term "transformation" may seem philosophically neutral. If pressed, we might consider it vaguely Darwinian. But to Heidegger it would still bear the imprint of Aristotelian science, with its distinction between form and matter, and this distinction itself has to undergo "transformation" in Heidegger by his consulting a painting.[18]

Another illustration of the problem the historian encounters here is "translation" itself, which is no more a philosophically neutral procedure than measurement. In my third volume, I shall point out how "translation" (in its ordinary, so-called literal sense of translating something from one language to another) is envisaged very differently in Husserl's philosophy-as-rigorous-science from the fashion in which it is envisaged in Heidegger's thinking, affiliated as it is with poetry. If I anticipate this issue now, it is because "translation" is often used in an extended "metaphorical" sense (that is, etymologically speaking, "trans-lated" sense), according to which the problems of one philosopher are translated by another philosopher from that philosophy into the language of his own philosophy. And in fact Husserl did use this idiom of the relation between his philosophy and Heidegger's. In a marginal entry on his copy of *Being and Time*, Husserl dismisses Heidegger's "entire problematic" as a "translation" (*Übertragung*) of his own. It is, he insists to himself, "my own theory." But he is not simply accusing Heidegger of plagiarism. With Heidegger's "translation," Husserl warns, his phenomenology also loses "its entire meaning." This loss is dramatized by Husserl's exploiting the etymology of *Über-tragung* as "trans-lation": "H[eidegger] *transponiert oder transversiert* . . . the phenomenological into the anthropological." [19] This transposition or transference, we shall later see, Husserl considers perverse because it involves a shift in *level*, which entails a shift in *subject*. These shifts deprive phenomenology of its entire meaning as a rigorous science; they transform phenomenology into the merely empirical science of anthropology. In Husserl, phenomenology, as a "transcendental science," occupies a higher level than any empirical science.

Affiliates

I have observed that a specific illustration of the change by which philosophy is coming to its end, according to Rorty, is the break that took place between Husserl and Heidegger. I have also indicated some of the shifts which this break involves even though we are in no position yet to decide in what sense what they add up to might count as the end of philosophy. These are shifts in *subject*, in *level*, and in *affiliation*.

I am postponing further illustration now of the shifts in *subject* and in *level*, for the shift in *affiliation* is the most obvious. Rorty, however, is not sufficiently discriminating with respect to it. Why should we allow philosophy to be brought to a dim end by relinquishing the conceptual scrupulousness that has traditionally been associated with philosophy? Why should we resign ourselves to so broad and loose a conception of the successor subject as Rorty's "philosophy-as-literature" and not discriminate further? "Philosophy-as-science" is almost as loose a rubric; it overlooks the extent to which philosophers committed to "philosophy-as-science" have concerned themselves with explicating the sense in which philosophy is scientific. Their various attempts at discrimination might be taken as a precedent for a comparable attempt to be more specific than the rubric "philosophy-as-literature" encourages us to be.

A possible first move is to recognize how the specific conception of "philosophy-as-science" that is proffered by a philosopher may depend in part on his taking one specific science rather than another as an affiliate. Thus Husserl takes geometry as the relevant affiliate for philosophy in order to distinguish philosophy from an empirical science which generalizes from experience. The geometer deals with the properties of a triangle as an "essence," that is, as an essential structure: this is to be distinguished from the triangle he clumsily draws on the blackboard; in conducting his demonstration, he disregards the wobbles in its lines. The phenomenologist, in Husserl's view, proceeds in comparable fashion in analyzing the essential structure, for example, of an act of perception.

I would suggest that "philosophy-as-literature," like "philosophy-as-science," is too sweeping. Indeed, Heidegger is specifically concerned to emancipate poetry from literature.[20] There are also other genres besides poetry which can replace science as an affiliate for philosophy, even within the confines of the history of phenomenology. If the relevant affiliate for Heidegger is poetry, in Sartre it is literature (which he defines more specifically as the novel); in Merleau-Ponty, it is painting.

The process of discrimination can be pursued further. Sartre has a different conception of poetry from Heidegger's and a different conception of painting from Merleau-Ponty's as well as Heidegger's. The process can be pursued still further. Heidegger makes philosophical claims on behalf of Hölderlin's unique role as a poet. Partiality to Tintoretto is (I shall argue) a feature of Sartre's philosophy. Tintoretto was not a landscape painter; Merelau-Ponty, however, is partial to landscape painting, and his philosophy confers on Cézanne almost as special a place in painting as Heidegger does on Hölderlin in poetry. Have I left philosophy far behind in favor of personal predilections? This is a question to which I have promised to return. But for the present, observe that Merleau-Ponty is preoccupied in painting with the rendering of depth, while his conception of "the vertical" is crucial to his philosophy. Moreover, he can move readily from the philosophical to the pictorial conception. Thus he is criticizing Sartre as a philosopher when he criticizes him for describing a "world that is not vertical but . . . flat. . . . Ultimately for Sartre there is no depth." [21]

Other Studies

Past changes in the history of philosophy have often been discriminated with some precision as tandem to specific accomplishments in a science. I cite a familiar example because it illustrates that philosophers who are alike committed to philosophy's "scientific character" may yet differ as to which science is its appropriate affiliate. When John Stuart Mill sought to transform the scientific utilitarianism he had inherited from his father and from Bentham, he explained, "I did not at first see clearly what the error [of my father], might be," but then "at last it flashed upon me all at once in the course of other studies." His "father was wrong" in having "taken as the type of the deduction, not the appropriate process, that of the deductive branches of natural philosophy [that is, Newtonian physics], but the inappropriate one of pure geometry." [22]

In *Human Nature and History* I borrowed Mill's phrase "other studies" to cover what I an now referring to as "shifts" in the affiliated subject. What Mill was seeking a scientific affiliate for was primarily political philosophy. I undertook to demonstrate how varied the "other studies" were which have been found relevant to political philosophy during its history. My argument was that if Mill's discovery of his father's error took place in the course of "other studies" besides political philosophy, it would be an error for the historian of political philosophy to assume that it has a subject matter which can be nailed down and held fixed throughout its history. This is not an error that a historian of any sophistication is likely to make. But the historian of political philosophy does tend to try to hold onto his subject matter as he makes his way through history; he tends not to pursue the implications imported from what he regards as alien subject matters.

Yet issues over the subject matter of political philosophy can be handled far more expeditiously by the historian than issues over the subject of philosophy at large. This is why I undertook my first illustration of the problems of the historian by considering how the subject matter of political philosophy shifted with successive philosophers, and why I was able in *Human Nature and History* to take in more historical scope—in fact, much of the history of political philosophy. Confronted now with the less tractable issue of the subject of philosophy at large, I have to restrict myself to a brief stretch of the history of philosophy.

There are two other respects in which my earlier analysis is relevant here. First of all, it illustrates that shifts in *subject* and in *affiliation* are traditional proceedings in the history of philosophy—that is, they are traditional features of the way in which a philosopher has proceeded from a previous philosophy (or philosophies) to arrive at his own philosophy. Still these two shifts initially attracted our attention here inasmuch as they seemed involved in arriving at the end of philosophy, at least to the extent that this eventuality is illustrated by Heidegger's relation to Husserl.

I have proposed to assess this eventuality by raising a question: How does the way in which philosophers have traditionally proceeded from previous philosophies differ from the way in which a thinker proceeds from previous philosophies when he is ostensibly reaching the end of philosophy? Or, more specifically, if shifts in *subject* and *affiliation* are traditional proceedings, how do they differ when they are undertaken by Heidegger, Derrida, and Rorty? The answer to this question I postpone, since we need to become clearer about the proceedings traditionally employed, including proceedings that have not yet been examined.

Another reason for recalling my earlier history is to press in particular the issue of affiliation. If Mill's Newton is to have a place in the history of philosophy, are Heidegger's Hölderlin, Sartre's Flaubert, and Merleau-Ponty's Cézanne to be denied places? If the places occupied by Mill's Newton, by Hume's Newton, by Locke's Newton, and so on, are to be distinguished, should not distinctions be drawn to locate Heidegger's Hölderlin, Sartre's Flaubert, and Merleau-Ponty's Cézanne more precisely?[23] If little effort is usually made to do this, it may be because a philosopher who is committed to philosophy as a scientific subject is tempted to dismiss Heidegger's later philosophy as poetic and Sartre's philosophy as literary. Similarly, when Merleau-Ponty defended his major work, the *Phenomenology of Perception,* he was met by the protest, "I can see your ideas being expressed in a novel, in painting, rather than philosophy." [24]

The proponent of philosophy as a scientific subject needs to be reminded that he is still able to maintain some distinction between this subject and other sciences. Husserl may bring out the sense in which his philosophy is a rigorous science, as compared with the empirical sciences, by an analogy between phenomenology and geometry as an "eidetic science" (that is, as a science of essences), but the two sciences are not to be confused, for geometry is a deductive science and Husserl's phenomenology is not. Similarly, the fact that Heidegger's philosophy is "coordinated" with poetry does not thereby render it poetic. When Heidegger enters "the dialogue between poet and thinker," he stresses their affiliation: they " 'dwell near to one another' " but they still remain " 'on mountains farthest apart.' " Heidegger is quoting Hölderlin, but before entering this dialogue, he has decreed as a philosopher that "like is only like insofar as difference allows." [25] Sartre's philosophy can be distinguished from his literary works, and Merleau-Ponty's from a novel or a painting.

Intervention

This process of discrimination I began in order to back up my suggestion that it is not necessary for the historian to resign himself to the refusal to discriminate which is implicit in Husserl's metaphor of the innundating "torrent of philosophy which renounces its scientific character." In fact, he does not mention Heidegger by name in *The Crisis of the European Sciences,* the unfinished work (with which "the dream is over" fragment is associated) that employs the metaphor of the "torrent." There is no evidence of which I am aware that Husserl bothered to read "Hölderlin and the Essence of Poetry" (1936), the essay in which Heidegger undertook his "dialogue" with the poet. Even the title of Heidegger's Hölderlin essay would have left Husserl indifferent if, indeed, it did not exasperate him. From Husserl's perspective, poetry was not the sort of thing to which an "essence" could be attributed.

At the same time, Husserl's philosophical indifference was matched by Heidegger's. As I have noted, Heidegger no longer mentions Husserl or phenomenology in his lectures, any more than Husserl mentions Heidegger in *Crisis*. Such conduct on the part of philosophers who had previously collaborated invites the intervention of the historian to "come between" them and try to bring out what was implicitly at issue. I have just offered a partial explanation from Husserl's side. But since Heidegger has a different philosophy, there has to be a different explanation from his side. It is especially needed if the historian suspects that Heidegger's continuing preoccupation with the concept of "essence" during the 1930s might to some extent carry over from Husserl.[26] If, nonetheless, Heidegger does not refer to Husserl, there is the explanation which I have already offered: Heidegger no longer sees Husserl's phenomenology in Husserl's own terms but, instead, as illustrating the philosophical tradition as a whole, going back ultimately to its founder, Plato. He therefore finds no reason to linger with Husserl. Indeed, as soon as Heidegger comes to envisage a perspective from which the history of philosophy can be embraced as a whole—precisely because it is coming to its end—he becomes primarily interested in the philosophers involved in its ending—in his view, Nietzsche and Hegel—as well as in Plato, the philosopher involved in its beginning.

I offered some of this explanation earlier to set the stage for my own undertaking as a historian—as compared with Heidegger's. I explained how he loses interest in his own place in the history of phenomenology, and in his own relation to Husserl, once he has discovered himself assigned a place at the end of the history of philosophy as a whole. But I would restore him to his place in the history of phenomenology, where he would retain his relation to Husserl. For the time being, the justification for this undertaking of mine is, as it were, merely historical: the emergence of Heidegger's view of the history of philosophy as a whole is itself an episode in the history of phenomenology, granted that with the emergence of this view Heidegger leaves Husserl and phenomenology behind.

By remaining within the confines of the history of phenomenology, I can achieve a certain economy of exposition. At any rate, I can avoid some of the complications posed by the attempt to take Nietzsche and Hegel as candidates for the end of philosophy—complications which are due not only to the intrinsic difficulties of their philosophies, and to the very great differences between them, but also to the difficulties posed by Heidegger's interpretation of them and by Derrida's interpretation of Heidegger's interpretation.

I can remain within the confines of the history of phenomenology, for both Heidegger and Derrida regard not only Husserl but also Sartre as traditional philosophers. Presumably, they would pass pretty much the same judgment regarding Merleau-Ponty, though Heidegger has paid little attention to him.

Relating

While remaining within these confines, my broader concern is to present certain general problems which might be faced in any history of philosophy but which in any case dictate how I shall go about this particular history. First, I acknowledge that the relation between two philosophies appears differently from the perspective of either one and thus requires the historian to supply an account of the relation from both sides. This may seem obvious. But, in fact, most of the applauded ventures in the history of philosophy today do not do justice to the problems of the relations between philosophers, either because they cover too many philosophers to get down to details about their relations, or because they stick to an individual philosopher, subordinating his relations to other philosophers to the exposition of his.

One reason for finding such monogamy unsatisfactory is almost as elementary as the reaction, "If I had another life to spend, I'd be glad to spend it with Mary Lou." But my reason for bringing up the matter is that many of these applauded ventures seem condemned to infidelity. Rorty has asked whether or not "understanding a [past] philosopher in his own terms" is "something distinct from, and prior to, the difficult achievement of relating his thought to what we ourselves might want to say."[27] I would offer a stronger argument than Rorty's. I don't regard the relation to what we might want to say as an achievement; rather, it is inescapable. At a minimum, relevance to what we want to say tends to determine our selection of this particular philosopher or, at least, of some one thing he said to the neglect of something else.

Even if we want to say nothing and remain silent because we are merely attempting to understand the past philosophy, our attempt is itself a philosophical performance which can hardly be assumed to be prompted simply by that philosophy (for example, by the conception of understanding that is integral to that philosophy rather than an imported conception of our own). Thus we find ourselves in a situation in which we are not simply confronted by a single philosophy but by the relation between philosophies, however inarticulate and rudimentary our own may be.

If there is no escaping on our part the relation between philosophies, it should be worthwhile to examine the relations that have held between past philosophies that are more articulate and less rudimentary than our own. For this examination might in turn enable us to assess more adequately the kind of relation that may hold between what another philosopher has said and what we might want to say.

A further argument for examining the relations between philosophers would stress the fact that no philosophical issue of any scope receives an adequate statement as the outcome of a single philosophy; rather, it is an issue because it is at issue between philosophies, and as such can be better understood in terms of the broader relations between them. Consider an example of Rorty's: "You will not know much about what the dead meant prior to figuring out how much truth they knew." [28] It is hardly necessary to seek out with Heidegger the assistance of a poet in order to be dubious about this quantitative conception of measurement. As soon as one starts figuring out, issues encroach which are involved in the differences between our conceptions of meaning and of truth and his.

My final argument is that I don't believe we should allow the dead, and what they meant, to be unalterably contemporary with us. However inescapably what we might want to say intrudes on what they said, the historian should put up a certain struggle on their behalf, trying to come to recognize that there may once have been a time when philosophy had not yet progressed to its present culmination. This was one reason why I began my own undertaking here in the history of philosophy with a reminder of the talent Stendhal displays when he reports a decisive battle from the perspective—or lack of any later perspective—of someone who was a participant. Waterloo was not simply a battle fought without tanks and air support. And the historian of philosophy should not advance his undertaking by discrediting the combatants as deprived of his superior intellectual equipment.

I am not denying that a contemporary philosopher may relate his thought to some congenial past philosopher in order to get some philosophical mileage of his own out of the relationship. This is of course a legitimate undertaking, much as a painter may exploit some affinity with a past painter. To be an artist, he need not immerse himself in the Pelican History of Art series. But my complaint is that there is nothing seriously comparable today in the history of philosophy to this series of volumes on the history of art, either in the number of movements and periods which are covered, or (even more obviously) in the number of readers such volumes command. I also would suggest that there is no strict correlation between the merits of any of these volumes and the number of its references to how an artist today might want to paint or engage in some other art. The merits depend rather on how well the relations between past artists themselves are handled in terms of their own works.

I am not denying the historical relevance of retrospect. After all, Husserl's retrospect on philosophy-as-rigorous-science is embodied in the title of this volume—*The Dream is Over*. Hume may have awakened Kant from his dogmatic slumbers, and so far I may seem to have been arguing simply that it is important for the historian to recognize that what Kant woke up to in his own philosophy was not what Hume himself had wanted to say. But it is also true that Hume's philosophy is not quite the same for us since Kant; nor Hegel's philosophy since Marx and Kierkegaard; nor (I would add) is Husserl's since Heidegger. What I am proposing is that when the historian focuses on the relation between Hume and Kant, between Hegel and Marx or Kierkegaard, he should envisage the relation in each case from both sides, as I have begun illustrating in the instance of Husserl and Heidegger.

Linkups

That we cannot get very far along in the history of philosophy without dealing with the relations between philosophers is more obvious than are my reasons for selecting Husserl and Heidegger to illustrate the general problem of dealing with these relations. My original reason for selecting Husserl and Heidegger was that Heidegger's break with Husserl seems to have been involved in the emergence of Heidegger's end-of-philosophy perspective. I pointed out that it would be more feasible to decide what is to count as the end of philosophy if we determined how Heidegger's break with Husserl differs from other breaks in the relations between philosophers where philosophy's coming to an end was not imminently at stake.

Though I am moving on to the general problems of dealing with the relations between philosophers, I shall continue to exploit Rorty as a foil since I shall return to the problem of the end of philosophy and probably no other English-speaking philosopher has been more influential in announcing it than Rorty. But pause now and consider the philosophers he links up when he argues on behalf of this perspective: "Whether or not we are in fact at the end of an era . . . will depend . . . on whether Dewey, Wittgenstein, and Heidegger are taken to heart." Rorty's justification for selecting them is that they are "the three most important philosophers of our century." When he accordingly takes them to heart, he discovers that they are in "agreement" on matters which portend that philosophy is coming to an end.[29]

Questions as to the relative importance of philosophers (especially those as close to us in time as this trio) I regard as relatively unimportant. But since Rorty brandishes his list, I have to observe that it is striking that None of the three ever found it significant for the statement of his own philosophy to agree or disagree with either of the other two.

Of course, I am not suggesting that Rorty should have been inhibited from pursuing some argument of his own by linking up philosophers who were unresponsive to one another. This may well, from Rorty's perspective, make the "agreement" he finds between them all the more impressive. All that I am trying to bring out now is the different fashion in which I would compile historical evidence, on the ground that the history of philosophy is not the linking up of philosophies like beads on some string of the historian's own devising. Or, to borrow a metaphor from Husserl, it is "not in front of us like a warehouse containing its assembled wares." I grant that it is not unusual for an historian to become a forklift and move previous philosophies around as if they were crated and could be shunted out of the way or in the direction he would have philosophy go.[30]

Sometimes, however, it is worth recognizing that almost any philosopher conceived his philosophy with some sense of its relation to other philosophies. Whenever this philosopher found it significant for the statement of his own philosophy to agree or disagree with another philosophy, we have evidence as to the relation between them, which has a certain prima facie advantage as philosophical evidence. For these statements are not merely about another philosophy; they are, implicitly at least, statements of the philosopher's own philosophy, which is available to the historian if he would track down their implications. Since they are only *prima facie* evidence, I am not suggesting that the historian should simply compile statements philosophers have made about each other. This evidence must also be sifted by going beyond their explicit statements of disagreement or even agreement, which do not necessarily exclude misunderstanding. But even a misunderstanding may be more readily pinned down on the basis of explicit statements.

I also am not suggesting that disagreement with a previous philosophy need be a primary motive for undertaking a philosophy. In Chapter 1 we shall see Husserl adopt as the principle of his philosophy "To the things [*Sachen*] themselves." Heidegger retained this principle in *Being and Time* (and it is an important respect in which he continued to regard his philosophy as phenomenological), although later, in "The End of Philosophy," he revised it to the singular: "To the subject [*Sache*] itself." Husserl considered that with his adoption of this principle he was shelving all disagreements between philosophers in favor of dealing directly with philosophy's "subject"—"the things themselves." All that I am maintaining is that however directly a philosopher may deal with his subject, his dealings with it can net disagreements with other philosophers, including disagreements over the question of what the subject of philosophy is. Thus even so slight a matter as Heidegger's altering Husserl's plural *Sachen* to the singular *Sache* betrays the shift in *subject* he would carry out.

Obviously, the historian cannot get through the history of philosophy by interpreting philosophers' statements about their agreements and disagreements with other philosophers. Unresponsiveness to other philosophers is common, as is evidenced by Rorty's Dewey, Wittgenstein, and Heidegger. My plea is only that explicit statements are a more reliable place for a historian of philosophy to begin working out his procedures for dealing more generally with the relations between philosophers.[31] The art historian can legitimately compare paintings by painters who never saw each other's canvases. Yet few comparisons can be as reliable, or illustrate more reliably the problems of making comparisons, as those which are based on a later painter having "quoted" in his work an earlier painting, adapting the "quotation" to his own style.

Even for more general historical purposes, there are reasons for selecting the relation between Heidegger and Husserl for detailed examination, quite aside from its pertinence to the shifts in *subject* and *affiliation* that may add up to the end of philosophy. Of course, the closeness of the relation, followed up by a break, is not itself unprecedented—rather, a fairly standard performance. Famous instances one might adduce are Plato and Aristotle (if more were known of their relation) or Hegel and Schelling. But, first of all, there is perhaps no precedent in the history of philosophy where two philosophers, both as prominent as Husserl and Heidegger, collaborated so closely when both were mature. Indeed, the relation was not broken off until after Heidegger had written *Being and Time,* which he continued to regard as his major work for the rest of his career. Not only was it dedicated to Husserl, but Heidegger also explained in the introduction, "The following investigation would not have been possible, if the foundation had not been laid for it by Edmund Husserl."[32] The relation was not one-sided: Husserl was wont to say to Heidegger, "You and I are phenomenology."[33] At the same time, each provides some *prima facie* evidence as to what was at issue in the breaking off of their relation.

The Lineup

There is a second reason for the historian to select Husserl and Heidegger in order to work out procedures for dealing more generally with the relations between philosophers. Though the relation between Husserl and Heidegger was itself remarkable, what is equally remarkable is that, after a rupture so complete, the relation survived in their successors. Thus the relation between Husserl and Heidegger is not just the relation between their philosophies as they had set them forth. In fact, the relation between their philosophies became more crucial for their successors than it had been for Husserl and Heidegger themselves.

In each successive generation there has been at least one prominent philosopher who in the course of elaborating his own philosophy has found it necessary to repair—or, at least, reassess—the relation between the philosophies of Husserl and Heidegger. This succession provides an exceptional proving ground for the historian to test exactly how to deal more generally with the relations between philosophies.

Consider the lineup, beginning with Husserl and Heidegger themselves. Husserl (at least in the view of the successors we shall be examining) founded phenomenology when he ushered in the twentieth century by publishing in 1900 the first volume of the *Logical Investigations*.[34] From then on, in each succeeding generation at least one philosopher of worldwide renown has turned up to contribute to the momentum of phenomenology. Heidegger was thirty years Husserl's junior, having been born in 1889. Sartre, born in 1905, became the dominant figure in the French intellectual scene for a generation after World War II. A larger crowd, it has been claimed, turned out for his funeral than for de Gaulle's. (Could any English or American philosopher compare attendance at his funeral with that at Churchill's or Eisenhower's?) And if allowance has to be made for the French *faiblesse* of paying attention to their intellectuals, it also remains the case that even outside of France, Sartre has been read by more people than any other philosopher of this century.

To try to single out later philosophers who have contributed to phenomenology itself or to its continued vitality may seem invidious. But French contributors would have to include Sartre's colleague Merleau-Ponty (born in 1908). Hans Georg Gadamer (born in 1900) should certainly be mentioned, because he has probably exercised more influence outside of Germany than any other German philosopher of his generation, unless we count Jürgen Habermas as a philosopher rather than as a social theorist, and he too has been concerned with Husserl and Heidegger.[35] After the death of Merleau-Ponty and Sartre, Paul Ricoeur (born in 1913) came to exercise more influence, at least in the United States, than any other French philosopher of his generation. Although the leading French philosopher of the next generation, Jacques Derrida (born in 1930), is not a phenomenologist (on certain occasions, at least, he even denies he is a philosopher), he identifies his own university generation as thinking of "Husserlian phenomenology" as "inescapable." He himself still regards it as "a discipline of incomparable rigor," but we have heard him admit to "relying at decisive junctures [in his interpretation of Husserl] on themes of Heidegger's." The care with which he has sifted details of the texts of both Husserl and Heidegger has helped keep them alive— or has at least accorded them an "afterlife."[36] In summary, there is a remarkable accumulation of evidence regarding the relation between Hus-

serl and Heidegger which is distinctively philosophical in the fashion I
have already indicated: its implications can be tracked down in successive
philosophies themselves.

When I recognize the importance of the relation between Husserl and
Heidegger, not only to Husserl and Heidegger but even more so to their
successors, I am recognizing what the historian does sometimes with regard to the relation between painters. On the one hand, the art historian
may generalize:

> An older view of Mannerism . . . conceived of it as the style of the
> imitators of Michelangelo. That view is no longer valid, . . . but it
> reminds us of the role of Michelangelo in relation to the whole
> style. . . . In Rome, where his authority had earlier been shared with
> Raphael, it was the latter's example . . . which was in general more
> influential in the first phase of the Mannerist style.

On the other hand, the art historian may interpret specific works in terms
of debts to two preceeding artists: "In these [frescoes] Salviati seeks
strong development of plastic forms on Michelangelo's example, and a
distribution of them into space by means that recall the mode of Ra-
phael." [37]

Relevance

This analogy of mine to the history of art may bring to mind a possible
misgiving that I have not acknowledged about my approach. In concentrating on the relations between philosophies, I shall usually neglect (as
S. J. Freedberg usually does in the history of art from which I have just
quoted) other relations historians often find relevant. I am not denying
that philosophies are significantly related to their economic, political, and
social circumstances. But let me refurbish my analogy. No art historian is
likely to deny that the Black Death or the Sack of Rome or the Counter-
Reformation effected certain changes in style. Still, it is necessary to determine exactly what these changes were if one is to explain them as effects. Indeed, despite the general relevance of economic, political, and
social circumstances, explanations that resort to these circumstances
often demonstrate their specific irrelevance by failing to describe accurately the very changes in art or philosophy they purport to explain. Or
some shove of circumstances is brusquely substituted for a close analysis
of what actually changed in the style under investigation. Of course, it
also can happen that such explanations might alert art historians to a
change in style they might otherwise have been less prompt to observe. In
handling the relation between Husserl and Heidegger, it would be un-

thinkable to overlook Heidegger's becoming a Nazi as furnishing possible evidence of the character of his philosophy. That Husserl's nationalism, which became fervent during World War I, is comparably relevant to his philosophy I would doubt.

The validity of my analogizing the history of philosophy to the history of art cannot be predetermined. I have offered this analogy because visual evidence is more vivid than intellectual evidence—or, at any rate, is so today—at least when the intellectual evidence is contemporary philosophy. But if philosophy is a science, or affiliated with a science, my analogizing has no philosophical warrant. Conversely, if philosophy is affiliated with painting, as it is for Merleau-Ponty, then my analogy obtains philosophical force.

In any case, the analogizing carries a certain relevance at another juncture. Despite the transformations that have taken place in science during this century, no one is talking about the end of science. This may merely mean that scientists are less solemn or less frivolous than philosophers. But there has been much talk about the end of art and the end of the novel. It can be argued that a definite answer to the question of the end of art or of the novel may be less worthwhile than the comparisons the question can encourage between traditional and contemporary art or between traditional and contemporary literature. The case of philosophy is perhaps similar. Yet so long as these comparisons are worth entertaining, the continuity with tradition gainsays proclamations that an end has been reached in any abrupt and simple sense.

There is another possible misgiving about the relevance of my approach. When I select the history of phenomenology to illustrate the general problems of dealing with the history of philosophy, it can be objected that no particular stretch of the history of philosophy can yield an adequate illustration of all the relevant problems. I quite agree. Indeed, to the extent that I come more closely to grips with the history of phenomenology, my analysis becomes increasingly couched in terms specific to phenomenology and less readily translatable to any other stretch of the history of philosophy.

However, I would recall my argument that the break in the relation between Heidegger and Husserl would seem to deserve particular attention because it seems to have been involved in Heidegger's eventually reaching the end of philosophy—which would be the most remarkable of all breaks. But whether or not this ultimate break is occuring, the locating, delineating and explaining of breaks which have taken place in the relations between philosophies is a general, recurrent problem in the history of philosophy. Indeed, in any kind of history there is a problem as to how the breaks by which it is punctuated are to be adjusted, as discontinuities, to the continuity that any historian presumes when he embraces the history of whatever he takes as his subject.

. . . .

In Part 1 I shall take up episodes in the history of phenomenology which illustrate certain breaks, and I shall show the extent to which they can be explained in terms of the shifts I have discriminated so far. In Part 2 I shall distinguish between a history of philosophy in which these shifts are worked out, and an intellectual history which handles the relations between philosophers by charting the sequential flow of influences from one to another.

In Part 3 I shall resume my analysis of the breaks, but by finally singling out shifts in *method*. On the one hand, what I take as predominantly at issue between our four phenomenologists are the differences of method which are involved in the promotion of the other shifts. On the other hand, I shall point out that Heidegger and Derrida repudiate philosophy's traditional commitment to a method. Not even deconstruction is presented by either of them as a method. I shall suggest that this repudiation might be taken as a demarcation of the end of philosophy, but it seems to have been the least examined by historians. Commitment to a philosophical method is particularly characteristic of phenomenology, and the differences of method among our four phenomenologists are particularly illuminating with respect to the operation of philosophical method and the implications of its repudiation for the end of philosophy.

O N E . S H I F T S

ONE

The Subject of Phenomenology

> The summons "to the subject itself" is renewed in
> Husserl's . . . Philosophy as Rigorous Science
> —Heidegger

Proliferation

I am sorting out certain ways in which a philosopher may proceed from another philosophy (or philosophies) to arrive at his own philosophy. Two broad ways have so far been sketched: the move may be carried out by a shift in the *subject* of philosophy; additionally, there may be a shift, which may accompany the first shift, in the subject with which philosophy is *affiliated*. These two proceedings came up initially for analysis as ways in which the end of philosophy was reached, as least as this eventuality is visualized by Rorty, who found them both illustrated by Heidegger's break with Husserl. Yet these shifts are also, I have argued, traditional proceedings.

I concentrated earlier on the second shift as the more obvious; I turn now to the more difficult issue of the subject of philosophy. It comes up as a matter of principle in the relation between Husserl and Heidegger. When Heidegger revised Husserl's principle from the plural, "to the *Sachen* themselves," to the singular, he attributes the revised version to Husserl: "The summons 'to the subject [*Sache*] itself' is renewed in Husserl's treatise, *Philosophy as Rigorous Science*." [1]

It might be protested that if my attention were not restricted to phenomenology, it would soon become evident that the subjects handled by philosophy are hopelessly miscellaneous. There is certainly something to this protest, especially if one of the characteristic developments in our time is taken into account—the proliferation of more or less segregable subject matters that are still considered philosophical. Besides such traditional subject matters as those of political philosophy and aesthetics there are more recent arrivals, such as the philosophy of literature, the philosophy of the novel, the philosophy of feminism. The list could be longer and undoubtedly will continue to lengthen. Is philosophy then giving up the ghost—or at least the *Geist*—which when it deployed itself throughout Hegel's philosophy kept matters under architectonic control? Certainly, the proliferation of these subject matters—however invigorating their treatment is for philosophy—weakens the concept of a subject which is philosophical as such: we may, accordingly, have to concede that the end of philosophy is being reached, in that any claim by a philosopher on behalf of the comprehensiveness of his subject is thereby rendered anachronistic and thereby, too, any attempt such as mine to discern what is at issue in competing claims. Conversely, so long as large-scale shifts in *subject* can still be traced, philosophy may be gaining a reprieve from mere proliferation.

Dismemberment

In any case, a distinction can be drawn between, on the one hand, the tendency, which has become pronounced in our century, to dismember philosophy as a subject by the proliferation of its subject matters and, on the other, the traditional proceeding whereby a philosopher dismembers a previous philosophy by discarding as largely irrelevant to his own purposes a certain portion of that philosophy (or philosophies) while retaining another portion as relevant. Such dismemberment may yield *prima facie* evidence of a shift in *subject*.

When I quoted Heidegger's acknowledgement of his debt to Husserl in *Being and Time,* I did not notice that he singled out a particular work of Husserl's: "The following investigations would not have been possible if the foundations had not been laid by Edmund Husserl, with whose *Logical Investigations* phenomenology reached its breakthrough." [2] Something is askew here in Heidegger's relation to Husserl, for Heidegger is writing in 1927, and way back in 1913 Husserl published *Ideas I,* which he regarded as superseding the *Logical Investigations,* published as they had been at the beginning of the century.

How does Heidegger justify his selection of the *Investigations?* Out of Husserl's own mouth, as it were. In the foreword to the second edition, which was published concurrently with *Ideas I* in 1913, Husserl stresses "the impossibility of lifting the *Investigations* to the level of *Ideas.*" He adopts the idiom of "breakthrough" for the *Investigations,* to convey the impression of how far he had progressed beyond them in *Ideas I*, explaining that they were merely a " 'breakthrough', not a culmination, but rather a starting point." [3]

If Heidegger has preempted the idiom with which Husserl had put the *Investigations* in their place, it was perhaps in an effort to get around *Ideas I*, which Heidegger does not mention in his acknowledgment. Thus the implication could easily be read into the acknowledgment that the *Investigations* were a "breakthrough" which needed to be followed up not by *Ideas I* but by *Being and Time*, especially since Heidegger adds:

> What is essential in phenomenology does not reside in its *actuality* as a philosophical 'movement'. Higher than actuality stands *possibility*. We can understand phenomenology only by grasping it as a possibility. [4]

This assertion sounds rather tactless, but it also can be read as tactical: Heidegger is breaking through into his own phenomenology. Presumably, "actuality" and "possibility" are italicized by Heidegger to caution us that they are terms to be understood in the setting of the analysis he himself will give of the distinction. Such an analysis is to be expected in a work on time. In fact, *Being and Time* will accord priority to a future possibility over what is actually present. [5] Thus the analysis still to come will in effect reinforce the implication that what Husserl has actually accomplished is to be superseded by the new possibility opened up for phenomenology by Heidegger. [6] If Husserl's *Logical Investigations* are still salvageable, it is because (Heidegger will later explain) they "remain, as it were, philosophically neutral." [7] Thus they could be followed up, without inconsistency on Heidegger's part, by the philosophy of *Being and Time*.

Though I can't pursue the argument here, I am dubious about the neutrality Heidegger would accord the *Investigations,* even with respect to the distinction between "actuality" and "possibility" to which Heidegger's follow-up is geared. Husserl's principle, "to the things themselves," accords priority to them as immediately given and, thus, accords priority to actually present experience as "the ultimate source of validation" in phenomenology, so that appeal to it becomes "The Principle of All Principles" [8]; in contrast, Heidegger (as we have just seen) accords priority to the future. In short, the relation between Husserl and Heidegger implicit in Heidegger's distinction has to be assessed by considering not only how this distinction is implemented in Heidegger's own philosophy but how it implicitly raises an issue between their two philosophies.

Cartesianism

There are personal and practical reasons why Heidegger dodged *Ideas I* rather than explicitly criticizing it: his sense of obligation to Husserl, his recognition that Husserl would not be receptive to his criticism, his hope that Husserl would support him as the successor to the chair. I shall not speculate.

What we can be sure of are Heidegger's criticisms in *Being and Time*. Their target is Descartes, but he is, in effect, a stand-in for Husserl, who had followed what he called "the Cartesian way" in *Ideas I*.[9] Heidegger had already explicitly criticized Husserl as a Cartesian in his 1925 lectures, which amount to a preliminary draft for *Being and Time*.[10] Husserl was probably unaware of the criticism, since these lectures were not published until long after his death. In "The End of Philosophy" (1964) Heidegger publicly identifies Husserl as a Cartesian:

> For Husserl the *Cartesian Meditations* were not only the subject of the lectures in Paris in February 1931. Rather since the period following the *Logical Investigations* their spirit accompanied the impassioned course of his philosophical investigations to the end.[11]

Observe that Heidegger extends Husserl's Cartesianism back before *Ideas I* to "the period following the *Logical Investigations*" (1900–1901). One possible explanation is that Heidegger is thinking of Husserl's lectures *The Inner Consciousness of Time,* which went back to 1904–5, for this was material between the *Investigations* and *Ideas I* with which Heidegger has some familiarity. Husserl had him edit these lectures for publication. If this is the explanation for Heidegger's periodization of Husserl, their title is suggestive. For Heidegger would have found "inner consciousness" irrelevant as a *subject*.

Irrelevance

Let me pause here to make the more general point that I am using Husserl's relation to Heidegger to illustrate. I am not referring to a subject in the casual, nondescript sense of something treated. That further probing is required to reach the *subject* in my sense is implied by Heidegger's emphasis, taken over from Husserl, on "the subject itself." Heidegger further emphasizes (in the lectures he gave during the summer of the year *Being and Time* was published) a procedure which he labels "phenomenological construction." He explains that it must intervene, since "we do not simply find Being [the subject of philosophy for Heidegger] in front of us. . . . [I]t must be brought into view by a free projection [*Ent-*

wurf]."[12] The idiom "in front of" suggests that Heidegger may be rejecting Husserl's "principle of principles," whereby "the things themselves"
are disclosed in their immediate givenness—a givenness which Husserl
considers comparable to the immediacy with which something is seen.

Heidegger's procedure of projection is directed instead toward possibilities that will emerge only as the subject is "brought into view," or
constructed. For the present, I am not concerned with Heidegger's procedure of construction or the procedures which must intervene in Husserl—
the eidetic and phenomenological reductions—if immediate givenness is
to be ensured. I am concerned only with the temporal implications of the
shift in *subject* in Heidegger. When Husserl asked Heidegger to edit the
manuscripts in which he analyzed *The Inner Consciousness of Time,* it
was because Husserl supposed that Heidegger's perusing them would advance his concurrent work for *Being and Time.* But Heidegger demonstrated their irrelevance to the subject he was treating in *Being and Time*
by begging off the assignment until he had that work ready for publication. And then when he did take on the manuscripts of Husserl's lectures,
he further demonstrated their irrelevance to his purposes by not bother-
ing with much editing. Husserl was disappointed, too, in Heidegger's perfunctory preface.[13] Perhaps one reason Husserl found it perfunctory is
that in it Heidegger refers to the *Investigations* instead of tying the lectures in with *Ideas I,* which Heidegger does not even mention.

Years later the irrelevance of the *subject* of the *The Inner Consciousness of Time* was again demonstrated by Heidegger's contribution to the
festivities in 1969 marking the thirtieth anniversary of Husserl's death.
What does Heidegger have to offer in the final—and presumably climactic—sentence in his tribute? It is the claim that *Being and Time* "proceeded in a direction which always remained alien to the investigations of
Husserl on the inner consciousness of time."[14]

Probably Heidegger dismissed these investigations as irrelevant to his
purposes not just because the future did not enjoy there the priority he
himself accorded it but, more broadly, because the subject with which
Husserl was dealing was "the inner consciousness of time." Heidegger's
own subject in *Being and Time* is not "the inner consciousness." Initially
it is "being-there," and by analyzing "being-there" as being "outside itself"—"in the world"—Heidegger undercuts the distinction between
"consciousness" as "inner" and what is "outside" of consciousness. Thus
his treatment of time becomes an "ex-sistential analysis." Temporality
becomes "the *ekstatikon* in the strict sense . . . , the primary 'outside of
itself.' "[15]

Those of us who were brought up on so-called analytic philosophy
may still believe that progress is being made when a distinction is drawn

that a predecessor did not see. But the undercutting of a distinction, such as Heidegger's here, is also a traditional philosophical proceeding—one of the ways in which one philosopher can proceed from a previous philosophy in order to arrive at his own philosophy.

Parasitism

A general point can be made now in a preliminary fashion. Whatever is at issue between two philosophers, I have proposed to assess from the side of each of their philosophies, and I have illustrated my procedure with respect to the treatment of time implicit in Heidegger's upholding the priority of "possibility" over "actuality," as applicable to the relation between his philosophy and Husserl's. With this focus of mine on the relations between philosophers, what happens to the autonomy which a philosopher usually seeks for his philosophy?[16] I am merely observing that there are also respects in which any philosophy is usually "parasitical" (to borrow a term from Derrida), so that its elucidation is facilitated by taking into account its relation to another philosophy, though a philosopher's conception of his relation to another philosopher is likely to be much more a feature of his own philosophy than a genuine concession to another philosophy. This I've just tried to illustrate by Heidegger's conception of his relation to Husserl.

The illustration can be carried a step further in a fashion which suggests that the issue of irrelevance is more complicated than I have so far acknowledged. Since Heidegger is undercutting the distinction between "inner" and "outside," there would be less relevance in his wielding the characterization "outside" in expounding the "ex-sistential" character of his own analysis if Husserl (and Descartes before him) had not firmed up the distinction. In other words, it is not just the subject of philosophy for Heidegger (and how it is "brought into view" by Heidegger, or "constructed") that is to be taken into account but also how its "construction" might be regarded as a "reconstruction" of an earlier treatment. But this term "reconstruction" Heidegger would hardly endorse, so I shall retain my own previous terminology: a shift in *subject* takes place in Heidegger from Husserl, or (to retain Heidegger's conception of the subject Husserl treated) from the subject that was "handed down" by the Cartesian tradition of modern philosophy.

Existentialism

If Husserl's philosophy after the *Investigations* had become unacceptable to Heidegger because of its Cartesianism, it became thereby more acceptable to Sartre. In fact, one piece of Sartre's own explanation of the initial attraction Husserl had for him was that Husserl's "philosophy . . . was more accessible [than Heidegger's] by virtue of its appearance of Cartesianism. I was 'Husserlian' and would remain so for a long time."[17] In Sartre's major "Husserlian" work, *L'imaginaire,* he credits phenomenology's crucial insight not to Husserl himself but to Descartes. Sartre starts out by explaining that "it is necessary to repeat here what has been known since Descartes, that a reflexive consciousness provides us with data which are absolutely certain."[18] The implication is that Husserl— and Sartre after him—are merely repeating the Cartesian appeal to what is immediately given to consciousness as determining the legitimate scope of phenomenology as a *subject.* Sartre is endorsing the Cartesian Husserl that Heidegger rejected when he rejected *Ideas I,* which was a work in which Husserl himself had followed what he called "the Cartesian way."

Toward the end of Sartre's life, *Ideas I* was the only work of Husserl's that Sartre remembered having read during the year 1933–34, which he spent in Berlin, working on phenomenology. Sartre recalls how "he had to get it completely inside of him."[19] This is a quite casual application of the "inside"/"outside" distinction, yet it is clear that it no longer applies simply in the technical sense in which "consciousness" as "inner" constituted the scope of Husserl's *subject.* Instead, it has something of the moralistic, individualistic flavor that Sartre's later existentialism will display when he succumbs to the influence of Heidegger.

For the present, however, we are considering Sartre's initial relation to Husserl independently of his later relation to Heidegger. In the process of getting *Ideas I* "completely inside of him," Sarte admits that the work had to be "dismembered and deboned."[20] Although dismemberment can take different guises (such as I am now illustrating with Husserl's successors), it is usually a brutal operation. If a philosopher takes another philosopher so seriously as to try to get that philosophy inside him, then it is no longer the same philosophy; its original structure is crushed as he digests it. So bloody a proceeding can bring the historian of philosophy (especially if he has some respect for the original philosophy) close to nausea. But he must overcome his revulsion and engage in patient comparative anatomy of the two structures. The only structural feature I am singling out now—and that only very broadly—is the *subject* being treated by the respective philosophers.

Merleau-Ponty also cannibalizes Husserl, though in what may seem a kinder and gentler fashion.[21] But it is still dismemberment. When Sartre returned from deboning *Ideas I* in Berlin, he tried to interest Merleau-Ponty in it, though without much success. The Husserl who later did command Merleau-Ponty's interest he labeled "the last Husserl"—that is, the Husserl whom Merleau-Ponty interprets as having taken in *Crisis* "the life-world" as his *subject*. Merleau-Ponty identifies this "last Husserl" as repudiating both the "logicism" of his first period (that of *The Logical Investigations*) and the "idealism" of his second period (that of *Ideas I* and the *Cartesian Meditations*). With the "Husserl of the last period" Merleau-Ponty arrives at a philosophy which he does not hesitate to label "existentialism."[22] It is the philosophy which in his view Heidegger, Sartre, and he himself all shared.

However, this dismembering of Husserl into discrepant periods suggests that "the last Husserl" of Merleau-Ponty's could not have all this much in common with the previous Husserls we have encountered in Heidegger and Sartre. Merleau-Ponty's label "logicism" for the Husserl of the first period is hardly compatible with Heidegger's claim that the *Logical Investigations* "remained, as it were, philosophically neutral." Merleau-Ponty's distinguishing "the last period" from the Cartesian second period is at the same time not compatible with Heidegger's characterizing Husserl as a Cartesian "to the end." What these three successors of Husserl then share with each other in the way of phenomenology may also become dubious. And what we should be looking for is how the breaks they successively introduce in the elaboration of Husserl's own phenomenology may betray differences in the successive *subjects* each adopts for his own phenomenology.

The Wrap-Up

With Derrida, the obvious break is with Sartre's and Merleau-Ponty's interpretations of Husserl. When Derrida has announced a somewhat ambiguous endorsement of Husserl—"I still see phenomenology today as a discipline of incomparable rigor"—he quickly adds, without any ambiguity, "Not—especially not—in the versions proposed by Sartre or by Merleau-Ponty, . . . but rather in opposition, or without them."[23] Derrida has, in fact, proceeded more without them than in explicit opposition.

His implicit opposition extends to their having broken up Husserl's phenomenology into periods. Thus Derrida's break with their interpretation amounts to a protest against Heidegger's interpretation as well. This is how Derrida begins his major work on Husserl:

> *The Logical Investigations* . . .have opened a way in which, *as everyone knows* [my italics], phenomenology has plunged. Up until the fourth edition (1928) there is no fundamental displacement, no challenge that is decisive. Some revisions, certainly, and a powerful effort at explication—*Ideas I*. . . . In *Crisis* and the texts associated

with it (particularly in the "Origin of Geometry") the conceptual premises of the *Investigations* are still in force, notably [*notamment*] when it is a matter of all the problems of meaning and of language in general.[24]

Is this elimination of the breaks, the periodization, which had been detected in the elaboration of Husserl's phenomenology by his previous successors itself "philosophically neutral" (to borrow the appraisal with which Heidegger severed the *Investigations* from the works which followed)?

I cannot pursue this question very far here, since Derrida is not himself a phenomenologist. His rejection of phenomenology is itself a shift in *subject*. We can see Derrida pivoting when we reach "notably." What he is prepared to notice, take note of, are "the problems of meaning and of language in general." Problems of meaning were Husserl's problems, but Derrida is making a transition from these problems when he conjoins problems of language. He then makes the break, and reaches his own *subject*, when he goes on to emphasize that "Husserl has deferred . . . any explicit reflection on the essence of language *in general*."[25] Given these circumstances, he is tempted by a certain kind of interpretation: to wrap up Husserl's phenomenology, by picking it up from both ends of "his itinerary," so that it is entirely confined in between. Accordingly, Derrida selects for interpretation (in contrast with his phenomenological predecessors) the first section of the first of the *Logical Investigations* and one of the last of the writings associated with *Crisis*—"The Origin of Geometry."

As I've indicated, Derrida himself is largely beyond my concern in the present volume since he is not a phenomenologist. I am only exploiting his wrap-up to help me circumscribe the history of phenomenology I would offer by assigning phenomenology itself to a period. I am taking this history as beginning with Husserl's "breakthrough" in the *Logical Investigations*. I am accepting Husserl as the founder of phenomenology because he is accepted not only by Heidegger in *Being and Time* but also by Sartre and Merleau-Ponty, as well as by Derrida. None of them look back behind Husserl and Heidegger to Brentano of any other immediate predecessor of Husserl; all of them furnish, as I explained in the Introduction, what I am looking for—interpretations of Husserl and Heidegger which are philosophical in the sense that their implications can be followed out in their own philosophies. This history I am taking as coming to an end when Derrida breaks with phenomenology and sponsors in its place what I have risked calling a philosophy of language. I am allowing Derrida this authority because this break is a feature of the interpretations of Husserl and Heidegger which he furnishes and whose implications can be followed out in his own writings.

The Lurch

In order to complete this preliminary examination of the shift in *subject,* we need to consider the kind of break it is. Earlier I commented on how indispensable the concept of "break" itself is to the historian. He regularly finds himself seeking some adjustment between the continuity of whatever history he is tracing and its discontinuities. We ourselves have been utilizing the concept at different junctures. Differently located discontinuity was implicit in the different periodizations of Husserl's work adopted by Husserl's successors as each elaborated his own respective phenomenology. When we finally reached Derrida, these discontinuities were all discounted, but it became feasible for us to circumscribe the history of phenomenology as a whole. On the one hand, it began with Husserl's "breakthrough" in the *Logical Investigations.* On the other hand, it can be said to come to an end when it loses its predominance in Western Europe to those tendencies which can only very roughly be lumped together under the crude rubric of "philosophies of language."

From now on, I shall be concentrating on the breaks within this history that punctuate it—that is, on the breaks in the relations between the philosophers whom I am treating as belonging to the history of phenomenology. To sharpen the preliminary concept of a "break" for this purpose, I shall briefly consider the break between Husserl and Heidegger. I have already suggested that it is the most important break in this history, to the extent that it can be regarded as leading eventually in Heidegger to the end of philosophy.

The publication of *Being and Time* in Husserl's *Jahrbuch* was a dramatic moment: it "struck like lightning." Georg Misch continues his appraisal: "The rudder of Husserl's *Jahrbuch* was wrenched with a lurch in a new direction [*mit einem Ruck in eine neue Richtung gerissen*]."[26] The only comparably dramatic moment in the history of the *Jahrbuch* had been its launching in 1913 with *Ideas I.* Husserl had steered it through the intervening years, but now he had lost hold of the rudder, not only with *Being and Time* but also with the spreading influence of Heidegger on the articles appearing. Husserl gave up the *Jahrbuch.* He must even have felt disoriented himself, or he wouldn't have read Misch's survey of contemporary German Philosophy (from which I have quoted), for previously in his life he had usually not found time to read the writings of his contemporaries.

Heidegger himself employs an idiom somewhat similar to Misch's in his winter lecture course that followed the 1935 summer course from which I quoted earlier to illustrate the shift in *affiliation* in his philosophy from science to poetry and the concomitant transformation of the concept of "measurement."²⁷ In the winter course, he again imposes a firm distinction between philosophy and science:

> To the sciences there is always an immediate transition and access [*Eintritt*], starting from everyday representation. If one takes everyday representation as the measuring stick of all things, then philosophy is always something out of wack [*Verrücktes*]. This shifting [*Verrückung*] of the attitude of thought can be carried out only with a lurch [*Ruck*]. In contrast scientific lectures can start immediately with the presentation of their subject.
>
> Philosophy, however, entails a continuous shifting of location. . . . Hence one does not know for a while which way to turn. So that this unavoidable and often helpful confusion does not get out of hand, there is need for a preliminary reflection on what questions should be asked.²⁸

I have myself not started out immediately with a presentation of the subject of philosophy (or of phenomenology) but, rather, with a preliminary reflection with which I am now raising questions about the shifts in *subject* that it may be necessary to take into account in dealing with the relations between philosophers. In extending Heidegger's appraisal of philosophy to the history of philosophy, I have different purposes from his, which I shall later concede. But when it is a matter of what one might oneself want to say (to recall the issue raised by Rorty), as compared with the philosopher one is expounding, there can be advantages in sticking with him (and even adopting some of his terminology) if one eventually would determine exactly where one would part company with him.

The "lurch" of a shift in *subject* may be more traditional than Misch may have recognized, dazzled as he still was by the lightning. Indeed, the shift in *subject* with which Husserl had founded phenomenology was also a "lurch." The principle that (as we have seen) he adopted in the *Investigations* was "to go *back* to 'things themselves' [*auf die 'Sachen selbst' zurückgehen*]."²⁹ He was pitting this shift in *subject* against the direction taken by the Neo-Kantians (the then-dominant school in German philosophy) whose slogan was "Back to Kant."

Versäumnis

My present purpose in citing Heidegger's *Verrückung*, Husserl's *zurück*, as well as Misch on the *Ruck* of *Being and Time,* is to provide more justification than I was able earlier for my using the more vigorous terms "shift" or "break," rather than the weaker "change," for the operative factors I would single out in the relation between philosophies.

What is at stake is more than terminological. Whenever a shift in *subject* takes place, a gap opens up in retrospect in the preceding philosophy, where the philosopher had failed to treat this subject. We have watched this happen when Derrida accuses Husserl of having "deferred, from one end of his itinerary to the other, any explicit reflection on the essence of language in general." Similarly, Heidegger starts out in the first section of *Being and Time*, "The Necessity, Structure, and Priority of the Question of Being," by asserting, "This question today has been forgotten" and by explaining that "a dogma has developed which not only declares that the question about the meaning [*Sinn*] of being is superfluous but even sanctions its omission [*Versäumnis*]."

I prefer the German because the translation of *Versäumnis* as "omission" does not convey the further implications of *Versäumnis*, namely, evidence of the "negligence" of the previous philosophers—of their "failure" to treat the subject they should have treated.[30] Any important philosopher usually sees himself not just as putting forward his own philosophy, by first determining what the subject of philosophy is; he first comes up against what has previously been taken to be its subject, and his shift in *subject* is to rectify the *Versäumnis* of some question by a previous philosopher or previous philosophers.

Direction

Heidegger complains not only of the *Versäumnis* of the "question of being" in previous philosophers but also, when he makes the transition to his analysis of "The Formal Structure of the Question of Being," that the question is "directionless" (*richtungslos*).[31] Not only has the necessary subject, Heidegger is implying, not been treated, but we also do not know in which way to turn in order to treat it.[32] This idiom of direction Misch may have picked up when he commented on the "lurch in a new direction" which took place with the publication of *Being and Time*. Later in life, Heidegger relies on the same idiom, when he ends his tribute to Husserl with the declaration that *Being and Time* "proceeded in a direction which always remained alien to the investigations of Husserl on the inner consciousness of time."[33]

The additional emphasis of "lurch" is needed to suggest how "alien." More is involved than an easily negotiated change in direction by which the successor would rectify the *Versäumnis* in a preceding philosophy. For the *Versäumnis* is not intrinsic to the previous philosophy, in the sense that it cannot be rectified unless the previous philosophy is in effect superseded by the succeeding philosophy. A previous philosopher, if he is still around to protest, is unlikely to resign himself to the charge that he lacks a sense of direction in his philosophy. Indeed, we have already heard Husserl complain that "Heidegger . . . has not understood . . . [the] direction" in which he [Husserl] had proceeded." Accordingly, Husserl interprets Heidegger as having "interpreted my phenomenology backward from the level which it was its entire meaning to overcome."[34]

Exposition

When the "entire meaning" of a philosophy is jeopardized by its translation into terms of another philosophy, it is clear that a historian who would deal with the relation between the two philosophies is in trouble. So I postpone further exposition until I have dealt with some problems of exposition.

My reader has probably already been able to imagine more straightforward ways than mine of expounding a philosopher. At one familiar extreme, there is the hit-and-run exposition in which the expositor makes off with only what he can make use of at the moment to advance some argument of his own. At the other familiar extreme, the expositor can attempt a linear exposition that follows closely in the steps of the argument the philosopher is advancing. Either procedure proves next to impossible if one would deal with the relations between two philosophers. Moving back and forth between their philosophies is not as simple as crossing a street from one sidewalk to the other sidewalk. For philosophers are not likely to start from the same point in their respective philosophies or to proceed from this point on in the same direction.

Thus, for example, Husserl's starting point in the first section of the first chapter of the first of the *Logical Investigations* is the "sign." Despite the debt Heidegger acknowledges to the *Logical Investigations,* he does not reach "signs" until section 17 of *Being and Time,* where he duly refers to the first of the *Investigations.* But he has long since adopted a different starting point from Husserl, and what Heidegger has accomplished in *Being and Time* up to the point where he introduces "signs" effects decisively his handling of what had been Husserl's starting point: this the expositor has to take into account.[35] For if an expositor is to do justice to the relations between two philosophers, his exposition must expose their respective positions on a topic which was important enough to one of them to take it as his starting point but not of comparable importance to the other.

At the same time, if the expositor is to do justice in some measure to each of the philosophers, his exposition cannot be hit-and-run. He cannot yank the evidence for a shift roughly out of its context. He must take enough of the context with it to indicate the direction in which the philosopher himself is going. But the pieces of context the expositor retains may often seem like clutter.

Matters become more complicated when the exposition is coping with more than two philosophers. Thus, for example, we have heard Derrida admit that in his deconstruction of Husserl he is "relying at decisive junctures on themes of Heidegger's." Yet Derrida selects as the starting point of his deconstruction Husserl's own starting point, the "sign," despite the fact that this is not a decisive juncture for Heidegger. Moreover, it does not even remain a decisive juncture for Husserl in his later works. Yet for Derrida it remains the starting point for Husserl's phenomenology as such, including these later works. Its remaining a decisive juncture for Derrida is to be explained less by reference to the subject to which Husserl commits himself in phenomenology than to the subject to which Derrida is committing himself in his own writings.[36] Thus I am anticipating that in the longer run a great deal is at issue between Husserl, Heidegger, and Derrida with respect to the starting point each has selected, yet I am not justifying this anticipation by tracking down the substantive implications of any of their selections.

Zigzag

Dismay over this lack of straightforwardness in my exposition may be due in some measure to the misconception that history should be straightforwardly chronological. But this is feasible only if the historian has officiously intruded retrospectively and has straightened out matters which were obstreperously crooked at the actual time. In the next chapter I shall take up the question as to why I did not start out my history by tracing the chronological development of Husserl's phenomenology, and I shall deal with other problems of chronology in Part 2.

For the present I borrow a term Husserl employs in defending his own lack of straightforwardness: "zigzag." My rationale for zigzagging is similar to Husserl's. He points out how "we must initially operate with methodological resources . . . which can only subsequently be given a . . . definite form."[37] Moreover, as we acquire these methodological resources, "we are led back again and again to our original analyses."[38] But my methodological predicament as a historian is more complicated than Husserl's. He is departing from the sequence which the subject he is treating seems to require. But I am, in the first place, dealing with a lurching shift in *subject* from one philosopher to another. I am up against philosophers who are adopting different starting points in order to get at their different subjects and then proceeding in different directions in treating these subjects: these are some of the differences with which I would deal, in the second place, by acquiring methodological resources in the form of a progressively more definite analysis of the "shifts" I find at issue. Indeed, since I am dealing with the differences between philosophers, I cannot even stick with the sequence to which any one of them is wedded. Instead I can only stick with it long enough to begin to see where each is going, and then I have to double back to follow out the direction in which another philosopher has proceeded. In other words, I am conducting a series of forays, each of which is justified partly by the philosophy I am raiding and partly by my attempt to acquire methodological resources that will enable me to deal with other philosophies along with his—philosophies which are incompatible with each other as well as with his.

To a considerable extent the justification for my procedure is to bring out these incompatibilities. Thus the philosophers themselves are often at such cross-purposes that they cannot accept the differences in direction that separate them. When Husserl had Heidegger collaborate with him in 1927 on the article "Phenomenology" for the *Encyclopedia Britannica*, he admits that the article "cost me a great deal of effort, mainly because I again thought through from the ground up my fundamental direction, and took into account the fact that Heidegger . . . has not understood this direction."[39] Meantime, Heidegger also sought to come to some understanding. He viewed the article as an "opportunity to characterize the fundamental tendency of *Being and Time* within the transcendental problematic"—presumably Husserl's.[40] But Husserl felt unable to use any of Heidegger's formulations as contributions to the article, and when he read *Being and Time* itself more carefully, he decided, "I cannot include the work within the framework [*Rahmen*] of my phenomenology."[41]

The term "framework" is too static (as also is "structure," though I shall continue to use this term) and does not do justice to the way each of them is moving, with the shift in *subject*, in a different direction. They are even able to use a curiously identical idiom to designate each other's movement as in the wrong direction. Husserl visualizes Heidegger as "falling back" from "the distinctively philosophical level" which he (Husserl) had reached; he characterizes Heidegger's fall as "anthropologism" or "psychologism."[42] Heidegger makes the same accusation against his mentor: Husserl "falls back" (*zurückfällt*) into "psychologism."[43]

Sartre puts his problem of direction more simply. When confronted by Merleau-Ponty's major work, Sartre confesses, "It is impossible for me to get my bearings in the philosophy of perception."[44]

Decisive Junctures

Given such differences in direction, especially when philosophers are so much at cross-purposes that both can use the same idiom to describe the other's different direction as the wrong direction, how is the expositor himself to get his own bearings? He has to zigzag in order to jockey for a position from which he can locate the "decisive junctures" in the relations between our phenomenologists—to borrow phraseology from Derrida that has no very special terminological significance for him in his dealing with the relation between Husserl and Heidegger. I am thinking of such junctures as Husserl indicates by referring to "the distinctively philosophical level." In my exposition, junctures are decisive not only for determining the relations between philosophers but also for working out my own procedures for analyzing these relations. They then require the kind of commentary I have just interrupted my exposition to give. Another illustration we have had of a decisive juncture is Heidegger's handling of "signs," though this is not a decisive juncture in his *Being and Time* itself but, rather, when his relation to Husserl is to be brought into focus. For this is the juncture at which Heidegger picks up the topic which had been Husserl's starting point in the *Logical Investigations*.

An even more striking discrepancy between philosophies, which I shall consider in my second volume, is illustrated by "the starting point" Sartre finds in Husserl for his own treatment of the imagination. It is found two-thirds of the way through *Ideas I*, and a great deal Sartre overlooks has already transpired. This juncture itself is certainly not decisive to the advance of Husserl's own analysis.

My interrupting my exposition for commentary may be as disconcerting as my zigzagging itself. I would not defend myself by boasting too close a comparison with the *Verrückung* which Heidegger commends as an "unavoidable and often helpful confusion." But there is a certain justification for the comparison: in Heidegger's case, the philosopher cannot make "an immediate transition and gain access, starting from everyday representation," as the scientist can; in my case, I cannot make an immediate transition from the first philosophy to the second, since it is usually problematic what any two philosophers have in common. Hence I cannot seek out some immediate access to the second in the first.

I have again adopted some of the terminology of the philosophy I am expounding, in order to comment on my own exposition. The point, as I have already explained, is to keep in as close touch with the philosophy as is feasible. Heidegger himself, when he adopted the term "phenomenological reduction" (the procedure, he must have known, Husserl was convinced Heidegger had never understood), admitted that he was "adopting a central term of Husserl's phenomenology terminologically, not with respect to the *subject* [*Sache*] referred to." Heidegger is drawing a familiar distinction, but in the context of two philosophies governed by the principle "to the *Sache* itself" he may also be drawing attention to the shift in *subject* that separates them. Just as the different implications of the same terminology two philosophers both use have to be tracked down in their different philosophies, so the different implications of the terminology I take over from them will emerge from my history and will come up for later commentary with respect to my own procedures.

The Level of Phenomenology

*Philosophy ... entails a continual shift of
location and level.—Heidegger*

Metábasis

In examining the problem of the direction in which a philosopher proceeds, I have thus far considered it to be a problem of starting point and of sequence: this approach has been an oversimplification. There is, as it were, a vertical as well as a horizontal dimension to the problem of direction, though the spatial metaphor itself is misleading in its pitting one dimension against the other.

The pivotal distinction in *level* which Husserl maintains is a distinction between "pure" (an "eidetic" or "transcendental") phenomenology and any empirical science. From Husserl's perspective Heidegger's perversity then was to interpret Husserl's phenomenology psychologically or anthropologically and, thus, to interpret it backward from the lower level which it was meant to overcome. Heidegger had thereby "fallen" from the distinctively philosophical level of "transcendental subjectivity"—the subject of pure phenomenology—to the level of "worldly subjectivity," which is the level of empirical science—of psychology or anthropology.[1] Such a shift in *level* is to Husserl a "shift to an undertaking of another kind [*metábasis eis allo genos*]," and he stigmatizes such a shift, we have seen, as "psychologism" or "anthropologism."[2] This is why he exploits the idiom of "trans-lation" to argue that Heidegger has "transposed or transferred ... the phenomenological into the anthropological."[3]

Something is more seriously askew here

in the relation between the philosophies than when Heidegger dodged *Ideas I* in favor of the earlier *Logical Investigations,* which Husserl himself regarded as having been superseded by *Ideas I.*[4] How could two philosophers be more completely at cross-purposes than when one interprets the other as having "interpreted [him] backward from the level" which it was the *"entire meaning* [of his philosophy] to overcome" (my italics)?

There is a danger of misconstruing so severe a reaction on Husserl's part to *Being and Time.* It was not sudden consternation on reading Heidegger's work. Thirty years before, Husserl had launched the *Logical Investigations* as an attack on "psychologism" as a *metábasis.* The reaction of a philosopher to other philosophies is usually a following out of deepseated implications of his own philosophy, rather than merely a direct response to their philosophies. Husserl's reaction cannot be understood except in terms of his own philosophy, especially since its "entire meaning" is at stake. Thus it can hardly be understood without much more exposition of his philosophy than I have yet undertaken. After all, Husserl is accusing Heidegger of not understanding his philosophy despite their having closely collaborated. But, at least, an argument I offered in my Introduction is reinforced and can be rephrased as a theme of this preliminary volume: one task of the history of philosophy is to understand the failures of philosophers to understand each other.

Philosophical History

Another generalization seems feasible with regard to *metábasis.* A philosopher, in elaborating his philosophy, makes some at least implicit commitment as to what is distinctively philosophical. The historian must be on the lookout for these commitments if his history is to be a history *of philosophy.* Otherwise, it may become a history of loose ideas in which there is no recognition of changes that have taken place in the conception of what is distinctively philosophical—that is (so far as my analysis has gone), shifts in the *subject* of philosophy and in the *level* at which this subject is located. Now that I am introducing this second factor, I can fill out the sentence in Heidegger with the phrase which I previously held back when I borrowed his phraseology: the history of philosophy is the "continual shifting of location and of level."[5]

We are not yet ready to take on the complications of Husserl's and Heidegger's interpretations of each other's philosophies. But an illustration of a shift in *level* can be elicited from Husserl's interpretation of his own philosophy. Accordingly, let me leave Heidegger to one side for the moment. In the foreword to the revised edition of the *Logical Investigations,* which was published the same year (1913) as *Ideas I,* Husserl draws attention both to his revisions and, in spite of them, to "the impossibility of lifting the *Investigations* entirely up to the level of *Ideas*."[6] In part 1 of *Ideas I* a shift in *level* takes place whereby Husserl would achieve a distinction between "matter of fact" and "essence" and, thus, between any empirical science and an eidetic science. This distinction I have already illustrated by phenomenology's affiliation with the eidetic science of geometry.

My interest in this distinction of level now is limited to its relevance to the interpretation of Husserl's own philosophy. Earlier, when I glanced at a contemporary debate over how to go about the history of philosophy, I undertook (in Rorty's phraseology) to interpret a philosopher "in his own terms." This is a vague formula. Something more definite can now be recognized—that a philosophy solicits a certain procedure for its interpretation, just as it rebuffs others. Of course, we need not respond to the solicitation or to the rebuffs. But if we do, we shall be in a better position to appreciate the failures of philosophers to understand each other. Our prime example has been Husserl's interpretation of Heidegger as a perverse misinterpretation of his own problematic—a verdict which Souche-Dagues has properly characterized as itself "a crude misinterpretation."[7]

I have put Heidegger temporarily to one side, but what I would recognize can be recognized in Husserl's own terms. Earlier we were confronted by the dismemberment of Husserl's corpus. Such dismemberment raises scholarly questions regarding the development of his philosophy. When I reach later phenomenologists who dismember his phenomenology into periods, or in effect reintegrate it (in the case of Derrida), for philosophical purposes of their own, my reader may have stifled a protest: Why did I not leave questions as to Husserl's development to the scholarly historian, who would pay impartial attention to all of Husserl's writings?

My initial answer is that ostensibly scholarly interpretation may not be entirely free from implicit philosophical commitments of its own, which are usually less available for our inspection than the commitments exhibited when the interpretation is backed up by a full-fledged philosophy.

In brief, I am proposing my own very different version of a distinction which Heidegger is drawing when he proclaims: "The history [*Geschichte*] of philosophy is not a subject for history [*Historie*] but for philosophy."[8] Heidegger is distinguishing between *Historie*, which is scholarly, and *Geschichte*, which is distinctively philosophical history, as he conceives it. I am not adopting his distinction nor trying yet to expound it; rather, I am designing a different distinction for my own different purposes. When I refer to my history of philosophy as philosophical, I mean this, in the first instance, only in the rudimentary sense that it is history in which the *prima facie* evidence for the relations between philosophers are their interpretations of each other's philosophies. But I further mean that it is a history in which this evidence is utilized as evidence for the shifts which I am sorting out in this preliminary volume.

Developmental History

Since I am accepting philosophers' interpretations as *prima facie* evidence for my history, it may seem puzzling that I have not resorted first to Husserl's own philosophy for an interpretation of its development before going on to his successors' conflicting interpretations. My procedure has a justification I am now ready to offer. With respect to the development of his philosophy, Husserl himself is not very helpful, because of the character of his philosophy. To interpret Husserl "in his own terms" is to recognize that his distinction between fact and essence applies to the interpretation of his philosophy as an eidetic science. Recall how it applies to the affiliate, geometry: the wavering lines which form the triangle drawn on the blackboard by the geometer are irrelevant to the essential structure of a triangle, and it is with reference to this essential structure that he conducts his demonstration.

Husserl applies a comparable distinction when he revises the first edition of the *Logical Investigations*. He asks,

> Was I entitled to mislead the reader once again through all my oversights, waverings, and self-misunderstandings, which, however, unavoidable and pardonable in the first edition . . . would yet put unnecessary difficulties in the way of a clear grasp of what is essential?[9]

This commitment of Husserl's to essential structure left him largely indifferent to the particular facts of the development of his own philosophy. He was often less aware of exactly what he had previously written than his research assistants,[10] and he did not usually provide us in his later analyses with the benefit of hindsight into what exactly he found amiss in earlier analyses. When the original analyses and their revised versions survive only in manuscript form (as they usually do), it is sometimes next to impossible for the most diligent historical scholarship to keep track of all the successive changes. This is why the foreword to the second edition of the *Logical Investigations* is a rather unusual document in Husserl. For he is faced, in the presence of his reader, with the task of revising earlier material which he had already published.

Dealing with Husserl's successors, we have become aware of how prone they are to dismember his corpus. But now I have to add that historical scholarship, which would seem qualified to pass judgment here, is at odds with Husserl's unremitting struggle to reach insights into what he held to be essential structures rather than to furnish episodes that could be lined up to compose the history of his development. I offer this "at odds" as illustrating how a philosophy may rebuff a certain procedure for its interpretation.

The Reductions

There is a second shift of *level* in *Ideas I*. While the outcome of the shift in its part 1 is a distinction between any empirical science and phenomenology as an eidetic science, the outcome of this shift in its part 2 is a distinction between any empirical science and phenomenology as a transcendental science. Each of these shifts is carried out by a "re-duction" in the etymological sense that consciousness is "led back": in part 1, consciousness is led back from acquiring knowledge of particular empirical facts (for example, by perceiving something) to knowledge of an essential structure (for example, of an act of perception as such); in part 2, consciousness is led back from the way in which it is ordinarily directed in acquiring general knowledge of particular empirical facts, until this ordinary direction is overcome and it is enabled to re-flect on the essential structure of its own acts. The first procedure Husserl calls "eidetic reduction"; the second, the "transcendental" or "phenomenological" reduction.[11] Both reductions have to be carried out if phenomenology is to become the distinctively philosophical subject that it is for Husserl. If he is sensitive in the second edition to "the impossibility of raising the *Investigations* to the level of *Ideas*," it is because he had not adequately maintained the distinctiveness of the eidetic level in the first edition and had not even discovered the phenomenological reduction as a procedure for reaching the transcendental level.

I postpone any clarification of these complex procedures (and of their relation to each other) in order to anticipate the most obvious respect in which the shifts in *level* they entail are relevant to the interpretation of Husserl. Here we encounter an exception to my generalization that Husserl was so indifferent to the particular facts of the development of his philosophy that he quickly forget them. He remained alert to these particular facts when they bore directly on the discovery of the distinctions of level which justified his indifference to particular facts. Thus Husserl was entirely able to recall when he was giving the lectures on *The Inner Consciousness of Time* that "he had not yet come upon the phenomenological reduction" but that these lectures were what urged him on "to make the discovery," which "he first got down on paper the following summer vacation."[12]

Earlier I gave a possible explanation of why Heidegger regarded Husserl's Cartesianism as going back to the period following the *Logical Investigations*—the fact that these lectures were on *The Inner Consciousness of Time* and were lectures with which Heidegger had some familiarity (even if had shirked his responsibilities as their editor, according to Husserl). But a likelier explanation (though the two are not mutually exclusive) is that Heidegger is thinking of Husserl's phenomenological reduction. Thus when Heidegger dodges *Ideas I* in favor of the *Logical Investigations*, one motive is to elude the phenomenological reduction. That this reduction is proposed in *Ideas I* may explain, too, why he regards the *Logical Investigations*, in contrast, as "philosophically neutral."[13] Conversely, when Husserl regards Heidegger as relapsing in *Being and Time* from the transcendental level, Husserl's explanation is that Heidegger had never understood the phenomenological reduction.[14]

Historical Stimulations

I am not trying to bring out what Husserl was aware of in his relation to Heidegger (or vice versa) just in order to follow up the claim in my Introduction that implicit in any philosophy is the philosopher's conception of its relation to another philosophy (or other philosophies) that he finds relevant to the elaboration of his own philosophy. The further claim can be made that what is implicit in a philosopher's conception of this relation may be some more general conception of the history of philosophy.

A debate as to whether or not Husserl did have a history of philosophy has gone on among scholars, perhaps largely as a result of Husserl's having written *The Crisis of European Sciences* in response to the charge he was "ahistorical"—an epithet which became attached to him (or, more annoyingly attached) once Heidegger had given a historical dimension to the phenomenology he had ostensibly taken over from Husserl.[15] At issue in this debate is, of course, what is to count as a history of philosophy, much as the debate over the end of this history turns on the issue as to what is to count as philosophy's end.

For present purposes, we need look no further than Husserl's comment to a student:

The study of the history of philosophy offers the phenomenologist many *Anregungen* ["stimulations"], once he has progressed a certain way. It is of interest to see in what *Schichten* ["strata"] the older philosophers ask their questions. One finds them of chief interest because of their naïveté.[16]

This naïveté Husserl would explain as their being so preoccupied with ordinary experience (or with the deliverances of empirical science) that they fail to distinguish the distinctively philosophical level or stratum. Thus the interest of the history of philosophy for Husserl is its illustrating the distinctions of level which are needed if philosophy is to become the subject it is, as an eidetic and transcendental science. Past philosophies then become of interest because they illustrate the difficulties that can be overcome only by maintaining these distinctions. When Husserl qualifies his endorsement of the history of philosophy with "once he [the phenomenologist] has progressed a certain way," Husserl is presumably thinking of some progress achieved in recognizing the need for these distinctions such that the phenomenologist is in a position to appreciate the dire consequences of the naïveté of the older philosophers.

Accordingly, Husserl has explained (in the sentence preceding the one I quoted) that the phenomenologist "is not impelled directly by an historical *Anregung*." One can guess that he regarded Heidegger as having been impelled directly by historical stimulations and, so, would also regard him as still at the mercy of the older philosophers who fail to recognize the needed distinctions of level.

The Psychology of Personality

There is one respect in which the issues of level at stake in the reductions bear on the conceptions of philosophy that come up in the present history of phenomenology. Husserl condemned Heidegger's relapse into "psychologism" as preoccupation with "the psychology of personality." Though Husserl interprets *Being and Time* as illustrating this relapse, a more plausible illustration, sufficient for present purposes, can be found in an earlier writing of Heidegger's:

> Philosophical thought is more than a scientific matter. . . . Philosophy lives in a tension with the living personality and draws content and its claim to validity from the depth of personality and its fullness of life. For the most part there lies at the basis of any philosophical conception the adoption of a personal position by the philosopher.[17]

To Husserl, a philosophical position is not a personal position and to conceive philosophy as drawing its content and its claim to validity from the depth of personality would be to violate the distinctions in *level* that the philosopher must secure with his reductions. To bring out the distinction, advantage can again be taken of the analogy between phenomenology and geometry: a psychology of personality might explain the ostentatious movements of a particular geometer's arm when he draws a triangle on the blackboard, but there is no "tension" in geometry between it and his "living personality." Analogously, Husserl claims that phenomenology does not "deal with the experiences of empirical persons" and "knows nothing . . . of my experiences or those of others."[18]

Just as the historian has to face up to differences in starting point and sequence between philosophers, so he has to face up to differences in the distinctions of level they draw. He has to ask: How much information regarding the personality of a philosopher (and the way it was shaped by his personal history) should be included in the exposition of his philosophy? The answer is not entirely left to the whim of the historian. It depends, for one thing, on how much information is available. If the philosopher himself (Sartre, for example) has made it available in considerable detail, this may be entreaty on his part for it to be used. Or there can be rebuffs: thus we have seen Husserl rule out as irrelevant his experiences as an empirical person. But my anticipating the example of Sartre indicates that the fixity of Husserl's distinction of level between the philosophical and the personal was not always maintained by Husserl's successors. Where and how the distinction is to be drawn between the philosophical and the personal is itself not just a personal issue but a philosophical one as well.

Existential Psychoanalysis

One of Husserl's "self-misunderstandings" in the first edition of the *Logical Investigations* was his rejection of a "transcendental ego." In *Ideas I* he discovered that the essential structure of consciousness was anchored at the transcendental level to this ego. Here we encounter a quirk in the history of phenomenology where phenomenologists are evidently at cross-purposes—a more serious quirk than Heidegger's clinging to Husserl's *Logical Investigations* when they had been superseded for Husserl himself by *Ideas I*. Sartre launches his career in phenomenology by rejecting the "transcendental ego," which Husserl himself had initially rejected but later retrieved.[19] Sartre then was left in his own philosophy with the self-consciousness of the particular, contingent individual.

I am not suggesting that Sartre gets by without any distinctions of level—no philosopher can. They are a dime a dozen in philosophy. The "tension" in which "philosophy lives" with "the living personality" (according to the early Heidegger) manifests itself in Sartre's existential dialectic in the guise of *interplay* between levels.[20] It is this *interplay*, along with the "tension" that produces it, which Husserl had tried in effect to eliminate by the fixed distinctions of level he would secure by his reductions.

One of Sartre's own distinctions of level is that whereby phenomenology supplies "first principles" to an "existential psychoanalysis." But this distinction is not Husserl's distinction, nor is it held as fixed by Sartre as Husserl's distinctions of level are. For example, among these principles which phenomenology supplies existential analysis in Sartre is the concept of an individual's "original choice of himself," but this reflexive choice is implicit in the apparent miscellany of his particular choices.[21]

This distinction of level in Sartre is not the same as the distinction of level in Heidegger, even though Sartre modeled his existential psychoanalysis on Heidegger's "existential analysis," as well as in competition with Freud. Here we encounter another quirk in the history of phenomenology, only this time three phenomenologies are at cross-purposes. Their divergencies provide an illustration of the kind of insight into the complexity of issues I would obtain with my focus on the relations between philosophers.

The quirk is that "psychologism" which Husserl accused Heidegger of is what Heidegger accuses Sartre of. In supporting his accusation, Heidegger cites Sartre's announcement in *Existentialism is a Humanism*: "We are at a level where there are only men."[22] (We are reminded of how Husserl accused Heidegger of relapsing to the level of "man" or "worldly subjectivity" from the level of "transcendental subjectivity.") Heidegger retorts on behalf of the *subject* of his own philosophy, "We are at a level where there is principally Being." One way in which this level can be reached is when we are exposed to anxiety: "We—the human beings we are—we slip away from ourselves. . . . This is why fundamentally it is not you or I that feels dislodged [*unheimlich*]."[23] Inasmuch as we are slipping away from the psychological characteristics that differentiate us as particular, contingent individuals, philosophy (as Heidegger conceives it) is essentially distinct from anything which would be regarded as a "psychology of personality."

The Contingent Individual

Anxiety is the phenomenon for which Sartre is most indebted to Heidegger. But in Sartre, unlike in Heidegger, one becomes an individual human being by virtue of exposure to anxiety, which encourages one to arrive (if I may borrow a phrase from the early Heidegger, whom Sartre probably never read) at "the adoption of a personal position." To indicate how uniquely personal this position is, Sartre revises Kafka:

> A merchant comes to plead his case at the castle where a terrifying guard bars the entrance. The merchant does not dare to go further; he waits and dies still waiting. At the hour of his death he asks the guard, "How does it happen that I was the only one waiting?" And the guard replies, "This gate was made only for you." This is precisely the case with the subject, if we may add that *each man makes for himself his own gate.*"[24]

Sartre's addition carries a reference to the individual's "original choice of himself"—a reference which was lacking in the original story, so that the merchant has had to ask the guard the question.

I borrowed the early Heidegger's phraseology "the adoption of a personal position" as also applicable to Sartre. But it did not have the philosophical ramifications that Sartre's conception of an "original choice" did, for with the shift of *level* in Sartre existential psychoanalysis is validated as a philosophically relevant discipline. I grant that Heidegger would disdain its philosophical relevance as evidence of Sartre's "fall" into "psychologism." But my present point is that this lapse into "psychologism" in Sartre's case (according to Heidegger), as in Heidegger's case (according to Husserl), cannot be dismissed as simply a lapse but, rather, brings into view a different range of philosophical issues, and to this extent it is a shift in *subject.*

Sartre's seeking support for his philosophy from Kafka may leads us to suspect that a concomitant of his shift in *level* may be his shift in *affiliation.* "Problems," Sartre explains in *What is Literature?,* "can be treated abstractly by philosophical reflection." But he protests, "We want to live them—that is, support our thinking by those fictional and concrete experiences which are novels."[25]

It is true that Sartre is intruding a distinction of level between philosophy as abstract and literature as concrete. Later we shall see that this distinction does not preclude *interplay* between the two levels. This *interplay* is the guise taken by the "support" that literature provides philosophy. When I focus in the Volume 2 on Sartre's relation to Husserl, we shall see how indispensable to the working out of Sartre's phenomenology are concrete examples. His career culminates in the three volumes on Flaubert—his longest work—in which he diagnoses the personality of a contingent individual and categorizes this diagnosis as "a novel which is true."[26] He is crossing the traditional line between the two genres: truth is not a claim which philosophers are wont to make on behalf of a novel, and most readers will respond to the claim by feeling that there is an unresolved "tension" between the two genres in Sartre. They are responding more or less to what I am characterizing as *interplay.*

The History of Philosophy

Since Sartre's philosophy accords a place to particular, contingent individuals, and their philosophical relevance is denied in different ways by both Husserl and Heidegger, the historian of phenomenology encounters the problem I have been approaching: Should he allow the particular individuals, which philosophers themselves are, to enter his history of philosophy, dragging after them pieces of their contingency? Or are these pieces to be discounted as philosophically irrelevant gossip?

Heidegger comes out, in effect, against their entry. For example, he promptly disposes of Aristotle's life when lecturing on Aristotle's philosophy: "Aristotle was born, he worked, he died." [27] No mention of Aristotle fleeing Athens lest it sin against philosophy twice or of his tutoring Alexander the Great. Similarly, Heidegger has tried to be as reticent about his own life, pushing his work out in front of it.

Consider, in contrast with Heidegger's treatment of Aristotle, Sartre's treatment of Descartes:

> The absolute is Descartes, the man . . . who lived in his own time, who thought from day to day with the means that were on hand, who . . . knew Gassendi, Caterus, and Mersenne, who loved in his youth a girl who was cross-eyed, who went to war, got a servant pregnant, who attacked not the principle of authority in general but specifically the authority of Aristotle. [28]

Since Sartre relies on Descartes's biographer, Baillet, for some of this information, it is clear that it obtains its relevance less from Descartes's own philosophy than from Sartre's. His absolutizing of Descartes as a particular individual is consistent with the twist Sartre has given in his philosophy to Kafka's story. Indeed, in *The Words,* in the ten volumes of *Situations,* in interviews and elsewhere, Sartre has deployed almost boundless information regarding the particular contingencies of his life— diligently abetted by Simone de Beauvoir.

The question is not whether the historian should attempt to include in his history such information as Sartre alludes to in the case of Descartes and provides outright in his own case or, rather, whether he should disregard such information, as Heidegger would in the case of Aristotle or himself. Whatever the information the historian may wish to include, he should be attentive to the philosophical weight that the philosopher himself attached to it, for this will have tended to shape the information.

This information is not a matter merely of "the facts." It has to be recognized that philosophical issues do not remain at the distinctively philosophical level which may have been upheld by some preceding philosopher. At issue is how the philosophical level is distinguished from and related to the personal level, and the relations here determine what is selected as philosophically relevant at the personal level. To employ the idiom of the most impressive exponent of personal relevance, "The person of an abstract thinker is irrelevant to his thought. An existing thinker . . . in presenting his thought . . . sketches himself." [29] What the thinker includes (or leaves out) in this sketch is not just a personal but a philosophical decision. Thus the term "personal" itself remains vague in its coverage until some philosophical discrimination has taken place.

Personal Relations

The preliminary effort at discrimination that I would make now is prompted, in the first instance, by my own focus as a historian on the relations between philosophers, since this renders more acute the question of the philosophical relevance of the personal relations between Heidegger and Husserl, on the one hand, and between Sartre and Merleau-Ponty, on the other.

Perhaps Heidegger's most blatant delinquency in relation to Husserl was his failure to pay a visit during Husserl's protracted final illness. When Heidegger dismisses this as a "human failing" (*menschliches Versagen*),[30] it may not be entirely irrelevant to recall his distinction between the personal characteristics of a man and the structure of his "being-there" that is disclosed with his exposure to anxiety. "Fundamentally, it is not you or I that feels dislodged," and therefore the personal relation between the you and the I is presumably no longer fundamental. Does "human failing" cover too his "stupidity" in joining the Nazi party and his continuing to pay his dues until 1945?[31] Is "human failing" the kind of colloquialism that it is a "human failing" to resort to when clearly one has not done the right thing—a resort that doesn't implicate the essential structure of one's "being-there"?

Overcoming some of the vagueness of the rubric "personal" can begin (as have my previous efforts at discrimination) with comparing philosophers who are to enter my history. Merleau-Ponty, as contrasted with Sartre, places an emphasis on personal relations. That this emphasis is philosophical is suggested by one of Merleau-Ponty's favorite citations from Husserl: "Transcendental subjectivity is intersubjectivity." [32] Unfortunately, this citation is not found in Husserl himself, and its absence illustrates that the philosophical use one philosopher makes of another philosopher is hardly ever pure scholarship.

The bogus citation does not indicate that Merleau-Ponty is restoring the transcendental ego; in fact, he endorses Sartre's refutation. But Merleau-Ponty's phenomenology is not first personal, as Sartre's is, with each individual waiting at his own self-made gate. [33] "Our relations to ideas, Merleau-Ponty explains, "are inevitably and justifiably our relations with other persons." [34] The "inevitably and justifiably" are the trademark of a philosophical claim: what transpires at the level of "ideas," which Husserl would segregate as the strictly philosophical level, should not be abstracted from the philosopher's relations to other persons, and these may include other philosophers.

Jean Hyppolite, a friend of both Sartre's and Merleau-Ponty's, points out that in interpreting Merleau-Ponty's phenomenology, "As much as on the influence of Husserl, . . . we must insist on the living dialogue, never interrupted, with Sartre." [35] But this dialogue involved Merleau-Ponty's upholding the experience of dialogue itself, as over against the dueling that goes on in Sartre's philosophy between the individual and the other. [36] Merleau-Ponty comments, "Between the other or myself one must choose—it is stated." [37] This statement Merleau-Ponty would attribute to Sartre, though he is not actually named. The choice itself would be consistent with the clipped way, at the beginning of the memorial essay Sartre wrote on Merleau-Ponty, that Sartre separates himself from the friends he has lost: "They were they; I was myself." [38] But in Merleau-Ponty's philosophy, "I borrow myself from the other." [39] In the experience of the dialogue, "we are for each other collaborators in a perfect reciprocity." [40] It is when "I experience the presence of others in myself and of myself in others" that I also "understand at last the meaning of Husserl's enigmatic proposition: "transcendental subjectivity is intersubjectivity." [41] Observe that this experience of overlapping personal relations is indispensable to understanding the meaning of a proposition.

The *interplay* that goes on in Merleau-Ponty between the philosophical and the personal level is illustrated by his essay on Husserl, despite the fact that Husserl would never have tolerated any such *interplay* in his philosophy. This essay was Merleau-Ponty's contribution to a volume commemorating the hundredth anniversary of Husserl's birth, and in the essay he apologizes for the "temerity of a contribution" on the part of someone "who never knew daily intercourse with Husserl nor listened to his lectures." This apology may seem merely *pro forma* recognition that former students of Husserl were also contributors. But I find the essay evidence that Merleau-Ponty is philosophically committed to *interplay*, so that he soon becomes entangled in elaborate adjustments:

> Nevertheless, perhaps this essay has its place alongside other approaches. For to the difficulties of communication with a work is added, for those who knew the visible Husserl, those of communication with an author. Certain memories provide here the assistance of an incident, of a conversation short-circuited. But others would rather mask the "transcendental" Husserl, the one who is now being solemnly installed in the history of philosophy—not that this is a fiction but because it is Husserl delivered from his life. . . . Husserl present in person could not, I imagine, leave in peace those surrounding him: all their philosophical life must have been for a while in this extraordinary and inhuman occupation of being present at the continual birth of a thought, of lying in wait for it day after day, of helping it objectify itself or even to exist as communicable thought. How then, when the death of Husserl and their own growth had turned them over to adult solitude, could they easily rediscover the full meaning of their former reflections . . . ? Having initially invested philosophy completely in phenomenology, do they not now risk being too severe toward it at the same time as toward their own youth, and to reduce to what they have been in their original contingency and in their empirical humility certain phenomenological themes which, in contrast for the foreign spectator, retain all their prominence?[42]

The *interplay* between these successive adjustments cannot swing the balance finally in Merleau-Ponty's favor, for the prominence these particular themes enjoy with him is in turn contingent upon his being a foreign spectator.

In tracing the shifts in level which have punctuated the history of phenomenology and which reach a remarkable low with the sinuous dips in the passage from Merleau-Ponty, I may seem to have entirely lost sight of the end of philosophy. It is, in fact, not a prospect which ever perturbed or enticed Sartre and Merleau-Ponty. However, the point that can be made is that it is hard to imagine that dispute over the relevance or irrelevance of the personal will not survive the end of philosophy: it will, no doubt, still be a problem with respect to whatever undertaking may succeed philosophy.

Metaphysics

Philosophy that is coming to an end Heidegger conceives as having been metaphysical. The end of philosophy that we previously encountered in

Heidegger when we compared him with Husserl was the end of philosophy as "rigorous science." But (to oversimplify matters for preliminary
purposes) it is philosophy as metaphysics which prepares the way in Heidegger for its supersession by the sciences.

In his lecture "What is Metaphysics?" Heidegger was not yet ready
to define metaphysics as the philosophy that is coming to an end. But my
present concern with that lecture is with the shift of level in it which renders the personal philosophically irrelevant. When Heidegger selected
this question for his inaugural lecture in July 1929, on succeeding to Husserl's chair, he may have intended to emphasize the distance between his
philosophy and Husserl's. Husserl did not identify phenomenology as
metaphysics. Indeed, for him "phenomenology is antimetaphysical." [43]
This pronouncement I am quoting from Husserl's manuscript for the article on "Phenomenology" which he wrote for the *Encyclopedia Britannica*. The pronouncement drew a protest from Heidegger, when Husserl
submitted the manuscript to him, in what was Husserl's last significant
attempt to secure Heidegger's collaboration and vindicate his confidence,
"You and I are phenomenology." [44]

We cannot be sure that Heidegger intended in this lecture to emphasize the distance between himself and Husserl. One reason I went on in
the last section to Merleau-Ponty was to suggest that Husserl's presence
in Heidegger's audience on the occasion of the inaugural lecture would
have been philosophically relevant to Merleau-Ponty, given the attention
he paid in his commemorative essay on Husserl to those who had, like
Heidegger, enjoyed personal relations with Husserl. In contrast, that Heidegger was succeeding to Husserl's chair, that Husserl himself was his
"fatherly friend" (as Heidegger called him), was of no philosophical relevance to Heidegger himself. He avoided any reference to his predecessor
in his lecture. Such a reference might have been normal personal courtesy,
but it became philosophically irrelevant in a lecture in which, with our
exposure to anxiety, "We . . . slip away from ourselves," and it is no
longer a matter of "you or I." [45]

Toward the end of the lecture, its implications for the distance between Heidegger and Husserl may perhaps be implicit in the claims, "No
scientific rigor can hope to equal the seriousness of metaphysics. Philosophy can never be measured by the standard of the idea of science."
"Rigor" and "the idea of a science" may seem commonplaces, but they
are criteria to which Husserl regularly repaired in exalting phenomenology. Moreover, Heidegger's claims precede the climactic paragraph in
which he cites Plato's *Phaedrus,* first in Greek. The citation would usually
be translated, "For, my friend, there is by nature something philosophical
in the way the man thinks." The man in question is a particular individ-

ual, Isocrates—a personal friend of Phaedrus's. But Heidegger follows up the Greek with a German translation in which "my friend" is discarded and, with it, Socrates' own personal relation to Phaedrus. At the same time, the specific reference to Isocrates as an individual is discarded in favor of a reference to man as the "being-there" into which any individual is "transformed" when he undergoes the shift in *level,* whereby he is "transposed" beyond himself as an individual with the exposure to anxiety which accompanies the posing of the question, "What is Metaphysics?" [46]

Our interest at present in the lecture is limited to its implications for how a historian of phenomenology is to handle the relations between Husserl and Heidegger. If the historian were confined within the constraints of Heidegger's philosophy (even when it later becomes a history of philosophy), he would overlook the fact that Husserl was present at the lecture. But my history of philosophy is philosophical not in the sense that it accepts the constraints of any philosophy being expounded; it accepts only the obligation of bringing out what these constraints are and how they change with the shifts in *subject* and in *level* that take place as we move on from one philosophy to another. In this fashion, more of an understanding can be gained as to what is at issue between different philosophies with respect to what philosophy itself is.

The Terrain of
Vulgarization

I regarded Heidegger as background for what
seemed to me to matter, Sartre.—Beaufret

Floruit

It is not only the way in which personalities
and personal relations are transcended in
both Husserl's and Heidegger's philosophies
but also the apparent completeness of the
philosophical break between them which
renders their relation difficult of access. Husserl does not explicitly refer to Heidegger in
his last work, *The Crisis of European Sciences and Transcendental Phenomenology,*
while for nearly thirty years Heidegger does
not offer any references to Husserl that
would yield *prima facie* evidence as to the relation between their philosophies. However,
this was the period when phenomenology extended its influence worldwide, and its most
influential exponents, Sartre and Merleau-
Ponty, restored in their own phenomenologies the relation between Husserl and Heidegger that Heidegger himself was no longer
acknowledging, at least not in his writings.

The historian then faces the question of
what historical sequence to follow. Encouraged by the precedent of Fabrice, I propose
to follow a sequence that would restore, in
outline at least, the experience of living
through this period. But let me first state
more generally the problem of historical sequence.

Earlier, I anticipated a protest to the effect that a proper history of phenomenology
should be fundamentally chronological, taking up the more influential proponents of
phenomenology in their chronological sequence. This sequence could be determined

either by the dates of birth of the four most influential phenomenologists who are under consideration here or by the dates when their major works were first published. These two sequences happen to coincide, and I offered this lineup in my Introduction.

However, the history of philosophy is not simply a history of those who have produced a philosophy; there is also the history of the reception of each philosophy, for by and large the history of philosophy includes only those philosophies which have had some impact, have exercised some influence. Here might be mentioned the sequence in which each of our four phenomenologists *floruit* for us. The evidence is provided by the dates when their major works were translated into English. Husserl's first strictly phenomenological work, the *Logical Investigations* (1900–1901), had to wait until 1970 for an English translation; Heidegger's *Being and Time* (1927), until 1962. But Sartre's *Being and Nothingness* (1943) was translated in 1956. The length of time which elapsed between original publication and English translation is *prima facie* evidence as to the demand for, and the accessibility of (two factors I shall not try to distinguish), the philosophies themselves to an Anglo-American audience. But our access to these philosophies is a matter of less consequence in the history of philosophy, since phenomenology has hardly flourished in England or America to the extent it has in Germany and France. I'll regain our perspective briefly in my third volume.

Translatio Imperii

What does concern the historian more is the translation of German phenomenology into French. In 1939 Sartre announced that "the publication of *What is Metaphysics?* is a *historic* event."[1] When he underlines "historic," he is drawing attention to his using the term in the special philosophical sense that Heidegger had conferred on *Geschichte*. We may be perplexed with Sartre's announcement, inasmuch as Heidegger does not deal with the "historic" in "What is Metaphysics?" But the "historic event" that Sartre is referring to is not the publication of Heidegger's "What is Metaphysics?" but of the translation of Heidegger into French to which the translator, Henry Corbin, gave this title, although the book also included other selections from Heidegger besides the inaugural lecture, in particular, Heidegger's analysis of "historicity" (*Geschichtlichkeit*) in *Being and Time*.

What Sartre is stressing is not just that his own German was not quite up to reading Heidegger in the original but that the translation was a "historic event, in which I had my part in contributing to its production." For he belonged to a French "public" that was "waiting for" Heidegger to be translated. Merleau-Ponty will go even further, when he speaks on behalf of himself and "a number of contemporaries" who have "the impression, on reading Husserl or Heidegger, not so much of encountering a new philosophy than of recognizing what they were waiting for." [2] Their having been "waiting for" it determined in considerable measure what they got.

What historians usually take pains to comment on here was how France, liberated from Germany by the war, surrendered to German philosophy, remaining dominated by it for more than a generation. But the comment oversimplifies. [3] The Sartre who in 1939 has already read Husserl and is waiting for the translation of Heidegger is a soldier who had just been drafted for a war that has not yet been fought. And when he was taken prisoner and was asked by a German officer if there was anything he wanted, requested a copy of *Being and Time.*

What I find more relevant than this minor adjustment in chronology is that after the war the prevailing interpretation of Husserl and Heidegger, and of their relation, was dominantly French. Even in Germany, Heidegger's acceptance by the French mitigated the taint of his Nazism. In fact he almost could be said to have become a *Re-Import* into Germany. At least this is what Habermas does say took place, even if to say it, he has to resort to an English idiom. [4]

There was in effect a *translatio imperii* in phenomenology during this period when phenomenology flourished—a "transference of authority" to the French. Derrida is more specific: this postwar period he characterizes as an epoch in the interpretation of Heidegger when Corbin's "translation" of Heidegger's *Dasein* ("being-there") as *réalité humaine* "dominated by virtue of the authority of Sartre." [5] That Derrida first offered this assessment of the epoch in a paper which he presented in the United States in 1968 suggests he may have thought that the authority of Sartre, and of his interpretation of Heidegger, might not yet be ebbing there as rapidly as it was in France.

In alluding to this epoch as a *translatio imperii* from Germany to France, I was recalling a more global precedent, when Rome, having conquered Greece, surrendered to Greek philosophy. At least many of its elite did, and many of the elite in Paris similarly surrendered to German philosophy. The result of this proceeding in ancient Rome was the formation, in considerable measure, of our philosophical tradition itself. Elsewhere I have analyzed Cicero's *translatio* of Plato, and Augustine's *translatio* of Cicero (as well as of Neoplatonism) when the authority of Rome became the authority of the Roman church. With this *translatio* came the *translatio reliquarum* from East to West. Sartre and Merleau-Ponty similarly proceeded from German philosophy to reach their own

French philosophies, leaving to the historian the question of what "remains" of what was originally Husserl or Heidegger.

This, I grant, was a transaction on a much smaller scale, and its result has been much less durable as a tradition. Centuries passed before Greek philosophy began to recover from its Latin interpretation; it took only a generation for Husserl and Heidegger to begin to recover from Sartre and Merleau-Ponty. But Frenchman—prominently, Derrida—played as considerable a role in this recovery as German philosophers did.

The French Connection

During the postwar epoch when (according to Derrida) "the authority of Sartre" tended to dominate the interpretation of Heidegger, Heidegger himself, as I have indicated, did not discuss publicly his relation to Husserl. One reference to Husserl by name appears in the "Letter on Humanism": "Neither Husserl nor Sartre (so far as I can see) recognize the essentiality of the historic in Being." [6] There is unintended irony in Heidegger's linking Husserl and Sartre in this respect, for we have just watched Sartre (in a wartime journal not published until after Heidegger's death) turn to Heidegger for the concept of the "historic," which we shall later see he recognized he could not obtain from Husserl. But my only present point is that Heidegger is linking Husserl and Sartre without acknowledging there had ever been any link between himself and Husserl.

The "Letter on Humanism" was addressed "To Jean Beaufret, Paris" and published in French (because of his Nazism, Heidegger was not allowed to publish in Germany) before it was published in Switzerland and imported into Germany. It seems no accident that when Heidegger eventually does discuss his relation to Husserl, it is almost always when he is addressing a non-German audience. The first discussion is in a "Dialogue with a Japanese Scholar (1959); the next, in his "Letter to Father Richardson" (1963), who was an American Jesuit. Further discussion of Husserl himself appears in "The End of Philosophy," which was first published in French (1964). The previous year, Heidegger offered a muted account of his relation to Husserl, but its occasion was a tribute not to Husserl himself but to the publisher of Husserl's works and Heidegger's *Being and Time*. The exception that proves the rule is Heidegger's very brief, indeed perfunctory, contribution to the celebration at the University of Freiburg of the thirtieth anniversary of Husserl's death.[7] In 1973 Beaufret organized a seminar in which Heidegger finally attempted to specify the decisive importance Husserl's thought had for him. This attempt is striking, because it was (so far as I'm aware) Heidegger's last sustained public effort to elucidate his own thought. But the request to make this attempt was (I strongly suspect) due to Beaufret himself, who organized the seminar for a non-German audience.

This history I have been tracing of Heidegger's relation to Husserl is a history in which the relation was first of all Frenchified and then internationalized. Meantime, the fact that there was no published reference by Heidegger to Husserl after *Being and Time* until the "Letter on Humanism," suggests that Husserl's thought no longer remained of decisive importance to Heidegger. Recall the scope he gave himself with the concept of "possibility." Consider, too, Gérard Granel's appraisal: "*Being and Time*, aside from occasional assertive moments (whose suppressed brusqueness itself creates problems), is immersed in a kind of fuzziness [*flou*] with respect to what has to do with its relation to Husserl's phenomenology." [8]

Relations

I have suggested before that Heidegger's relation to Husserl perhaps belongs rather less to the history of Heidegger's or Husserl's own thought than it does to the history of phenomenology—that is, to the history of what phenomenology became when it was imported into France (where Sartre and Merleau-Ponty elaborated their own version of phenomenology by reconciling, each of them in a different fashion, Husserl and Heidegger) and then was reimported into Germany, and at a time when Heidegger was as unreconciled to Husserl's phenomenology as Husserl had become in the 1930s to Heidegger's.

Should a historian who would maintain a focus on the relations between philosophers and make as much use as feasible of how they themselves conceived these relations, as I proposed to do in my Introduction, begin with Husserl's and Heidegger's conceptions of the relations between their philosophies? On Husserl's side, we do have his marginal comments on *Being and Time*, but they are rather skimpy and also involve (as we have already heard Souche-Dagues point out) "crude misinterpretation." Are we then to turn to Heidegger's references to Husserl in *Being and Time*, which (as Granel has observed) are "fuzzy," except when they are of "suppressed brusqueness"? Or should we instead first make use of the extensive commentary Sartre's and Merleau-Ponty's philosophies yield on Husserl and Heidegger and the relation between them?

No single contention provides the clincher as to where to begin, so perhaps this claim itself should be dramatized by doing violence to the standard procedure of following chronological sequence, as I myself did with the lineup in my Introduction. Where to begin, I am suggesting, depends to a considerable extent on the historian's purposes and on how the philosophies in question lend themselves to his accomplishing these purposes. In this regard he can weigh the relative accessibility of the evidence. Since I am seeking my evidence primarily from the philosophies themselves, their own relative accessibility as philosophies is a pertinent consideration. I have already deployed chronological evidence (dates of English translations) that Sartre's philosophy proved more accessible than Husserl's or Heidegger's. Even nowadays, when Sartre's philosophy is very much out of fashion, it is still more familiar than theirs.

The historian needs to acknowledge a distinction between the evidence that happens to be available to him and how this evidence happened to become available. I propose not just to take advantage of the familiarity of Sartre's philosophy but also to explain how it attained its familiarity, insofar as this can be explained as the deliberate result of Sartre's own philosophical effort. Of course I am not denying that Sartre's philosophy first having become familiar and then having gone out of fashion is much more the result of the vagaries of fashion than of his own deliberate effort and that these vagaries require a very different explanation from that which I am offering.

Sartre's own comment on accessibility was that Corbin's translation, which rendered Heidegger accessible to a French public (including Sartre himself), was itself "historic" in what Sartre took to be Heidegger's special philosophical sense of *geschichtlich*. My comment, then, is not just that Sartre's philosophical "translation" of *Being and Time* into *Being and Nothingness* (I am taking "translation" in the special philosophical sense I derived earlier from Husserl) was a rendering of Heidegger as well as Husserl that was more accessible to the public (not merely in France but even throughout the world) than were Heidegger's philosophy as well as Husserl's. My further comment is that *Being and Nothingness* is also a more accessible illustration of the problems posed by such "translations" from one philosophy to another than the "translation" of Husserl's own philosophy that Husserl accused Heidegger of having offered in *Being and Time*. This is why I shall pay more preliminary attention in this present volume to *Being and Nothingness* than to *Being and Time* or to any work of Husserl's. It is not because I rate Sartre's philosophical competence as approaching that of either Husserl or Heidegger. We shall later see that when Sartre was writing *Being and Nothingness,* he warned de Beauvoir it might well give the impression *"Quelle salade!"* since he had relied so extensively on his predecessors in order to state his own philosophy. Thus it provides extensive evidence as to the relation between his philosophy and Husserl's and Heidegger's philosophies.

Via

There is, however, a difficulty I shall face in dealing with the relations between Sartre and Husserl: Husserl did not respond to the works Sartre published before Husserl's death in 1938. Husserl was too old and sick to notice a Frenchman who was young and not yet known as a philosopher. But we do have Heidegger's response to Sartre's conception of the relation between Heidegger and himself—the conception which Sartre began elaborating in 1940 with his reaction to the Corbin translation of 1939 as a "*historic* event." Here we have the kind of *prima facie* evidence which is desirable in determining how a relation is perceived from both sides.

In order to understand Heidegger's response to Sartre's conception of his relation to Heidegger, we need first to recognize how authoritative Sartre's role was. As late as Heidegger's eightieth birthday, in 1969, French journalists interviewing Heidegger speak for their generation when they recall for his benefit how "it was *via* [*à travers de*] Sartre's work, *Being and Nothingness,* that many discovered you in France after the Liberation."[9] Heidegger admitted to having read the work but promptly changed the subject.

To proceed toward a philosopher *à travers de* another philosopher is a traditional proceeding. But we are perhaps too inclined to think of the access route as something medieval, when philosophers proceeded toward Plato *à travers de* Plotinus or Augustine, or toward Aristotle *à travers de* Averroës, and so on. (I cite the case of Aristotle because Heidegger himself sought to get back behind the medieval Aristotle, who had been a feature of his scholastic education, to his Greek predecessor.) We are less likely to think of this access route being traversed in our own time when the relevant texts are available.

To illustrate the access route that was traversed *via* Sartre toward an eventual understanding of Heidegger, which those who arrived there regarded as being in Heidegger's own terms, it is worth taking as a representative traveler Jean Beaufret, to whom Heidegger addressed his "Letter on Humanism." For it was in this letter that Heidegger tried to straighten out the relation (or, rather, asserted the lack of relation) between Sartre and himself. Furthermore, Beaufret was to become the disciple, regardless of nationality, whom Heidegger found the most understanding. Their relation is one of those stories which is best begun at the end. When Heidegger, late in life, was consulted regarding a difficulty in his philosophy, he deferred to Beaufret, who happened to be present, "Ask him, he understands my philosophy better than I do."

Beaufret had not understood it that well at the time he formulated the questions Heidegger answered in the "Letter," for they were clearly inspired by familiarity with Sartre rather than with Heidegger. But before I let Beaufret himself tell the story, I should point out, having myself argued that personal reference has no place in Heidegger's philosophy, that the "Letter" is not strictly personal. The title does include the subscription "To Jean Beaufret, Paris," but since there is no street or institutional address to ensure delivery, this subscription can hardly be intended just to create the illusion that this sixty-six-page work is a personal letter or to serve as evidence that Heidegger, deprived of any authorized role, had been reduced to expanding his ideas through personal communications. I take it that Heidegger may be emphasizing that he is addressing a French audience, perhaps even seeking out a French audience, at a time when he was bitter about being deprived of a German audience by the interdiction (implemented by the French occupying forces) against his teaching or publishing in Germany.

Beaufret's journey toward an understanding of Heidegger had begun long in advance of his pilgrimage in 1945 to the ski hut at Todtnauberg where Heidegger spent much of his time while he was debarred from teaching. Beaufret's first contact with phenomenology had been in 1939, when Merleau-Ponty had shown him a text of Husserl's that he had just typed up. But Beaufret had not been particularly responsive. He reports that the "decisive episode" which brought him round was his reading Sartre's essay "Intentionality, a Fundamental Idea of Husserl's Phenomenology," which was published that same year.[10] As a result, Beaufret immersed himself in *Ideas I,* as Sartre himself had done during the year in Berlin when he wrote "On Intentionality." Thus Beaufret came to Husserl, as well as Heidegger, *via* Sartre.

As for his initial response to Heidegger, Beaufret had read Corbin's translation of "What is Metaphysics," which was the first essay of Heidegger's to appear in French (1931), but he admits, "I understood nothing of what he was saying."[11] Beaufret had sought Heidegger's attention by sending him, before Beaufret paid his first visit, in 1946, the articles he had published on existentialism in 1945. There Heidegger would have read, "No one has understood Heidegger better than Sartre."[12] Such an affidavit on behalf of Sartre's understanding, Heidegger could have taken as evidence of "the almost insurmountable difficulty," of which he later complained, in obtaining an "understanding" of his philosophy.[13]

It should be added that Beaufret's own concern then was not just with understanding Heidegger's philosophy. "For a long time," Beaufret recalls, "I regarded Heidegger as background for what seemed to me to matter—Sartre. And when I made my trip to Freiburg, it was still with curiosity with respect to what had made *Being and Nothingness* possible." [14]

Access Routes

The detour Beaufret took in reaching Heidegger must have been a not uncommon French experience, and the same route was often followed elsewhere. The relation between Heidegger and Sartre was one in which Sartre initially occupied the foreground and Heidegger the background. This is the access route I am following myself, not just because it was the usual route but because following it helps bring into focus the problems entailed in one philosopher's understanding of another philosopher.

During this initial period *Being and Time* was likely to be read so as to better understand, *via* it, *Being and Nothingness*; later, *Being and Nothingness* is more likely to have been read on the way to understanding *Being and Time*, until finally *Being and Time* itself moves into the foreground and Sartre is relegated out of the way.

Such reshuffling of the relations between philosophers may seem merely a matter of intellectual fashion and not philosophically edifying. But a philosophy is not simply a freeway. Its viability, how it is understood, to some extent depends on the route which provides access to it. This is one reason why I have picked up Rorty's innocuous-sounding problem of "understanding a philosopher in his own terms" and why I keep coming back to it in the context of my own concern with the relations between philosophers. [15]

More might be said on behalf of paying attention to the traditional proceeding whereby one philosophy is approached *à travers de* another philosophy. Access routes are not a feature just of the history of philosophy. They are so inescapably a feature of human experience that novelists are often at pains to devise them. Henry James confesses that he is "addicted to seeing through." He repudiates "the mere muffled majesty of . . . 'authorship,'" in favor of his "preference for dealing with my subject matter, for 'seeing my story,' through the opportunity and the sensibility of . . . some person who contributes to the case mainly a certain amount of criticism and interpretation of it." Instead of providing us with his own "impersonal account of the affair in hand," we are provided with some "person's access to it, and estimate of it contributing thus . . . to intensification of interest." [16]

Admittedly, James is a devious writer, so his commitment to a *via*, to what he too calls "access," is hardly surprising. But the history of philosophy is also devious. Reconsider how access was gained to *Being and*

Time during the first two periods I have distinguished. Initially, our representative traveler, Beaufret, had no access to Heidegger: we have heard him confess that when he read Corbin's translation of "What is Metaphysics?" in 1931, "I understood nothing of it." But Beaufret did think he achieved access to Husserl *via* Sartre when, in 1939, he read Sartre's "Intentionality." Next, consider Sartre's own case. In 1931 Sartre could hardly have avoided reading Corbin's translation of "What is Metaphysics?" for it appeared in the same review as a portion of the work with which Sartre expected to launch his career—*La légende de la vérité*. But Sartre confesses, "I read 'What is Metaphysics' in *Bifur* without understanding it." [17] This is the same confession as Beaufret's. Sartre did think he had gained access to Heidegger in the complete Corbin anthology of 1939. Then he read *Being and Time* itself in German after he became a prisoner in 1940. His understanding of Heidegger became a widely utilized access route to Heidegger with the publication of *Being and Nothingness* in 1943. But late in his life Sartre would look back and confess, "However, I understood Heidegger *via* Husserl much more than in his own terms." [18]

If I have traced this history from 1931 on, it is not just because 1931 was the date of the first translation both of Heidegger ("What is Metaphysics?") and of Husserl (*Cartesian Meditations*) into French. I began with this date because that same year marked for Heidegger the break between him and Husserl: that year Husserl had publicly criticized Heidegger's philosophical work, and Heidegger took it personally.[19] Thus 1931 can be said to be the end of the relation between Heidegger and Husserl themselves and the beginning of the history of their relation in France.

The climax of this history is the publication of *Being and Nothingness* in 1943—the year when the French began understanding the relation between Heidegger and Husserl *via* Sartre and, thus Heidegger *via* Husserl.

How does Heidegger respond to *Being and Nothingness* as an access route to *Being and Time*—the access route which Beaufret and other Frenchmen had traveled? He does not respond. One possible motive is that he wants to disregard Husserl, *via* whom Sartre had approached him in *Being and Nothingness*. Instead Heidegger selects for response a public lecture of Sartre's, *Existentialism is a Humanism* (1946), in which is no allusion to Husserl.

Husserl is so prominent in *Being and Nothingness* that Heidegger could hardly have handled the interpretation meted out to him there without coming to grips with the way he was brought into relation to Husserl. I have already presented ample evidence that Heidegger was at that time dodging the question as to his relation to Husserl, and I have mentioned that the one passing reference to Husserl by name in the "Letter on Humanism" is offered as if the philosophy in *Being and Time,* which Heidegger would rescue from Sartre's interpretation, had never been written with an acknowledgment that "the foundations" had been "laid" for it by Husserl.[20]

We are reminded again by the "Letter" of the problems posed for the historian by Heidegger's persistent lack of philosophical interest in Husserl's "crude misunderstanding" of him, as Souche-Dagues characterizes it. It seems plausible, then, to begin by isolating instead, as Heidegger does in the "Letter," some of the problems posed by what Heidegger regards as Sartre's crude misunderstanding of him. This misunderstanding receives an explanation from Heidegger in the more general terms of his own philosophy, just as Heidegger's misunderstanding of Husserl is explained by Husserl in the more general terms of *his* own philosophy—that is, as "psychologism" or "anthropologism."[21]

The Public Place

In the "Letter on Humanism," Heidegger complains that "the market of public opinion demands ever new 'isms.'"[22] Sartre can hardly escape this complaint, since *Existentialism is a Humanism* would seem to market two for the price of one. But Heidegger's complaint is not whimsical. Because what is at issue for him in the "Letter" is Sartre's interpretation of *Being and Time,* Heidegger's analysis in *Being and Time* of the domination of "the everyday understanding" by the impersonal "anyone" (*das Man*) takes on special relevance. In this analysis he elaborates the existential category of *Öffentlichkeit* ("public accessibility" or "obviousness").[23] One of its subcategories is "everyday talk," which is not restricted to oral communication but "extends to what gets written."[24]

This analysis comes close to providing one possible account of what I shall label "vulgarization"—a traditional proceeding not to be disdained, for it is one of the most influential in the history of philosophy, partly because it is designed to extend the influence of a philosophy.[25] I call this proceeding "philosophical" to indicate that what I have in mind is not what is done to a philosophy by "the vulgar" themselves, the general public, but what is done to a philosophy by another philosopher—in Heidegger's criticism, to his philosophy by Sartre. I have begun with Heidegger's criticism because it shows that a philosophical account of the proceeding can be offered.

I am intervening here as a historian because Heidegger overlooks the fact that Sartre had offered an alternative philosophical account of "vulgarization"—that is, an account in the setting of his own philosophy:

> Either one must maintain a doctrine at a strictly philosophical level, and leave it to chance for the doctrine to exercise an influence, or ... because the philosophy [Sartre's philosophy] would be a commitment [*engagement*], one must accept vulgarizing a philosophy, on condition that the vulgarization not distort it. Of yore, philosophers were attacked only by other philosophers. The vulgar understood nothing, and couldn't care less. Nowadays, philosophy is made to descend to the public place.[26]

Sartre accepts the shift to this lower *level*—to what he calls the "terrain of vulgarization."[27] In borrowing "vulgarization" as a label from Sartre, I would relieve it of some of its usual pejorative implications, in order to apply it to a shift in *level* which can be distinguished from the shift (which I have already sorted out) to the empirical level, as involving "psychologism" or, more specifically, some concessions to "the psychology of personality." I would distinguish the two shifts, even though they may overlap from Heidegger's perspective.

A properly philosophical level (for example, Husserl's transcendental level or his eidetic level) is a traditional philosophical distinction, and I have recalled, as the most familiar version, the distinction of the metaphysical level from the empirical. But vulgarization, I have admitted, is usually regarded as befalling a philosophy from the outside. Nevertheless, on the one hand, in Heidegger's case, the vulgar are, as it were, recast philosophically as *das Man,* and Heidegger finds in Sartre an illustration of a philosophy that is "publicly accessible" and, as such, not properly a philosophy. On the other hand, in Sartre vulgarization is accorded philosophical legitimacy.

Between the accounts our two philosophers would give of this new shift in *level,* there is another broad difference. Heidegger assumes in *Being and Time* that it is virtually impossible for the understanding of a philosophy to escape distortion insofar as the philosophy becomes "publicly accessible" or "obvious." In contrast, the attempt to be understood publicly is deliberate on Sartre's part, and he assumes that the descent "to the public place" need not "distort" his philosophy.

The Wrap-up

There is one final episode I must consider in the history of the dawning of the recognition in France that Sartre had vulgarized Heidegger's philosophy. Earlier I considered the effect of Heidegger's own recognition in the "Letter on Humanism" that his philosophy had been vulgarized by Sartre: it relegated Sartre out of the way as an access route to Heidegger's philosophy. The damage it did to Sartre's reputation as a philosopher was not without a certain irony. For I have shown how Sartre's *Being and Nothingness* contributed to Heidegger's rehabilitation from the taint of Nazism—first more in France, later in Germany. That Heidegger's "Letter" contributed decisively to the process by which *Being and Nothingness* lost favor (and Sartre himself became philosophically a "has been") is indicated by the way in which the only philosopher (if he is a philosopher) whose influence today comes anywhere near to approaching what Sartre's once was—Jacques Derrida—deals with Sartre: Derrida sees Sartre almost entirely in terms of his failure to understand Heidegger and faults the authority Sartre's failed understanding exercised in France during the postwar epoch. We have already heard Derrida speak for his generation, insisting that the version of phenomenology to which they could respond was Husserl's own and "not—especially not—in the versions proposed by Sartre or by Merleau-Ponty, . . . but rather in opposition to, or without, them." [28] Derrida is equally opposed, or indifferent, to Sartre's and Merleau-Ponty's interpretations of Heidegger.

Further rerouting is involved in the step Derrida takes beyond Heidegger's. Whereas Heidegger criticized *Existentialism is a Humanism* as a vulgarization (in my terminology) not of *Being and Nothingness,* as Sartre himself had presented the lecture, but of *Being and Time,* Derrida extends this criticism: *Being and Nothingness* itself becomes a vulgarization of Heidegger, Derrida thereby carries out a proceeding vis-à-vis Sartre which is similar to that which we watched him carry out vis-à-vis Husserl. He wraps up the dominant philosophy of the epoch in France previous to his own generation, as he would wrap up Husserl's corpus, which that previous generation had dismembered.[29]

Since Derrida is wrapping up in order to advance to his own philosophy of language, he focuses on a particular word, stigmatizing as "monstrous" the "translation," which we have seen Sartre had accepted from Corbin, of Heidegger's *Dasein* ("being-there") as *réalité humaine.*[30] That "this translation," comments Derrida, "dominated *via* [*à travers de*] the authority of Sartre—this gives much to think about regarding the reading or not reading of Heidegger during this epoch."[31]

Derrida does not share with us much of the much we are given to think about. He only observes that the translation has "imposed on Heidegger's thought, as it is formulated in the word *Dasein*, a violence which is inadmissible, because it flattened and normalized monstrously the novelty of his thought."[32] Monstrous normalization suggests some kind of vulgarization, and flattening suggests that a distinction of level is being violated, whatever satisfaction Derrida may normally take in deconstructing such distinctions himself.

I shall not take time out to anticipate how Derrida, in his own epoch, has suffered at the hands of some of his followers, for he has been at the mercy of monstrous vulgarizations which attribute to him, and apply, the doctrine of an infinite plurality of possible readings, without admitting that violence is ever inadmissible.[33] Instead I have shown how, in the cases of Husserl and Heidegger, certain successive readings of them and their relation have gained significant prominence in France, and I have singled out certain shifts as factors broadly determining these readings.

I would only add now that it's hard to believe that if philosophy is coming to an end (thanks in part to deconstruction), whatever undertaking is scheduled to replace it (for example, deconstruction) will not be susceptible to the traditional proceedings of vulgarization. Accordingly, it's just as hard to believe that philosophy's replacement won't require some account of how such vulgarization or normalization can take place—an account comparable to the one which Heidegger gave of Öffentlichkeit when he himself was still a philosopher, and on which he is still willing to rely in the "Letter on Humanism," even though he there presumably has reached, or is reaching, the end of philosophy.

FOUR

: *Nazism*

Heidegger has a double responsibility: for what he
said in 1933 and for what he did not say in 1945.
—Robert Minder

The Descent

It seems manifestly perverse of Heidegger to
have attacked Sartre's *Existentialism Is a
Humanism* rather than the work Sartre had
written for professional philosophers. I have
suggested that Heidegger may have preferred
the public lecture, in which Sartre indulged
in "isms," because it lent itself to an attack
couched in terms of Heidegger's analysis of
Öffentlichkeit. Another possible reason, I admitted, was that Sartre did not refer in the
lecture to Husserl, and Heidegger was apparently reluctant at that time to become involved in a discussion of his own relation to
Husserl.

A possible reason why Sartre himself did
not refer to Husserl was that criticism of
him, especially by French Communists, focused on his debts to Heidegger as a Nazi. By
descending to the "terrain of vulgarization"
in the lecture, Sartre was trying to initiate
a dialogue with the French Communists,
which would enable him to become a fellow
traveler. The historian may well be tempted
to claim that if Sartre, after establishing his
philosophical credentials with *Being and
Nothingness*, descended to a political terrain
where he vulgarized his major work, so also
did his critic Heidegger, for after having established his philosophical credentials with
Being and Time, he vulgarized this work in
his Nazi discourses. I grant that the differences between their philosophies (as well as
between Nazism and Stalinism) preclude any
close comparison here. Of course, Sartre

never joined the Communist party. Heidegger did join the Nazi party, in 1933, after he became rector of the University of Freiburg, but I think it fair to say that he became a fellow traveler, indulging in what one of the Nazi leaders called his "private National Socialism" while continuing to pay his party dues until nearly the end of the war.[1]

A difference which might seem to impede the comparison is that where Sartre is loquacious, Heidegger is taciturn. Sartre supplies us with an explanation—which, however awkward, can still pass as philosophical—for his descending to "the public place"; and in his political journalism he had a ready justification for every political stance he took. But Heidegger never supplies (at the time or in retrospect) an explanation comparable to Sartre's for his descent from *Being and Time* to his public discourses. Even though he confidently applies his analysis of *Öffentlichkeit* to the vulgarization of *Being and Time* that he finds in Sartre's *Existentialism is a Humanism,* he never applies it to his own vulgarization of *Being and Time.*

It is true that there are no references to Sartre's politics in the "Letter on Humanism," any more than to Heidegger's own Nazi politics, though Heidegger must have known that something of this sort would be expected of him in his first postwar work. However, there is one slight—but not insignificant—change in the reference to *Öffentlichkeit* from his handling of the category in *Being and Time:* Heidegger refers to "*Die Diktatur der Öffentlichkeit.*"[2] It had not been a dictatorship in *Being and Time.* The change suggests that Heidegger is not unaware that his support of the Nazi dictator may have been on the mind of his French audience. But the implications are unclear. Is Heidegger implying that the Nazi dictatorship itself embodied or implemented *Die Diktatur der Öffentlichkeit?* There is no evidence for this interpretation. Is he implying that *Die Diktatur der Öffentlichkeit,* illustrated by the dedication of Sartre's pamphlet to "isms," is somehow more execrable, or at any rate more fundamental, than any merely political dictatorship? Is he bitter over his exclusion from publication at a time when Sartre was enjoying unprecedented public vogue as a philosopher? We cannot spell the implications out.

Heidegger's evasiveness is closely associated with his taciturnity. As Robert Minder puts it, "Heidegger has a double responsibility: for what he said in 1933 and for what he did not say in 1945."[3] I am concentrating on what Heidegger did not say in 1945 and later, not just because it would seem he could have said something more consequential than he did, about what he had said in 1933 but more because his taciturnity, which seemed initially to us to impede the comparison with Sartre, might become a sort of pivot for a certain comparison. There is perhaps a sense in which Heidegger's postwar refusal to explain his dedication to an "ism" in 1933 might itself receive pretty much the same explanation from Heidegger as Sartre's dedication to "isms"—the explanation Heidegger obtains from the category of *Öffentlichkeit,* as applied in his analysis of "everyday talk" in *Being and Time.* For Heidegger seems to have believed that were he to have spoken out at length about what he had said from 1933 on, his comments would have inevitably been distorted and misunderstood in a fashion not very dissimilar to the way in which *Being and Time* itself was distorted and misunderstood by Sartre, at the behest of *Die Diktatur der Öffentlichkeit.* Thus Beaufret, having on one occasion lept to Heidegger's defense, "was earnestly begged by Heidegger, as soon as Heidegger had heard of it, never from then on to intervene in this fashion, and that it was not just a matter of wasting one's time but of lowering oneself by replying seriously to Heidegger's detractors."[4] In other words, Heidegger's detractors can be assigned to the vulgar level but not (it would seem) the propagandistic discourses of Heidegger's to which his detractors call attention. Presumably, they have also betrayed their vulgarity when they call attention as well to his taciturnity—for example, about Auschwitz.[5]

Breaks

I am not trying to reach an overall assessment here of Heidegger's conduct. I have elicited the issue of his taciturnity as a juncture at which his philosophy would seem to justify his conduct in a fashion that has apparently not been noticed by commentators.

To this extent I have already rejected the claim of many of his apologists that his personal conduct was irrelevant to his philosophy. Thus, so astute a scholar as Pierre Aubenque concludes that there is no relation between Heidegger's previous philosophical writings (notably, *Being and Time*) and his Nazi discourses, that instead "there is really a break [*rupture*] of style, of level, of thought—between Heidegger's philosophical works before 1933 and his discourses of 1935 having reference to circumstances."[6] With such a *rupture,* these discourses can hardly retain any philosophical relevance. It is true that in Heidegger's philosophy in general no clear relation between philosophy and circumstances is elaborated, but it is also true that no clear distinction between them is made. The distinction here is Aubenque's own intrusion.

Another distinction favored by Aubenque and many others who would salvage Heidegger as a philosopher is between his philosophy and his conduct as merely personal in its implications. This distinction is also

Heidegger's regular resort, as when he disposes of his Nazism as "the biggest stupidity of my life." [7] So blanket a dismissal would seem to forbid any discriminating assessment of what he said at that time and implies that it need not be explained by reference to his philosophy.[8] After all, "stupidity" is a merely personal attribute. But the distinction between the philosophical and the personal is itself a philosophical distinction of level, one which we earlier watched exposure to anxiety impose in *What is Metaphysics?* I made use of a comparison with Sartre to argue that the distinction is not philosophically inevitable. Now I would add that a philosopher has to take philosophical responsibility for the distinction and its implication, if only to determine more exactly the dimensions of the area where he can commit big stupidities that have nothing to do with his philosophy.

Without recognizing that it is Heidegger's distinction, another of his friends falls back on it as if it were a colloquial, readily understood distinction. (I would add that, unclarified, it would seem to remain of the sort that is a feature of "everyday talk," which in Heidegger is a manifestation of *Öffentlichkeit*.) Heinrich Petzet writes that Heidegger's Nazism was a "personal error, which in fact had nothing to do with Heidegger's world-changing thought." [9] To the distinction between the philosophical and the personal, Heidegger himself gives an additional twist. He almost implies that it is the unimpugnability of his thought which prompts attacks on him personally, for he cites Valéry: "He who cannot attack a thought, attacks the thinker." [10] Here again the result of the twist is that Heidegger's detractors become guilty of philosophically unwarranted conduct, inasmuch as they are violating the philosophical distinction between the philosophical and the personal.

Heidegger offered the Valéry citation to Erhart Kästner, who was involved in arranging for Heidegger the interview in *Der Spiegel* regarding his political conduct; Kästner hoped such an interview would "put an end to the entire litter of crazy slanders." In assessing the arrangements, Dominique Janicaud asks "if it was right of Kästner to 'force Heidegger's hand' to the extent of limiting completely the interview's objective to a personal defense." He does not absolve Heidegger of responsibility: "But Heidegger, having carefully gone over the text afterward, could himself have given more depth to its presuppositions and its perspectives. . . . Nothing precluded his preparing in addition a 'philosophical testament.' Thus he has deliberately chosen to shelter himself in some fashion behind the occasion [of the interview] in order not to say anything more." However, Janicaud does not recognize that Heidegger was taking shelter behind his own philosophical distinction between the philosophical and the merely personal. In fact, it is a little difficult to imagine Heidegger so blending the philosophical with the personal as to prepare a "philosophical testament."[11]

Dummheit

At least one ardent defender of Heidegger has found the distinction between the philosophical and the personal intolerable. This is how François Fédier visualizes the distinction as being drawn: "But—it may be objected—what is at issue is not Heidegger's *thought;* it is his *person,* his history as individual, his inclinations—in short, all that focusing exclusively on his work leaves in the shadow." Fédier reacts vehemently:

> I ask, Has the objector reflected on what such a separation between "life" and "thought" (if it were possible) would mean? Has the question of the articulation between an ignoble life and a sublime work been raised clearly?[12]

Since Fédier has thus repudiated any separation between the two levels, he has to deal with the fact that their separation seems to be implied by Heidegger's "the biggest stupidity." Fédier reports that Heidegger's phrase has been disdained as a vulgar colloquialism, unworthy of a serious philosopher, "more appropriate to the clumsiness of a child upsetting a jar of jam."[13]

Fédier would rescue Heidegger from this vulgarization. He argues that "translating Heidegger's *die grösste Dummheit* into French as *la grosse bêtise* (since this is a locution which designates . . . primarily childish behavior that lacks seriousness) demonstrates that one does not want to understand Heidegger."[14] What I myself would bring out with this relatively simple example of a single phrase is the facility with which the shift in *level* can be carried out. If *bêtise* depresses Heidegger's conduct to the personal level, where it can refer to the innocent clumsiness of a child, *Dummheit* can apparently be elevated to the philosophical level, as it is by Fédier when he takes a step beyond the problem of translation:

> There is in the *Critique of Pure Reason* a note of Kant's . . . where *Dummheit* is in question. Kant writes: "A lack of force of judgment is what is properly called stupidity (*Dummheit*); there is no remedy for such an infirmity. . . ." Heidegger's reference points are above all philosophical. . . . For Heidegger to say of his period as rector that it was "the biggest stupidity" of his life, does not mean at all that Heidegger is making light of his error but, to the contrary, that he is crediting it with its full philosophical scope.[15]

When this expostulation is taken in conjunction with the alternative interpretation of *Dummheit* as colloquial, we can see how easily the distinction between the philosophical and the personal can slip around. It also shows how indeterminate was the meaning of Heidegger's pronouncement. He himself having remained taciturn as to its implications, we have had to listen to his struggling expositors.

T W O · I N F L U E N C E

FIVE

Discipleship

*The influence of a philosophy on important
disciples permits . . . a more accurate assessment
than would the laborious study of a
conscientious commentator.* —*Levinas*

The Flow

I have not tried to botanize—to tabulate the
different species of vulgarization. I have indicated that I am not now directly interested
in what happens unmercifully to a philosophy at the hands of the public, which has to
be kept plentifully supplies (according to
Heidegger) with "isms," such as Sartre's *Existentialism Is a Humanism.* Since I would
focus on the relations between philosophies
themselves, I am for the present interested
only in what happens to philosophy at the
hands of philosophers. in my account of how
accusations of vulgarization punctuate the
relations between our phenomenologists, I
could have begun with Husserl's accusing
Heidegger of catering to his public. But I
concentrated instead on the more remarkable cases of Heidegger and Sartre, for both
of them could be said to have vulgarized their
own philosophies. Furthermore, while Sartre
deliberately vulgarizes his *Being and Nothingness* in *Existentialism Is a Humanism,*
Heidegger sees in this public lecture a vulgarization of his own *Being and Time,* and Derrida sees in *Being and Nothingness* a vulgarization (or normalization) of *Being and
Time.*

Vulgarization is a consequence of a philosophy exercising an influence, but inasmuch as vulgarization is also usually supposed to involve some sort of degradation of
the original philosophy, I have taken it up
first as a shift in *level* to be distinguished

from the shifts in *level* I considered in the preceding chapter, even though for Heidegger Sartre's vulgarization is in fact a relapse into "anthropologism," as are for Derrida Heidegger's Nazi discourses.

However, the broader phenomenon, for anyone who would focus on the relations between philosophies, is the flow of influences. The philosopher himself can be concerned with what happens when his philosophy flows beyond its own bounds and loses its native structure as it becomes an influence on another philosophy. His own philosophy he can then rescue by bringing this influence itself back within the scope of the philosophy for explanation, as is the case when Heidegger retrieves in the "Letter on Humanism" the account of "the publicly accessible" or "obvious" in *Being and Time* in order to explain Sartre's distortion of that work.

Since we have dealt with vulgarization as a phenomenon of the flow of influence, we have reached a juncture at which the historian of philosophy should clarify the character of his history by distinguishing it from intellectual history, as the genre to which the flow of influence can, to a considerable extent, be consigned. I don't propose to corral here the varieties and vagaries of intellectual history. I would only pick up Derrida's reference to the "authority" of Sartre as suggesting that some authority or authorities often become dominant in any epoch and that the intellectual (as well as the institutional) versions of this domination merit examination. Thus it is easy to visualize the history of phenomenology as the history of shifts in the authority whose influence is dominant. If this were all I sought as a historian, the history of phenomenology would become the history first of Husserl and of his influence, then of Heidegger's breaking away from this influence and becoming a dominating influence, then of Sartre's taking over from both Heidegger and Husserl, and then of Merleau-Ponty as influenced by Husserl, Heidegger, and Sartre, until Derrida and his contemporaries emancipate Husserl and Heidegger from Sartre's and Merleau-Ponty's influence. Such an outline, if filled in, might pass muster as intellectual history, though it might be difficult to keep it so routinized and to maintain such disdain for the issues dividing these philosophers.

The distinction I would draw between the history of philosophy and any such intellectual history is implicit in my analysis so far. A first step toward tracking down philosophical implications is to expose in the flow of influence the shifts I am sorting out. When these shifts take place as breaks in the relations between philosophers, they are also breaks which articulate the flow of influence from one philosopher to another. The history of philosophy can thus be kept from dissolving into that welter of influences which is intellectual history.

The Confusion

Before I go any further, let me allude to an episode I would consign to intellectual history, so that I can then go on to how I would track down its philosophical implications.

About the time Beaufret and other Frenchmen were making their pilgrimage to Todtnauberg to listen to Heidegger, a story got into circulation that Sartre, after his year in Berlin in 1933–34, went for the winter semester of the next year to Freiburg and that Heidegger, "when asked . . . about his early acquaintance with Sartre, did not at first remember him by name, but then identified him as 'the Frenchman who had always confused him with Husserl.' "[1]

Unfortunately, the story (told by the French cultural attaché in the French zone of occupation) is apocryphal. Apparently Sartre did consider staying a second year in Germany but gave up the idea. One possible reason was Simone de Beauvoir's ability to pull on the leash, though in most accounts of their alliance this leash did not exist, even then. Another possibly relevant factor is suggested by Sartre's admission: "I had definitely decided to familiarize myself with the love of German women, but I soon recognized that I did not know enough German to talk with them. . . . I remained completely dumb and did not dare to try anything."[2] To talk German philosophy probably requires rather more German than seducing German women. Meantime, Sartre's recourse was the French wife of one of his fellow students, and his intellectual activities too seemed to have been confined within the French Institute, where he dedicated himself to living again the life he had lived in the *École normale* in Paris.[3] In short, Sartre never visited Freiburg before the war, he never met Husserl, and he did not meet Heidegger until long after the war.[4]

Everything I have just reported belongs to intellectual history. Even though the story is not true, its being told and gaining currency are facts of intellectual history. That the story may have gained currency because Heidegger was not dealing with the relation between himself and Husserl at a time when the problem of this relation had been posed by Sartre's bringing them together in *Being and Nothingness* is also a fact of intellectual history. However, it is a fact which impinges on the history of philosophy, to which we have to resort for an explanation as to why Heidegger was not dealing with his relation to Husserl and as to how Sartre deals with that in *Being and Nothingness*.[5]

Sequence

In much of Part 2 of the present volume, I shall be canvassing episodes in intellectual history which impinge on the history of philosophy. In tracking down some of their philosophical implications, I am preparing to continue designing, in Part 3, a distinctively philosophical analysis, which I would characterize as history of philosophy rather than merely intellectual history and which is to be applied in Volume 2. Thus some further indications may be helpful now with respect to the sequence I am following. For, as I stressed earlier, sequence can present disconcerting difficulties to an expositor examining the relations between philosophies.[6]

In the Chapter 4 I was recalling the postwar epoch as Derrida demarcates it, where not only in France, but even around the world, Sartre occupied the foreground, while Husserl and Heidegger remained in the background and were not understood in what later came to be regarded as their own terms—in Derrida's idiom were "not read" or were read (in the idiom I have adopted) *à travers de* Sartre. This recollection, I have already anticipated, will provide some justification for my departing from the conventional chronological sequence and beginning my commentary in Volume 2 with the influence of Husserl on Sartre, Husserl's most influential disciple. The postwar reading of Heidegger would seem to bear out his warning that his philosophy encountered "almost insurmountable difficulty of understanding."[7] In contrast, Sartre's philosophy has emerged as more readily accessible (presumably, in part, because he was concerned to be accessible), and the relation to Husserl implicit in his philosophy should also be more accessible than Heidegger's relation to Husserl is in Heidegger's philosophy.

So far I have assumed that since Sartre brought Husserl and Heidegger together in *Being and Nothingness,* Sartre's relation to Husserl might be pretty much comparable with his relation to Heidegger. The difference I have acknowledged is that Husserl was not able to protest Sartre's interpretation of him, whereas Heidegger did. I have given Heidegger's protest precedence as possibly shedding some light on Sartre's relation to Husserl as well as to Heidegger. But we still have to examine from Sartre's side his relation to both Husserl and Heidegger.

In this examination, I shall follow a sequence which is authorized by a pronouncement of Sartre's in 1940 that "serious studies must begin with Husserl, the master, and later reach Heidegger, the dissident disciple."[8] This sequence Sartre himself had already followed when he made this pronouncement, so I find it authorization for me to examine first, and separately, Sartre's relation to Husserl before examining his relation to

Heidegger. What I would then get at next is the relation between Husserl and Heidegger in Sartre's *Being and Nothingness,* in order to show that it is not a simple confusion but is structured by Sartre's own philosophy.

The Encounter

Aside from the sequence Sartre endorses as a requisite for "serious studies," there is considerable evidence which seems to warrant the conclusion reached by Sartre's biographer Annie Cohen-Solal that from 1933 to 1939 Sartre did not read Heidegger but "read Husserl exclusively." [9] So let me pay almost exclusive attention to Sartre's relation to Husserl during this prewar period.

Earlier, I quoted Sartre on the voracity with which he consumed Husserl's works during his year in Berlin. In the notebooks he kept in 1939–40, Sartre recalls how

> Husserl had taken me over. I saw everything in terms of the perspectives of his philosophy. . . . I was "Husserlian" and would remain so for a long while. At the same time, the effort which I had expended to *understand*—that is, to break my personal prejudices and to grasp his ideas starting from his own principles and not mine—exhausted me philosophically, that year [in Berlin].[10]

Sartre adds that he spent four more years on Husserl, which brings us up almost to the outbreak of the war.

Sartre's last philosophical undertaking before the war was *Psyché* (a term he took over from Husserl without acknowledgment), but he decided that most of what he had written merely "repeated ideas of Husserl's which I had absorbed."[11] He salvaged only a fragment, which he published as *Sketch of a Theory of the Emotions* (1939).

Husserl's impact on Sartre is summed up by Cohen-Solal: "Sartre discovers, with Husserl, phenomenology, which will remain, forever, *the* encounter of his life: he will never give it up."[12] But more important for my present purposes than Husserl's enduring influence on Sartre is the completeness of Sartre's conversion to Husserl. That Sartre then had no comparable interest in any other philosopher is in sharp contrast with Sartre's readings in literature, which were wide and miscellaneous. His readiness to designate himself a "disciple" of Husserl is striking, since his commitment at that time was to be a "loner" (*l'homme seul*).[13]

It is not just that Sartre attempted, as we have seen, "to grasp [Husserl's] ideas starting from his own principles and not mine." The fact that Sartre, four or five years after his conversion, could discount most of what he had written as "pure Husserl, not at all original" suggests a degree of abnegation which would be unusual in any philosopher but particularly in one so prone to *contestation*.

Thus Sartre provides a remarkable specimen of discipleship, which is the simplest, most accessible of relations between philosophers, to the extent that a disciple is someone who has not proceeded (or not yet proceeded) from his mentor's philosophy to reach a separate philosophy of his own. Such discipleship on the part of a philosopher as prominent as Sartre will later become, is a rather unusual episode in the history of philosophy. More often someone gets underway as a philosopher because he is sensitive to unresolved issues between his predecessors, as is the case later with the Sartre who would resolve in *Being and Nothingness* the issues dividing Husserl and Heidegger. The relative simplicity of Sartre's initial relation to Husserl, especially if compared with his later relation to Husserl and Heidegger, is an extreme case of the influence of predecessor being all-embracing, and it is an exceptionally advantageous starting point for formulating some of the problems which the relations between philosophies pose for the historian.

Sartre's prewar *L'imaginaire* is the most suitable work for determining Sartre's initial relation to Husserl. Sartre himself acknowledges, "I wrote an *entire* book inspired by Husserl—*L'imaginaire*." [14] But the precise character of Sartre's initial relation to Husserl can be determined only by conscientious commentary on this specific work, and this commentary has to be postponed until Volume 2, since some more general problems of the relations between philosophers have to be brought out first in this preliminary volume for their bearing on how I should proceed in this commentary.

Via Levinas

One of the more general problems is illustrated by an obvious complication in the relative simplicity of Sartre's initial relation to Husserl. It could perhaps be delegated to intellectual history, but it does have philosophical implications. It is that Sartre's conversion to Husserl took place before he ever read a word of Husserl's. The conversion was triggered by a report on Husserl that was delivered over drinks by Raymond Aron, who was back from his fellowship in Berlin for the midwinter holidays: "Aron pointed to his glass. . . . You can talk about this cocktail, and it's philosophy." How intoxicating Sartre found the prospect of such a shift in *level* is evident from his reaction: "Sartre turned almost pale with emotion. For years this had been his fervent wish: to speak of things, as he came into contact with them, and that this would be philosophy." [15]

Sartre then rushed out to purchase the only full-length exposition of

Husserl available in French—*The Theory of Intuition in Husserl's Phenomenology,* a dissertation which Emmanuel Levinas had written under Husserl's supervision in 1928–29. Thus Sartre read Levinas in French on Husserl before he ever read Husserl himself. Indeed, Sartre never pretended that he had gained his initial access to Husserl directly. Instead he regularly admitted, "I came to Husserl *via (par)* Levinas." [16]

I have already illustrated that this kind of indirect access is a traditional proceeding. The "epoch" which Derrida delimits as a "not-reading" of Heidegger was a period when Heidegger was approached *via* Sartre—most strikingly in the case of Beaufret, since he later became so unreservedly a Heideggerian.

The deviousness of the *viae* by which access is gained to major philosophers can often be left to intellectual history, but a philosophical implication does attach to Sartre's access route to Husserl, at least for a historian focusing on the relations between philosophies and concerned in the first instance with how these relations are conceived by the philosophers themselves. Levinas himself had a conception of the relation between Husserl and Heidegger. He explains that his "objective" in the dissertation is "to grasp" Husserl's "fundamental and simple aspiration," and with this objective in mind he will "not hesitate to take into account the problems posed by philosophers who are Husserl's disciples and, in particular, Martin Heidegger, whose influence on this dissertation will often be recognizable." Indeed, Levinas believes that "the intense philosophical life which animates Heidegger's philosophy sometimes permits us to render more precise the contours of Husserl's philosophy." For Levinas is convinced as an expositor that "the influence of a thought on important disciples [*disciples de valeur*] permits without doubt . . . a more accurate assessment than would the laborious study of a conscientious commentator." [17]

I shall save most my own doubts until Volume 3, but at least this generalization can be taken as encouraging me to take into account the influence of Husserl's thought on as important a disciple as Sartre. But from the arguments for so doing which I have already deployed, it is clear that I have different criteria from Levinas as to how "precision" and "accuracy" are to be satisfied. Any major philosophy is complicated, and to attribute a "fundamental and simple aspiration" to him is to commit oneself to vulgarization, granted that it will spare one laborious and conscientious commentary.

It is true that Sartre was himself committed to vulgarization, at least for political purposes. But one characteristic of the kind of vulgarization I am now recognizing is its successiveness—one *via* after another *via*. Thus vulgarization can become an almost infinite regress. But once this regress has been sufficiently illustrated as a traditional proceeding, it becomes prudent for the historian of philosophy to cut it short at some point. This I shall soon do, by observing that even if Sartre "came to Husserl *via* Levinas" in early 1933 in Paris, by the next fall he was in Berlin devouring Husserl on his own. So I don't propose to try to determine exactly the significance of Levinas as an access route to Husserl. It will be enough, in Volume 2, to examine Sartre himself as an access route.

Mutual Students

Given what we have learned about Levinas, we should, before we return to France, make the transition from Husserl to Heidegger as it was made by philosophers in Germany. When Levinas was in Freiburg, he attended Heidegger's as well as Husserl's lectures. Husserl himself was not yet fully aware of the extent of Heidegger's defection, or at least he was not sharing his misgivings with students in residence. He was more frank with a former student at the distance of Poland, to whom he had written late in 1927, after the publication of *Being and Time,* that Heidegger's work . . . in method and content appears to be essentially different from mine." He wrote a month later, "I allow myself to become depressed by . . . the fact that my better students, . . . instead of finishing what I have started, time and time again prefer to go their own way. So also Heidegger." The hope lingered with Husserl of an access route: "Our mutual students" might provide a "bridge between us." [18] But this hope vanished too, as Husserl became aware that there was no warrant for speaking of "mutual students," since his were deserting him for Heidegger. If Levinas did not desert, this may have been in some measure because he was submitting his dissertation at the University of Strasbourg, where its sponsor, Jean Héring, had been a student of Husserl's in the pre–World War I generation. Perhaps Levinas can be regarded as having himself come to Husserl via Héring. Suffice to say that by the 1930s Husserl himself had come to view Héring as a vulgarizer who had tried to extract a philosophy of religion from phenomenology.[19]

Two matters can perhaps be explained by the fact that Levinas was not sensitive in 1930, as Husserl himself was, to how Heidegger's work was essentially different from Husserl's. Levinas even cherished the impression that Heidegger was a disciple of Husserl's, which (it is fair to stress) Heidegger never had been.

First of all, there is that interesting story that Heidegger, "when asked soon after the war about his early acquaintance with Sartre, did not at first remember him by name, but then identified him as 'the Frenchman who had always confused him with Husserl.'" It is hardly surprising that Heidegger had trouble remembering Sartre by name, since he had never met him. But if the story has any basis, it is possible that the student he identified as "the Frenchman who always confused him with Husserl" was Levinas. Would this originally Lithuanian Jew have been by then sufficiently Frenchified to be remembered as a Frenchman? He did give French lessons to Frau Husserl. Would Heidegger (whose peasant provinciality is something to which apologists for his Nazism sometimes call attention) have himself confused a Lithuanian Jew with a Frenchman? Whatever the answer to these questions, Heidegger's confusion over the confusor would have a certain appropriateness in view of Sartre's own emphasis that he had come to Husserl "*via* Levinas."

More important is that Levinas's insensitivity to the essential differences between Husserl and Heidegger may help explain Sartre's own prewar insensitivity. Cohen-Solal goes too far when she suggests that Sartre then "read Husserl exclusively." She cannot herself actually have read Sartre's prewar phenomenological writings, for in each of them Heidegger is mentioned. What is true is that Sartre, in making these references, assumes (like Levinas) that what Heidegger has to say is not only consistent with Husserl but is even of assistance in elucidating him.[20]

It was later when Sartre began rereading Heidegger in 1939 that he recognized there were differences between Husserl and Heidegger and that there was a place for a phenomenology which would adjust these differences. He reports this in the letter to Simone de Beauvoir which I have already quoted, and he explains he is entertaining an idea which will at last allow him to "reconcile Heidegger and Husserl."[21] The "bridge" Husserl hoped for from their "mutual students" was finally built by Sartre in *Being and Nothingness.*

Sartre might not have thought that they were reconcilable if he had not gained his initial access to Husserl *via* Levinas and then, as he himself admitted later in life, "understood Heidegger *via* Husserl much more than in his own terms."[22] Will I be risking a comparable failure of understanding when, in Volume 3, I finally respect conventional chronology by myself approaching Heidegger *via* Husserl? To minimize this risk, I have thus far been disregarding conventional chronology, in order to come to some preliminary appreciation of what it means to fail to understand a philosopher in "his own terms" as a result of coming to understand him *via* another philosopher.

However, the failure illustrated by Sartre (and by the "epoch" Derrida demarcates as dominated by the "authority " of Sartre) is more complicated, since Sartre (and this epoch) eventually arrives at an understanding of neither Husserl in his own terms nor Heidegger in his own terms. Instead, both of them are understood largely in terms of *Being and Nothingness,* not just in France but worldwide.

We need to see now that the problems of dealing with the relation between Husserl and Heidegger would not receive an adequate illustration from Sartre's relatively simple initial relation to Husserl. We need to take into account the complications illustrated by *Being and Nothingness.* There we need to begin with the way in which the relation between Husserl and Heidegger first assumed in France a different guise than it had initially for Levinas and Sartre. Thus our next concern is not with how Sartre reconciled Husserl and Heidegger. Rather, we must examine how he first discovered that Heidegger was no longer, as Levinas assumed, simply a disciple of Husserl's but "a dissident disciple," one whose differences with his master needed to be reconciled. When Sartre made this discovery, he also discovered that he was no longer himself simply a disciple of Husserl's.

Turning

I turned toward Heidegger.—Sartre

The Shift in Allegiance

I am not just piling up further evidence as
to the length of time it can take for a philosophy, as difficult as Husserl's or Heidegger's
to make headway against vulgarization (for
example, by Sartre) and become understood, each in its own terms. What I would
bring out is that the relation between Husserl and Heidegger, as conceived by their
successors (to whom, I stress again, their
relation was more significant than it was to
either Husserl or Heidegger himself), does
not remain a fixed relation. Derrida's comment on Levinas's dissertation is that "in
1930 Levinas turns toward Heidegger
against Husserl." But in 1930 Levinas is not
yet aware of his debt to Husserl's disciple
Heidegger as a shift in allegiance, and the
quotations I have already offered bear me
out.[1] Derrida is so sensitive himself to the
differences between Heidegger and Husserl
that he is seemingly reluctant to recognize the extent to which Levinas could initially overlook them. We have watched
Levinas turn "toward Heidegger" in his
dissertation, but his turning was not
explicitly for him a turning "against
Husserl." However, in later works Levinas
does become responsive to the differences.

What solicits the historian's attention
here is not that Levinas as an individual
turns "toward Heidegger" but that this turn
is taken by nearly all of Husserl's former
disciples. Thus this shift in allegiance
amounts to a broader historical pattern,

something more than an episode in the history of an individual philosopher.

To illustrate this broader pattern, some other philosophers besides Levinas might be mentioned, before I resume the exposition of Sartre as the most influential. The two disciples whose turning would have been the most distressing to Husserl (if he had been aware of it) were those of his research assistants—Ludwig Landgrebe and Eugen Fink. They also deserve mention as access routes in addition to those I have already mapped.

If Sartre can say that he came to Husserl *via* Levinas, Merleau-Ponty can be said to have come to Husserl *via* Landgrebe and Fink. As Husserl's last research assistants, they enjoyed a certain authority with respect to the interpretation of "the last Husserl" (in Merleau-Ponty's periodization). Only after Merleau-Ponty read their articles in the Husserl memorial issue of the *Revue internationale de philosophie* (which was published in 1939, the year after Husserl's death) did he become seriously interested in Husserl. The reference in these articles to unpublished materials led Merleau-Ponty to visit Louvain, where Husserl's "Jewish" manuscripts had been transferred on the eve of the war. Fink was on hand to transcribe these manuscripts from Husserl's difficult shorthand. Apparently, Merleau-Ponty was the first visitor from France. Fink gave him some guidance on how Husserl was to be interpreted. Landgrebe, who was to work with Fink on the manuscripts, had not yet arrived from Prague, but one of the reasons for Merleau-Ponty's visit was his desire to read *Experience and Judgment,* a work of Husserl's which Landgrebe had compiled. On occupying Czechoslovakia, the Nazis had destroyed all the copies in stock of this "Jewish" work, and Merleau-Ponty had been unable to find a copy in Paris.[2]

Defectors

When, after the publication of *Being and Time,* Husserl lamented the loss of his "better students" to Heidegger, he never anticipated that, after his death, he would lose Landgrebe and Fink. I grant that any philosopher is more likely to find a Judas among his disciples than a disciple who will recline comfortably in the bosom of his philosophy. And I am not implying that Landgrebe and Fink were anything but honorable men. Their personal fidelity to Husserl was beyond the shadow of a doubt. Fink stuck with Husserl even when the Nazi government stopped the funding for Husserl's assistant, and both Landgrebe and Fink went to work in the archives at Louvain at a time when this entailed considerable risk. But Husserl would never have confused such personal fidelity with philosophical allegiance. In 1931, during a conversation at which Fink was probably present, Husserl condemned two students who had defected to Heidegger, but he went on to assert, "Landgrebe will go the right way." [3] There is no doubt, however, that if Husserl had been alive to contemplate Landgrebe's or Fink's postwar writings, he would have had to conclude that their allegiance, too, had shifted toward Heidegger.

Nevertheless, by virtue of the authority they enjoyed as interpreters of a still largely unpublished Husserl, they remained in demand at Husserl conferences in France and Belgium after the war. Thus when Merleau-Ponty refers in his 1959 commemorative essay on Husserl to erstwhile students of Husserl's who had known "daily intercourse" with him and "listened to his lectures" (unlike Merleau-Ponty himself), he must have had in mind Landgrebe and Fink, as well perhaps as Levinas and Héring, for all those *viae* to Husserl were also contributors to the commemorative volume. [4]

In his contribution Levinas was more cognizant than he had been in his dissertation itself that "the confrontation" between Husserl and Heidegger had furnished in the Freiburg of 1928–29 "an important subject of reflection and discussion for those students then finishing up who had been trained by Husserl before coming to know Heidegger." [5] Levinas singles out Landgrebe and Fink by name, but he does not add that since that time they had turned (as Derrida says of Levinas) "toward Heidegger against Husserl."

We have already seen an instance of this turning in France, besides Levinas, in Beaufret. We heard him admit that when he first read Heidegger in 1931, "I understood nothing of what he was saying." [6] Instead, he became interested in Husserl as a result of reading in 1939 Sartre's essay "Intentionality: A Fundamental Idea of Husserl's Phenomenology." Having thus reached Husserl *via* Sartre in that essay, Beaufret's allegiance shifted to Heidegger *via* Sartre in *Being and Nothingness* (1943). Beaufret's shift is not surprising, since in *Being and Nothingness* the shift in Sartre's own allegiance had become manifest. Indeed, Beaufret's shift is philosophically less interesting than Sartre's—not just because Sartre provided stimulus for Beaufret's successive moves but because Beaufret can hardly be credited with ever arriving at a philosophy of his own. Instead he became completely the disciple of Heidegger and (to revert to one of the analogies I used at the beginning of this volume) "some sort of ambassador" to the French on behalf of Heidegger's higher philosophical authority.

Epochs

Although Sartre, in the Berlin essay he wrote on "Intentionality" in 1933–34, assumes that intentionality was as fundamental an idea to Heidegger as it was to Husserl, he was by 1939 becoming aware of the differences between them. In his wartime journal he reports, "I turned toward Heidegger." His turning can perhaps be said to have culminated in *Existentialism Is a Humanism* (if, with some skepticism, we accord this work the importance Heidegger does in his "Letter on Humanism," for the purpose of appraising Sartre), in which Husserl is not even mentioned.

Shifts in allegiance are more accessible than the other shifts I have been sorting out and, thus, often become punctuation marks in intellectual history. But more is at stake than a concession to intellectual history in my expounding these shifts. Derrida demarcates a postwar epoch when the predominant intellectual scheme was the"humanistic" or "anthropologistic" interpretation which was imposed on Husserl and Heidegger in France, although they had alike denounced it. In order to frame this epoch, Derrida holds the scheme fixed, as "common ground" (*le sol commun*) of the prevailing philosophies.[7] But there is no solid ground here. And I would, as a historian, reinstate the dynamics of the experience of those who lived through this epoch, which was marked by a shift in allegiance, on the part of an array of philosophers. Derrida does notice this shift in the case of Levinas, who is the French philosopher of the epoch in whom he is apparently the most interested (at any rate, more interested than he is in Sartre), yet he does not treat the shift as a more general feature of the epoch itself.

Distinctions can now be drawn with respect to the relation between Husserl and Heidegger in France which are comparable to the distinctions I drew earlier with respect to the shifting relation between Sartre and Heidegger in France. During the prewar epoch (aside from refugees who were aware of the "lurch" that *Being and Time* had been away from Husserl), there was no general attention to the differences between Husserl and Heidegger; during the war (and the postwar epoch on which Derrida comments), differences were recognized but were assumed by Sartre and by Merleau-Ponty to be reconcilable; during the third epoch, to which Beaufret and his followers as well as Derrida and his allies belong, the differences came to be considered irreconcilable.

Originality

*How can anyone resign himself to being the
disciple of someone else?—Simone de Beauvoir*

Disarray

Before continuing my analysis of the relations between philosophers, I must pause to
take into account a compunction which has
been dogging my steps since my Introduction: given my focus on these relations—and
now on the shifts in these relations—what
happens to the individual philosophy? Or to
put the question in a fashion congenial to
Sartre: What happens to the originality of
the individual philosopher?

This question became more acute when I
claimed that a case of discipleship presents
the simplest, most accessible of relations between philosophers. Sartre proved a suitable
candidate. He acknowledged himself a "disciple" of Husserl's and announced he was
prepared "to break my personal prejudices
and to grasp [Husserl's] ideas, starting from
his own principles and not mine."[1]

Nevertheless, originality remained for
Sartre an imperative criterion in assessing his
own accomplishment, and some implications
of this criterion can be explored much more
appropriately by reference to him than to
our other three phenomenologists. We have
watched him apply it by his discarding of
most of his major prewar undertaking,
Psyché, because it was "pure Husserl, not at
all original." When he became aroused by
Aron's report of Husserl, we saw that Sartre's
first move was to purchase the only work on
Husserl available in France, Levinas's dissertation. Sartre impatiently leafed through it—
a moment of "complete disarray" for him,

according to de Beauvoir, because he was alarmed by the thought that Husserl "has already discovered all my ideas." [2]

Simone de Beauvoir asks, "How can anyone resign himself to being the disciple of someone else?" And she asks this question more on Sartre's behalf than her own.[3] But the question itself was prompted by her reading an article of Fink's which had come out during the academic year that Sartre spent in Berlin, after the impact of Aron's report, studying Husserl and from which Sartre himself quotes in the essay *The Transcendence of the Ego* that he wrote that year. I can't be confident that de Beauvoir herself actually read Fink's entire article. Her question could have been prompted by Husserl's prefatory statement, in which he emphasizes how he had "guided Fink's philosophical studies from the very start of his career" and that he is "happy to be able to state that it contains no sentence which I could not entirely accept as my own." [4] Why Husserl would seek this kind of discipleship is a question that must be deferred to Volume 3. But it can be safely said now that Sartre was not that kind of disciple.

When Sartre recalls how "I wrote an entire book inspired by Husserl—*L'imaginaire*—he is not recalling complete abdication. For he adds that he was writing "against him too, but only insofar as a disciple can write against his master." [5] How far is this? There is clearly an adjustment here in their relation which will require, as I have already admitted, conscientious commentary in Volume 2. De Beauvoir assures us that in *L'imaginaire* "Sartre invented both method and content, obtaining all its materials from his own experience." [6] In Volume 2 I shall demonstrate that her boast on behalf of her man is not entirely warranted.

Freedom

It is Sartre's own commitment to his originality which compels him to set down in his wartime journal in 1940 a report on how he turned "toward Heidegger" by subsuming the specific issue of this turning under a general issue: "If one wants to understand the respective roles played [generally] by freedom and destiny with respect to what is called 'succumbing to an influence,' I can reflect [specifically] on the influence Heidegger has exercised on me." [7]

Sartre is writing in 1940: he has not yet written *Being and Nothingness* (1943) and is not yet the philosopher of freedom that he will go down as in the history of philosophy; nor is he the novelist of freedom that he will become when he writes his *Les chemins de la liberté* (the first two volumes of which were published in 1945). What does become clear in his 1940 report is that the "freedom" at stake is the intellectual initiative which he can regain despite Heidegger's paramount influence on him.

The issue is perhaps subtler than he himself explicitly acknowledges, for his formulation of the issue of influence itself is influenced by Heidegger. Sartre had no conception of "destiny" (except possibly in *Er l'Arménian,* which has not even to this day been published) until he encountered *Geschick* in his reading of Heidegger. The conception of "freedom" which he will adopt in the journal entry will also betray Heidegger's influence.

The general issue Sartre is raising of "succumbing to an influence" can interest the historian of philosophy from another angle. Such succumbing is the stock-in-trade of intellectual history, which is often the history of how anyone whose thinking makes a splash in history because others have succumbed to his influence had himself succumbed previously to influences. To the extent that the history of philosophy becomes absorbed in intellectual history, philosophers tend to become diluted into influences. A rough difference here between intellectual history and the history of philosophy is that a philosophy traditionally involves a more sustained effort to exercise intellectual initiative, in an area of greater scope, than is usually credited to other intellectuals. This is a difference which acquires philosophical significance in a philosophy such as Sartre's, in which a premium is put on originality, exercising initiative, freedom, and so forth. Hence "succumbing to an influence" becomes a philosophical issue for him. To put the issue more in my own fashion: Is Sartre merely a vulgarizer of Husserl and Heidegger, or is he in some respects original?

Contingency

If intellectual history has a role to play here in relation to the history of philosophy, it is to get the facts of influence straight—though which facts are philosophically significant is a matter determined by the philosophy in question. Take as a first illustration the way Sartre's conversion to Husserl has been handled, for this is an obvious occasion on which he was prepared to succumb to an influence.

I have already begun quoting an account provided by an eyewitness, de Beauvoir, and we have since seen she is alert to the threat to originality that discipleship presents. She recalls how, when Sartre first learned of Husserl from Aron, Sartre's leafing through Levinas's dissertation was a moment of "complete disarray" because he was alarmed by the thought that Husserl "has already discovered all my ideas." But this is her later account of the conversion. It is clear from her earlier account that what Sartre was alarmed about was not "all" his ideas but, specifically, the idea of contingency. "He felt a sudden shock finding in Levinas some allusion to contingency. Someone had cut the ground from under him. Reading further, he was relieved. Contingency did not seem to play an important role in Husserl's system." [8] By and large, de Beauvoir is an informant who is *bien rangée*. But in this instance, with the passage of time, one specific idea of Sartre's has become "all" his ideas.

Much worse is the way de Beauvoir's earlier account is embroidered on in the standard and acclaimed biography by Annie Cohen-Solal. The latter has Sartre

> leafing through Levinas awkwardly, almost devouring it, with the impression that with each page he is falling on something familiar which he recognizes: at first sight, in any case, Husserl frequently took up the concept of contingency. Thus it was that Sartre encountered Husserl: up until 1939, in philosophy, Sartre will read Husserl exclusively. [9]

"Awkwardly," "devouring," "each page," "familiar," "frequently" are all embroidery, since Cohen-Solal's narration is based on de Beauvoir's eyewitness account. There Sartre could not have read "each page," since he was "in such a hurry to get the information that, as he walked, he leafed through the book without even having cut the pages." [10]

Such embroidery on a source is something to which intellectual historians are sometimes prone. Here it hardly matters philosophically, since in this account (as in de Beauvoir's account) what does survive is the fact that Sartre felt that the originality of his most cherished philosophical concept was at stake. But if this is the case, it would seem to be worth determining (especially since this encounter with Husserl was "*the* encounter of his life," according to Cohen-Solal) to what extent Sartre was in fact original. The sort of phrase that would have disconcerted him at first sight (that is, in the early pages of Levinas's exposition) was the statement that "negation or contingency . . . is inherent in existence." [11]

Since this encounter was with a philosopher, Cohen-Solal might well have asked, Does Husserl (or even Husserl as expounded by Levinas) frequently take up the concept of contingency at second sight? He does not. This is a fact. But the philosophical issue is, Why not? Neither Cohen-Solal nor de Beauvoir bother to explain, so we are left with the impression that contingency was something he simply overlooked.

Husserl does not frequently take up the concept of contingency because what concerns him is not "existence" but the intuition of essential structures. He follows a procedure he calls the "eidetic reduction," by which our consciousness is "led back" from the existing particulars. They are, as such, contingent (for example, a particular act of perception by a particular person) and are eliminated from consideration in favor of how (for example) any act of perception is necessarily structured. Thus contingency could not play an important role in Husserl, and Sartre had every right to feel that his originality was intact vis-à-vis Husserl.

Of course, philosophical issues are often dissipated in an intellectual history. In the present instance, at the moment of Sartre's conversion to a philosophy, when "Aron pointed to his glass" and announced to Sartre that in Husserl "you can talk about this cocktail, and it's philosophy," Cohen-Solal has no interest in what the philosophy is. She plays up the dispute over what was in the glass:

> Apricot cocktail, or a simple glass of beer? The legend still hesitates on the drink which was a feature of the blessed day when Aron . . . expounded his recent philosophical discoveries. Simone de Beauvoir affirms that what was in question, beyond doubt, was an apricot cocktail; Raymond Aron, on his side, swears to the gods that it was only a glass of beer. Sartre, so far as I know, did not commit himself on the identity of the drink.[12]

A textual analysis of *Ideas I* reveals that a glass does turn up there in Husserl's initial inventory: "Immediately, physical things stand there as objects of use, the 'table' with its 'books,' the 'drinking glass,' the 'vase,' the 'piano,' etc."[13] But, unfortunately, this hardly settles the issue between Simone de Beauvoir and Aron over the identity of the drink.

Even more unfortunately, the *identity of the drink* is not the philosophical issue. What Sartre turned almost pale with emotion about is not pure Husserl. The *Trinkglass* belongs at the level of particular things around us, and of our particular acts of consciousness with reference to these things, before the eidetic and phenomenological reductions supervene to "lead" consciousness "back" from this level so that it can re-flect on the structure of any act of perceptual consciousness as identical for all such acts.

Husserl regarded this higher level that was to be reached as the level where a "pure phenomenological analysis" could be conducted. I don't want to go so far as to argue that when Sartre speaks of "pure Husserl" (and means primarily that there was no originality in the phenomenology he himself was then setting forth in *Psyché*), his usage has been contaminated by Husserl's. "Pure" is not a word that Sartre favors as a philosopher, except when it is Husserl's criterion that Sartre retains as applicable to the way in which Re-flection can emancipate consciousness—for example, from self-deception. In my Volume 2 my commentary on Sartre's prewar phenomenology will confirm that Husserl would have regarded him as having failed to carry through these reductions. In fact, we shall see that Sartre undertakes his analysis of imaginative consciousness without recourse to the phenomenological reduction and that the "leading back" in the case of the eidetic reduction is so minimal that Sartre can (as I observed earlier) "repeat . . . what has been known since Descartes, that a reflexive consciousness provides us with data which are absolutely certain." [14] Thus he prefers the expression "eidetic intuition" to "eidetic reduction," as we have seen.

Sartre's preference probably betrays what is original in his analysis vis-à-vis Husserl's. Instead of carrying out (or fully carrying out—any more precision must wait upon my second volume) Husserl's reductive shift in *level*, Sartre tends to remain at the level of particular things as we come into contact with them (in the phraseology of Simone de Beauvoir's report on his conversion). Thus Cohen-Solal's raising the question of "the identity of the drink" may be whimsical, but it is not entirely irrelevant in Sartre. In contrast, it is entirely irrelevant in Husserl, a failure to carry out the eidetic reduction, which eliminates all such *faits divers* from consideration, so that the identity which is allowed to survive is that of any act of perception, whose structure remains identical whatever the diversities of particular acts of perception.

Husserl himself mocked lingering at the level of particular things as "picture-book phenomenology" (*Bilderbuchphänomenologie*).[15] It was from his perspective a relapse from the distinctive level of "pure" phenomenology—one of those relapses to which the label of "vulgarization" might be supplied.

A supplementary or alternative explanation of why Sartre throughout his career usually refers to "eidetic intuition" or to "eidetic analysis" rather than to the "eidetic reduction," is the emphasis in Levinas's dissertation that Husserl's phenomenology was a theory of intuition. If so, it is an explanation which belongs to intellectual history rather than to the history of philosophy and, thus, provides an illustration of the distinction I would draw between the two. Access routes (*viae*) to a philosophy belong to intellectual history, though they may have philosophical implications. What matters in philosophy are issues, and in my Conclusion, which will be transitional to my Volume 2, I shall bring out the issue of principle which is motivating Sartre in his reluctance to leave behind entirely the level of contingent particulars, to the point that he was prepared to weaken the distinction of level that the eidetic reduction presupposes and enforces.

Shifts in allegiance can also hardly be accepted as philosophically pivotal, but they too may have philosophical implications. As I have suggested, when Sartre gained his initial access to Husserl *via* Levinas's *Theory of Intuition in Husserl's Phenomenology* and for a moment felt his originality threatened, it must have been because he had come across the statement there that "negation or contingency . . . is inherent in existence." Sartre was encountering a juncture (unbeknownst to himself) at which Levinas's exposition of Husserl had been contaminated by Heidegger—where (as Levinas put it generally) he did "not hesitate to take into account the problems posed by philosophers who are Husserl's disciples and, in particular, Martin Heidegger, whose influence on this dissertation will often be recognizable." [16]

Nausea

I am picking up again the question of Sartre's originality, for if it only briefly disconcerted him in relation to Husserl, it recurs later in relation to Heidegger. De Beauvoir overlooks it here, as does Cohen-Solal with her conclusion, which I have already quoted, that "up until 1939, in philosophy, Sartre will read Husserl exclusively." Perhaps Cohen-Solal did not herself read Husserl or Levinas or Heidegger. But she should have read Sartre's four prewar philosophical writings: if she did, she would have found references to Heidegger in them.[17] If she didn't, she must at least have read Nausea, Sartre's most famous literary work, and have had some familiarity with its most famous scene—the nauseous encounter with contingency in the public garden.

Reading Nausea should have disturbed her conviction that before the war Sartre read Husserl to the exclusion of Heidegger. Nausea, to be sure, has features which might seem "Husserlian," For example, the protagonist's description of things around him seems inspired by Husserl (even though it is "picture-book phenomenology"), and I shall examine it in my Volume 2. But the climactic episode in the novel, the hero's vision in the public garden of "being-there" as contingent, betrays Sartre's indebtedness to Heidegger. Hence three pages of this vision were offered as an appendix to the first scholarly work on Heidegger to be published in France, La Philosophie de Martin Heidegger (1942), by A. De Waelhens. Consider his explanation: "Allow me to cite here from Nausea, which translates with a force and clarity which cannot be equaled the central experience of Heidegger's philosophy." [18]

So strenuous a contention deserves comment. On the one hand, Sartre may still be trivially indebted to Husserl in this vision. At its focus is his experience of an individual tree, and this example had turned up in Ideas I, in Sartre's Berlin essay on intentionality in Husserl, as well as earlier in Sartre before he read Husserl. But there are no individual trees in Being and Time. On the other hand, though Sartre's debt to Heidegger in the vision is irrefutable, A. De Waelhens blurs certain relevant distinctions. The central experience of Heidegger's whole philosophy in Being and Time is anxiety, not nausea. What A. De Waelhens could not have known is that anxiety would become the central experience in *Being and Nothingness,* which was not published until 1943, the year after his book on Heidegger.

Moreover, though in *Being and Nothingness* anxiety jostles nausea to one side, nausea still remains a distinct experience, if diminished in its scope. Sartre describes it as an insipid [*fade*] taste . . . which stays with me in my efforts to get away from it." [19] Although A. De Waelhens's book on Heidegger shared in the vogue that *Being and Nothingness* lent to *Being and Time,* no one seems to have noticed that Sartre's brief description of nausea in *Being and Nothingness* is not simply a phenomenological description of an experience but is, rather, a translation from Heidegger of the "indifferent and pallid indeterminate lack of mood [*ebenmässig und fahle Ungestimmtheit*] which is often persistent and wherein being becomes satiated with itself." [20] Sartre's *fade* translates Heidegger's *fahle,* and the next phrase spells out Heidegger's "persistent" (*anhaltende*). Heidegger himself did not give a name to the experience he is describing. Sartre doesn't either, until after he has given his ostensible description. Then he adds, "This is what I have described elsewhere under the name of nausea." But Sartre does not admit that one place the experience, if unnamed, had been described elsewhere before was in *Being and Time.* Sartre is able to give it a name because he has made one adjustment, which might be rated a shift in *level:* what was entirely indeterminate in Heidegger becomes determinate as a "taste" in Sartre, and it is this determination which enables Sartre to identify it with nausea.

Biography

Since Sartre had, in *Nausea,* previously translated Heidegger (in A. De Waelhens's extended sense of "translation"), Cohen-Solal is flagrantly wrong in her conviction that before the war Sartre read Husserl to the exclusion of Heidegger. Conscientious commentary is rarely more futile than when it would buttress a protest against what a writer does to a philosophy when this writer is addressing the more or less general public. I have thus far restricted the attention I pay to "the terrain of vulgarization" only to those instances when that terrain is occupied by philosophers themselves—but I am now allowing myself this one exception. In the present instance there are certain philosophical points I want to make.

Sartre's life (and hence a biography of him) may seem to the general public very much more interesting (all those women . . .) than his philosophy. But if a biography is worth undertaking, some justice should be done to the preferences of the person undergoing the biography: Sartre's life was the life of someone who said of himself, "The only thing I really like to do is to be at my desk and write—preferably philosophy." [21] While I am granting that a philosopher at his desk is not of much public interest, what is philosophically interesting about Sartre is the *interplay* between his philosophy and his life. It is the philosophical character of this *interplay* which I have brought out by the shift in *level* which takes place in his philosophy in its relation to Husserl's with Sartre's repudiation of the transcendental ego and the rigid distinction in Husserl of the philosophical from the personal (in Husserl, the personal can be eliminated as merely contingent). Here it might be interesting to recognize (especially if one is writing Sartre's biography) that this shift in *level* may have lent encouragement to Sartre himself to undertake biography and autobiography—not to mention all the autobiographical evidence which he supplied to prospective biographers throughout his life. This evidence includes the 1940 report in the wartime journal which I mentioned at the beginning of this chapter. However, this report deserves a more careful examination if we would determine the circumstances under which Sartre turned "toward Heidegger against Husserl."

Immersion

History *was all around me, philosophically first of all.*—Sartre

Historicity

A feeling for contingency is hardly sufficient to encourage one to resort to biography or autobiography. Indeed, this feeling was involved in bringing to a halt the attempt of Sartre's protagonist in *Nausea* to write a biography. Nor is *Nausea* itself autobiographical; at least Sartre does not identify with its protagonist.[1] But when we go on from *Nausea* to *Roads of Freedom,* the sequence of novels Sartre began next, on the eve of the war, we encounter a protagonist who is a stand-in for Sartre himself, and we see the refurbishing as characters of members of his actual entourage.

Sartre soon dismissed the first novel in this sequence, *The Age of Reason,* as a "Husserlian work, which is rather disgusting when one has become a zealous convert to Heidegger."[2] In acknowledging this second conversion, Sartre is somehow able to overlook the zeal with which he had in *Nausea* transcribed as nausea what he took to be Heidegger's conception of the anxiety that a feeling of contingency promotes. For what preoccupies Sartre in his 1940 report of what has happened to him philosophically is Heidegger's conception not of contingency but of "historicity" (*Geschichtlichkeit*). This is the significant philosophical break in Sartre's career, instead of that indicated by Cohen-Solal's erroneous conclusion, "Up until 1939, in philosophy, Sartre will read Husserl exclusively."

In dismissing *The Age of Reason* as

"Husserlian," Sartre is characterizing it as "ahistorical," if I may borrow the term which had been used in Germany to dismiss Husserl as compared initially with Dilthey (and Hegel) and later with Heidegger.

The term "ahistorical" designates Husserl's failure to come to grips with history. But this metaphor is hardly vehement enough to apply to Sartre. It was history which "gripped" him. Later Sartre's doctrine will become total immersion in history. During his bitter dispute with Albert Camus, Sartre will mock Camus's statement, addressed to a Nazi soldier, to the effect that the soldier "was trying to 'make me enter history.' " Sartre ironizes:

> It's normal for Camus to lay down conditions before entering, . . . like the little girl who feels the water with her elbow, asking, "Is it hot?" You look on History with distrust, you insert a finger, which you pull back quickly, and ask yourself, "Does it have a meaning?" [3]

Sartre is implying that Camus was making a moralistic fool of himself by asking this question. But if we ask instead how history during the war became for Sartre more than a meandering of contingencies, how instead it came to have a meaning, it will soon be evident that the necessity of its having a meaning was provided less obviously by the actual history in which Sartre was immersed than by what Sartre took to be Heidegger's concept of "historicity."

Understanding

If Sartre's understanding of Heidegger in *Nausea* was an understanding of "the central experience of Heidegger's whole philosophy" (according to De Waelhens), it was not an understanding of the whole philosophy. This is apparent from the 1940 report: there Sartre lays out conditions for understanding which we can see he had not recognized before the war, when he wrote *Nausea*, but which now impel him to adopt Heidegger's philosophy of "historicity" and therefore to face the issue of "succumbing to an influence." This issue I have already anticipated, because it had already been posed for Sartre when he was converted to Husserl. But Sartre's conversion to Heidegger's philosophy of "historicity" posed it for him in different terms.

Before quoting portions of the report, I might observe that late in his life Sartre will recall that "there must have remained in me something of the professor for a certain length of time" and that "this was something that had to be smashed." [4] The pomposity of this report suggests he had not yet gotten around to smashing it, not even in a private journal:

It was *impossible* for me to study Heidegger earlier than I did . . . or to come to him with the intention of understanding. . . . The threats of the spring of 38, then of the autumn, slowly led me to seek a philosophy which . . . would enable me to hold out. I was in the exact situation of the Athenians after the death of Alexander, who turned away from Aristotelian science to assimilate the more brutal but more "totalistic" (*totalitaires*) doctrines of the Stoics and the Epicureans, who taught them to *live*. And then *History* was everywhere around me. Philosophically first of all: Aron had just written his *Introduction to the Philosophy of History,* and I was reading it. Then history surrounded me and gripped me as it did all my contemporaries. . . . I was still badly equipped with tools to understand it. . . . It was then that Corbin's book was published. Just when it was needed. Sufficiently detached from Husserl, desiring a philosophy that was "pathetic," I was ripe to understand Heidegger. . . . The "pathetic" of Heidegger struck home with its words of death, destiny, nothingness. . . . But above all it came at the right juncture. . . . I was waiting for *him* . . . , I wanted to be provided with tools to understand History and my destiny.[5]

Interplay

I would initially draw attention in this portion of the entry to how "history," if it was "everywhere around him," was "philosophically first of all." Sartre is distinguishing between the level of philosophy and the more immediately experiential level of living, and he is permitting *interplay* between these two levels. Some of the details of this interplay are worth enumerating.

1. The implications of Sartre's "turning toward Heidegger against Husserl" have gained in scope in two contrasting ways. On the one hand, they have gained historical scope from the academic history of philosophy Sartre had been saddled with—from the precedent whereby "the Athenians . . . turned away from Aristotelian science to assimilate the more brutal but more 'totalistic' doctrines of the Stoics and the Epicureans, who taught them to *live*." On the other hand, they gain affective scope in another entry, in which Sartre offers an explanation of why it was impossible for him to study Heidegger earlier than he did: "The essential fact was certainly the revulsion I felt toward assimilating this barbaric and unscholarly philosophy after the inspired academic synthesis that was Husserl's."[6]

2. However, Sartre's conversion to Heidegger did not take place di-

rectly: just as his access route to Husserl had been *via* Levinas, so it was via Aron's *Introduction to the Philosophy of History* that Sartre gained access to Heidegger's philosophy of "historicity." Throughout Sartre's career, there is often a certain indirect, secondary character about his relation to his German inspirers.

3. When Heidegger's philosophy provides Sartre with the "tools" for understanding the array of untoward experiences the war would mete out to him, we should recognize the twist given to the *interplay* between philosophy ("first of all") and history, for Sartre's adoption of the idiom of "tools" seems itself prompted by the prominence of manual tools in *Being and Time.*[7] But Sartre's philosophical "tools" are an idiom which Heidegger himself would have found an intolerable vulgarization—to intrude my own terminology. This is one illustration of how clean distinctions between the philosophical level and the lower level do not survive the *interplay* between levels.

4. There is, from Heidegger's perspective, further vulgarization in the shift in *level* with which Sartre adapts specific philosophical "tools" of Heidegger's. For example, in a letter written at this time Sartre proposes a "being-for-war" (*être pour la guerre*) on the model of Heidegger's "being-toward-death" (*Sein zum Tode*) and allows for variations in the personal reference which is not found in the model: "Each individual has his *own* war, as he has *his own* death; it is absolutely not a question of undergoing it as a cataclysm, but one has a being-for-war (which varies according to cases . . .), as one has a being-for-death."[8] In Heidegger himself, "being-for-death" is an essential structure, which does not vary according to individual cases.

5. There are additional shifts in *level* and *subject* which illustrate the difference between what will become explicitly Sartre's humanism (in *Existentialism is a Humanism*), in which "we are at a level where there are only men") and Heidegger's ontology ("We are at a level where there is principally Being").[9] Heidegger's "toward" (*Zu*) loses the distinctively ontological and temporal implications it has in *Being and Time* and becomes Sartre's psychologistic "for" (*pour*), acquiring voluntaristic implications.

6. Concomitantly with these shifts, the "tools" which are reported in the entry as having been provided for Sartre's understanding of his "being-for-war" become less distinctively designed for intellectual understanding (as compared with the "tools" Husserl could be said to have provided Sartre with earlier). Sartre's "pathetic" refers, after all, not just to *pathos* (presumably in the Aristotelian and Hegelian theories of tragedy) but also to the shift in *level* Heidegger had sought by rendering the

category of *Befindlichkeit* (the "affectivity," in Sartre's later translation, of how being-there "finds itself" there—"in-the-world"), which in Heidegger is "equiprimordial" with "understanding." [10]

7. The shifts in *level* from "being-toward-death" to "being-for-war" and from what was distinctively academic intellectual understanding in Husserl to the "pathetic" Sartre in turn imposes on "Heidegger's philosophy" as "his free taking upon himself of his epoch"—World War I and its aftermath—"which was a tragic epoch of *Untergang* and despair for Germany." [11] The difference here between Heidegger and Sartre, from the latter's perspective, is that history has not merely reproduced a comparable war experience in his case but also arranged that Heidegger's philosophical "tools"—forged during the first experience of world war—were available for Sartre's understanding the second time round. Again this would be vulgarization from Heidegger's perspective. He does not go in for such short-run epochs, and World War I and its aftermath are not mentioned in *Being and Time,* as if they were for him, as they are for Sartre, conditions for understanding what Heidegger understood in that work. The shift in *level* here in Sartre is completed in *Being and Nothingness,* for there he rejects Heidegger's "being-toward-death" (on which he modeled, in the letter, "being-for-war") but salvages a conception of "my war." [12] We have seen that "being-for-war" in the letter "varies according to cases" and so, presumably, can accommodate differences between World War I and World War II, as well as the different attitudes different individuals adopt toward the same war.

Academicization

Enough details have been sifted for us to appreciate how Sartre handles the issue he raised in launching his 1940 report:

> If I want to understand the respective roles played by freedom and destiny with respect to what is called "succumbing to an influence," I can reflect on the influence Heidegger has exercised on me. This influence sometimes has appeared to me recently as providential, since it has arrived to teach me authenticity and historicity at the very moment when the war was about to render these conceptions indispensable to me. If I were to try to figure out what I would have made of my thought without these tools, I would be overcome by retrospective fear. [13]

The influence to which Sartre has succumbed is not a historical destiny, in the first instance, but the influence of a concept of history (*Geschichte*) as "destiny" (*Geschick*). And he is asking, in the second instance, what role destiny played in his succumbing to this influence itself.

However, it is the role of freedom that is more threatened by "succumbing to an influence." Observe that what was threatened when Sartre succumbed to the influence of Husserl in 1933–34 was Sartre's originality, which was his own native concern. But Sartre's concept of "freedom" is no more his own free elaboration than is the concept of "destiny" with which it is linked. Not only is the idiom of "taking upon" a translation of Heidegger's *Übernahm*, but Heidegger has preceded Sartre in the exercise of this freedom. Heidegger's philosophy was "his free taking upon himself" of World War I, and Sartre follows him in now freely taking upon himself World War II. It might perhaps be added that Sartre's experience of this war was to a considerable extent reading and writing (the letters and notebooks I am quoting, as well as *Being and Nothingness*). His experience was "absolutely not a question of undergoing it [the war] as a cataclysm." [14] I am not sure he ever heard an enemy shot fired or a bomb dropped. Furthermore, with respect to his freedom, "Reading" to a considerable extent enjoyed precedence over "Writing." (This is the sequence of two titles under which his autobiographical *Words* is organized.) This precedence might be labeled an "academicization" of experience, using this label with a broader reference than Sartre's own reference to Husserl's philosophy as "academic" in contrast with Heidegger's "barbaric" philosophy. The label would also pick out a different sense in which "there must have remained in me something of the professor for a certain length of time."

Sequence

The professor was also a writer. The autobiographical report in the notebooks is crude as writing. Sartre may have been emboldened by what he took to be the crudity of Heidegger, since he was in effect reporting his conversion to Heidegger's philosophy. But later Sartre would become a subtler writer in his autobiographical *Words,* in which the stylistic attention that is lacking in the journal is paid to the way he employs words.

I offer this comparison to emphasize one respect in which the report in the journal cannot too easily be brushed aside. In *Words* philosophy takes precedence over Sartre's own history (in the usual chronological sense) in much the same fashion that "Reading" philosophy comes "first of all" in the report at a time when the war itself was still a phony war and Sartre not yet fully immersed in history. With reference to *Words,* Philippe Lejeune has posed the question "What sequence is one to follow, to tell the story of one's life?" as a "question" which "is almost always evaded, . . . as if it were not to be posed." It is usually assumed that fundamentally a "chronological sequence" is to be followed. Although "flashbacks" are permissible, the chronological sequence must remain fundamental, in order to give "the impression that a life is being lived." Otherwise, "the reader's distrust is aroused," and he suspects "artifice." (Earlier I tried to cope with the reader's distrust, as aroused by my own departures in the present volume from chronological history.) In *Words*, Lejeune argues, Sartre deludes us into thinking he is following the traditional chronological sequence (something I was not able to do), but while one finishes the book "believing that one has read a history, one has followed an analysis in which logical connections are disguised by a terminology which is chronological." In order to keep my emphasis on how in the report in the journal philosophy takes a certain precedence with respect to Sartre's "immersion" in "history" as it unfolds chronologically, I am drawing attention to Lejeune's comparable claim as to what is "the real sequence of *Words*, what, at the level of analysis, the narration is about which has made possible the writing of *Words*." [15]

I would add that the way history, which was "everywhere around" Sartre, was "philosophically first of all" is not in his report "disguised" by any convincing artifice, as in *Words*, and thus it seems incongruous with his own conviction of his complete immersion in history. When Sartre later rebukes Camus for failing to recognize this immersion, it is by relying on the metaphor of dipping merely an elbow or finger in. But when Sartre reports, "I was waiting for him [Heidegger]," because "I wanted to be provided with tools to understand history and my destiny," his extension of the scope of "tools" so that they become tools for understanding is hardly more consistent with complete immersion than is dipping, for it suggests an even greater separation between Sartre wielding the tools and what they are being employed upon.

My concern, however, is with the misunderstanding of Heidegger. Not only is Sartre misapplying Heidegger's conception of "tools" when he forges his own conception of "tools to understand history," but this misapplication is also inconsistent with the conception of affective understanding which Sartre also derives from Heidegger. For *Befindlichkeit* in Heidegger implies finding oneself there, not at a tool-wielding distance from what is "everywhere around me."

Sartre's even more fundamental misunderstanding was that what he was waiting for, and could get from Heidegger, was a philosophy of history. But what Heidegger provides as a philosophy of history is not entirely distinguishable from the philosophy of the history of philosophy it would become in his later works. And the history of philosophy as a discipline was of little interest to Sartre.

It is my interest here. And this is why I have been demonstrating that the history Sartre was immersed in was not raw and untreated. It had already been treated philosophically; consequently, in Sartre's retreatment of it, we encounter an episode in the history of philosophy involving the relation between philosophers.

Historical Considerations

There is another episode that I regard as a response to Heidegger, though Husserl was too bitter to mention him by name: "We must immerse ourselves in historical considerations if we are to be able to understand ourselves as philosophers and understand what philosophy is to become through us." [16] This behest (five years before Sartre's response to Heidegger but also unpublished at the time) is offered in the fragment that begins with the announcement "the dream is over," which has sometimes been taken as an announcement of the end of philosophy.

If I have postponed commentary on my epigraph until we ourselves arrived *in medias res*, it was because I wanted to have brought out first the "historical considerations" I would myself raise and to show how I would refocus the problems of understanding "ourselves as philosophers" on the failures of philosophers to understand each other. Husserl himself was simply mystified and demoralized by Heidegger's failure to understand phenomenology—Heidegger, someone brilliant who had worked closely with him.[17] Recall too Granel's appraisal of Heidegger's understanding of Husserl: "*Being and Time,* aside from occasional assertive moments (whose suppressed brusqueness itself creates problems), is immersed in a kind of fuzziness with respect to what has to do with its relation to Husserl's phenomenology." I was reluctant to tackle immediately problems created by brusqueness, especially when it was suppressed, and by fuzziness. Accordingly, I promptly switched from the relation between Husserl and Heidegger themselves to the relation between them in France, where previous failures to understand them and their relation were recognized in successive epochs—first, by Sartre's own wartime confession of his prewar misunderstanding of Heidegger and his relation to Husserl; and then, more notably, by Derrida, with his demarcation of the epoch in which Corbin's "monstrous" translation of the crucial term *Dasein* in *Being and Time* "dominated *via* the authority of Sartre."

Derrida's elucidation of this failure to understand is of interest to me because deconstruction (though it is a topic I am carefully postponing) is itself a way (or a variety of ways) of understanding philosophy and its history, and insofar as it is involved in philosophy's coming to an end, it should differ from the previous ways of understanding philosophy and its history, which remain confined within this history. Eventually, sifting these differences should contribute to defining deconstruction and the end of philosophy.

Ambiguities

Before resuming my analysis of Sartre's failure to understand Heidegger, let me bring in our fourth phenomenologist, in order to offer another comment on the character of my analysis of the history of philosophy itself. If I have so far left Merleau-Ponty largely to one side, this is not only because he comes last in the succession of our phenomenologists but also because he is often ambiguous (almost deliberately so, it would seem) and difficult to pin down, as is illustrated by a comment of his: "History never admits to anything [*L'historie n'avoue jamais*]." [18] This comment on the ambiguity of history I cite now because I take it to have been to some extent a response to the kind of unambiguous certainties which Sartre felt himself able to extract from history, as we are seeing in his 1940 report—though what Merleau-Ponty would be thinking of are the later verdicts of history which Sartre regularly dished out in what would become the ten volumes of his *Situations*.

Merleau-Ponty's comment I would extend from history to the history of philosophy, but without his note of defeatism, since I have some hope that I can, with my present undertaking, cut down the range of this history's ambiguities.

Let us review some of these ambiguities, overlooking those introduced by the *viae* which I have already tracked. Sartre has insisted on his immersion in history, but it is also his immersion in the philosophy of history which he finds conveyed by Heidegger's concept of "historicity." This ambiguity is complicated by a further ambiguity in Heidegger himself. For the philosophy of history in *Being and Time* to which Sartre responds will turn out in Heidegger's later works to be a philosophy of the history of philosophy, to which Sartre will remain indifferent.

Translation

In explaining Sartre's response to Heidegger's concept of "historicity," another *via* besides the Aron of the *Introduction to the Philosophy of History* should be taken into account. We have seen that Sartre, like Derrida, distinguishes two epochs in the understanding of Heidegger: the first (prewar), when he failed to understand Heidegger; the second, when he succeeded (or failed again, according to Derrida). [19] Sartre draws a sharp contrast between his failure in the first epoch (in 1934 in Berlin he had planned to read Heidegger "after Easter," but gave up) and his success in the second epoch (having "read him without difficulty last Easter [that is, in 1939, on the eve of the war] . . . without having made in the meantime any progress in my knowledge of German"). Corbin's translation facilitated his access:

> Certainly, if Corbin had not published his translation of *Was ist Metaphysik?* I would not have read it. And if I had not read it, I would not have undertaken last Easter to read *Sein und Zeit.* And certainly . . . the publication of *Qu'est-ce-que la métaphysique?* . . . really constituted for me an encounter.[20]

This portion of Sartre's report is confusing. In a footnote to the page I am quoting, he recalls, "I had read, without understanding it, in 1930 *Qu'est-ce que la métaphysique?* in the periodical *Bifur.* This footnote refers to Corbin's translation of *Was ist Metaphysik?;* in the text of his 1940 report, Sartre must be referring to the anthology *Qu'est-ce que la métaphysique?* This anthology included in addition to Heidegger's inaugural lecture other selections and, in particular, the chapter from *Being and Time* entitled "Temporality and Historicity." It is because the anthology included this chapter that the distinction between it and what had been translated before in *Bifur* has helped explain how Sartre succumbed to Heidegger's influence in two successive steps. As I indicated earlier, despite Sartre's disclaimer of any understanding, his attention had been drawn in 1931 to the inaugural lecture *Was ist Metaphysik?* if only because Corbin's translation appeared in the same issue of *Bifur* as a portion of a literary work by Sartre.[21] Here the evidence I presented was the influence on the nauseous reaction to contingency in Sartre's *Nausea* of Heidegger's analysis of anxiety as a reaction to contingency. But the decisive influence in Sartre's own view was the concept of "historicity," to which he was exposed only by the 1939 anthology.

Le Sursis

One reason I have concentrated on Sartre is that he provides the most manageable illustration of the shift in *affiliation.* If Heidegger can be regarded as in some sense still a phenomenologist at the time he became committed to "the dialogue between the poet and thinker," he was not himself the poet in this dialogue. Merleau-Ponty was not a painter. But Sartre was himself a writer of literary works. When he reports his 1939 shift in allegiance (in Derrida's phrase) "toward Heidegger against Husserl," we have seen it is to dismiss what he was then writing as "a Husserlian work, which is rather disgusting when one has become a zealous convert to Heidegger." We naturally surmised that Sartre was referring to some philosophical work of his, but he is actually referring to a novel, *The Age of Reason.*

The novel in which Sartre demonstrates his conversion and is responsive to Heidegger's handling of "historicity" is the novel which followed *The Age of Reason* and which was entitled *Le sursis.* Sartre's editor Contat explains that the title is taken from the French translation, published in 1943, of a novel on the eighteenth century which "Sartre had not read: the title imposed itself on him as expressing at once the situation during September 1938 [the Munich crisis] and the philosophical idea that is a major theme of the novel—that of human existence *en sursis perpétuel.*" [22] Even so astute a reader of Sartre as Contat does not notice that this philosophical idea is elaborated by Heidegger. *Sursis* is Corbin's translation of Heidegger's *Ausstand.* Heidegger introduces the term in analyzing that trait of "being-toward-death" whereby it is "not yet." Something is still "outstanding" which belongs to "being-there" but is "still lacking." Sartre clearly exploits this section 48 of *Being and Time* for his own analysis of "lacking" (*le manque*) in *Being and Nothingness,* even while repudiating Heidegger's "being-toward-death." [23]

The English translation *The Reprieve* translates the French title *Le sursis* but fails to translate the German behind it, and so weakens the implication of "being in suspense" (*être en sursis*—Corbin's translation), the sense that something is still impending. [24] It remains plausible, of course, that Sartre was encouraged to adopt the title from its previous use as the title of a novel. But since he hadn't read that novel, the title could have retained implications from what he had read in Heidegger, mediated by Corbin's translation. Contat does emphasize that Sartre borrowed the title from the novel "at a moment when the outcome of the war is still uncertain." In handling the Munich crisis in *Le sursis,* Sartre plays up the uncertainty of its outcome, not that the negotiations may succeed in achieving a "reprieve."

History could again (with Heidegger's and Corbin's assistance) function as a condition for Sartre's understanding Heidegger's conception of *être en sursis.* I return to Sartre's report: "The threats of the spring of 38, then of the autumn, slowly led me to seek a philosophy which was not only a contemplation [as was "the inspired academic synthesis of Husserl's"] but . . . wisdom, heroism, sanctity—anything which would enable me to hold out." [25] "Autumn" refers, of course, to the Munich crisis, whose "menace" would become the subject of *Le sursis*—the novel in which Sartre turned "toward Heidegger against Husserl."

NINE

Turning Point

The war really divided my life in two—Sartre

Periodization

At the end of my Introduction, I acknowledged that the problem of periodization
plagues almost any historian, including the
historian of philosophy. At the end of Chapter 6, I distinguished three periods in the
French assessment of the relation between
Husserl and Heidegger. I focused on the second period, because it began when the relation between Husserl and Heidegger became
a general problem, as Husserl's disciples
turned "toward Heidegger against Husserl."

In Chapter 7 I narrowed my illustration
of the problem of periodization to the relation assumed by Sartre between Husserl and
Heidegger. The period which begins with
Sartre's conversion to Husserl in 1933, and
ends with his becoming "a zealous convert to
Heidegger" in 1939, is not a period when
Sartre read Husserl to the exclusion of Heidegger (as Cohen-Solal claims) but a period
in which he (like nearly all of his French contemporaries) was insensitive to the differences between Husserl and Heidegger, despite his having been able to exploit in
Nausea (1938) the philosophy of contingency which Heidegger had elaborated.
What happened in 1939 was that Sartre not
only turned "toward Heidegger against Husserl" but also turned toward a different Heidegger—the Heidegger who had elaborated
a philosophy of "historicity," from which
Sartre was able to extract the concept of
being kept "in suspense" by history, as I explained in Chapter 8.

What I have not yet fully explained is how Sartre himself, as well as de Beauvoir and Cohen-Solal, could overlook his earlier debt to Heidegger. I believe that much of the further explanation needed is that an overriding effect of Sartre's wartime immersion in history, abetted by Heidegger's philosophy of history, was Sartre's becoming committed to a periodization whereby it was "the war" which "really divided my life in two." The war was "the real turning point [*le tournant*] of my life." [1]

What has to be kept in mind is not just the distinction, which I have stressed, between Sartre's earlier feeling for contingency and his later feeling for "historicity" but the sharpness, which came with his feeling for "historicity," of his feeling for the dividing line itself. Late in his life he reports that "what I see most sharply in my life is the break [*coupure*] whereby there are two periods almost completely separated, to such a degree that, being in the second, I no longer recognize myself very well in the first—that is, before the war." [2] This break is so sharp to him, in retrospect, that the war had also to become for him the dividing line between his having been a disciple of Husserl and his having become a "zealous convert" to Heidegger.

One of the disadvantages of being exposed to history is that one is exposed to its cunning and its ironies. Though Sartre had admitted before his death that he had become a "has been," [3] the irony since his death is that the prewar Sartre whom the postwar Sartre was no longer able to recognize very well now receives more recognition than the postwar Sartre. What is happening is (as Boschetti has put it) an "inversion of Sartre's own career. One returns . . . to the Sartre . . . who was . . . the disciple of Heidegger. To the public figure of the period after the war is now preferred the young Sartre revealed by his letters and the wartime notebooks." [4]

The Public

If I had not learned that I was in step with the Sartre now in vogue in our present period, I might not have felt justified in dragging my readers through the thickets of the notebooks in order to distinguish the two different periods of his life. The "public figure of the period after the war" is (I need hardly remark) the existentialist. So it might be asked, How much has been left to Sartre in the way of existential initiative after his succumbing to the influence of Heidegger *via* Aron's opportune *Introduction to the Philosophy of History* and via Corbin's opportune translation of the "Temporality and Historicity" chapter? Sartre himself recovers a certain initiative by suggesting that "if Corbin has translated *What is Metaphysics?* it is because I am (among others) freely constituted as the *public* waiting for this translation, and in this respect I am taking upon myself my situation, my generation, and my epoch."[5] The concept of "taking upon," as I have already indicated, is Heidegger's; the concepts of "situation," "generation," and "epoch" are featured in *Being and Time* and are found in the "Temporality and Historicity" chapter. Since in our present period, according to Boschetti, we have turned our back on Sartre "the public figure," there is perhaps a further irony that one fashion in which the Sartre "revealed by the . . . notebooks" does exercise his freedom and achieve originality, while otherwise succumbing to the influence of Heidegger, is with his conception of "freely" constituting himself "among others" as "a *public* waiting" (*public attendant*). This exhilarating conception is hardly compatible with Heidegger's conception of the bondage imposed by *Öffentlichkeit*, which will become a "dictatorship" in the "Letter on Humanism."[6]

Yet Sartre himself seems oblivious as to how extraneous to Heidegger his conception is, even though it nestles in Sartre's entry alongside conceptions he did derive from Heidegger—"situation," "generation," and "epoch." Earlier in his entry, Sartre simply reported, "I was waiting for him [Heidegger]." Since what has happened to this simple declaration in the later reformulation is largely due to the influx of jargon from Heidegger, we suspect that the model for Sartre's conception of being "freely constituted" as a "public" is the "taking upon" myself, which is a free operation in Heidegger and which turns up in the next clause of Sartre's sentence.

Sartre's originality might well seem too fumbling to be worth recognizing, did he not later elaborate a full-fledged theory of the role of the waiting public in producing a literary work:

> For the work to emerge, a concrete act is necessary, which is called reading. . . . But the writer cannot read what he writes. . . . In reading, one foresees, one waits [*on attend*]. . . . Readers are always ahead of the sentence they are reading in a merely probable future, which partly collapses and partly is consolidated as they progress. . . . Without waiting, [*attente*], without a future, without ignorance, there is no objectivity.[7]

That is to say, no literary work.

The writer himself cannot "wait" in the requisite fashion. He knows, or at least has to decide, what is going to happen. Thus he is dependent on the reader's collaboration for the creation of the work. At this juncture "the public" enters Sartre's analysis as *une attente*. It is defined as "an immense feminine interrogation, the *attente* of an entire society."[8] We recognize that "public accessibility" is as indispensable in Sartre as it is a menace in Heidegger.

Sartre's adoption of *What is Literature?* as a title for this theory may have been a reminiscence of the title *What is Metaphysics?* I don't know if Heidegger is aware of Sartre's theory when he suggests in the "Letter on Humanism" that Sartre is catering to "the market of public opinion." [9] In any case, a complicating factor is the shift in affiliation. For Heidegger draws an insurmountable distinction between literature (the affiliate of Sartre's philosophy) and poetry (the affiliate of Heidegger's thinking). The poems which Heidegger enlists in *What Invokes Thinking?* (*Was heisst Denken?*), he explains, "do not belong to literature." In discounting literature, Heidegger brings to bear the same criterion with which he had discounted Sartre in the "Letter on Humanism": the "destination" of literature is "to be accessible to a reading public [*einer Öffentlichkeit für das Lesen*]." [10]

Now that this denouement of the relation between Heidegger and Sartre has been anticipated, we can return to Sartre's 1940 report for one final irony. Sartre's last thought on Corbin's translation is to ask: "But why was the first translation of Heidegger and not of Husserl, . . . since, as a matter of fact, serious studies must begin with Husserl, the master, and reach Heidegger later . . . ?" This is the sequence, I observed, Sartre himself had followed. Sartre's answer is that Husserl "is not accessible to the general public." Heidegger, however, is: "Even though it cannot be understood by most of them, the 'pathos' of Heidegger makes a forcible impression, with the words 'death,' 'destiny,' 'nothing' tossed around. But, above all, he turned up at the right time." [11]

The unintended irony is double-edged. On the one hand, Sartre assumes that he, unlike the general public, understands Heidegger, and his assumption he would in part justify by having, "as serious studies must," approached him "*via* Husserl." But later in life, Sartre will be forced to recognize the extent to which during the war he had failed to understand Heidegger, and the reason he will give is that he had "understood Heidegger *via* Husserl much more than in his own terms." On the other hand, during the war Sartre saddled Heidegger with public and contemporary accessibility—a criterion which Heidegger's philosophy in *Being and Time* required him to repudiate and with which he will later saddle Sartre.

Solipsism

I am not implying that Heidegger made no discernible contribution to Sartre's wartime conception of "the public." So far in discussing Sartre's explanation of why the public was waiting for Corbin's translation of Heidegger, I have been concentrating on the fact that "above all, he turned up at the right time"—with most of his "Temporality and Historicity" chapter included in the Corbin anthology. I have accordingly stressed that Sartre was turning "toward Heidegger against Husserl" because Husserl was "ahistorical." I have not yet taken into account another factor—the "impasse" which Sartre admits in his 1940 entry he had reached in Husserl and which, to get out of, he had to turn to Heidegger. It was the problem of solipsism.[12] And what Sartre turned toward specifically here in Heidegger was the concept of "being with" (*Mitsein*), so that the former *l'homme seul* arrived (albeit in parentheses) at his own conception of himself as "(among others) freely constituted as the *public* waiting for this [Corbin's] translation."

By the time Sartre deals with the problem of solipsism in *Being and Nothingness*, a shift in *level* takes place, comparable to the shift which is implicit in his developing in the 1940 report a concept of "being-for-war"—"my war."[13] In *Being and Nothingness* he is insistent that "the relation of *Mitsein* cannot help at all to resolve the psychological, concrete problem of our recognition of the other."[14] Thus Heidegger turns out here to be only a way station, *via* which Sartre reaches his own analysis of our being "among others."

Even though Heidegger's *Mitsein* soon proves of no help, in the 1940 report it meshed with Sartre's historical experience of "being-for-war" as distinctively a social experience. The prewar Sartre, I have just recalled, thought of himself not as "among others" but as *l'homme seul*. If for Sartre "the war really divided my life in two," it was not only because it immersed him in history but also because this history was social history. He "made a transition from individualism and the pure individual to the social, to socialism."[15] And it is this respect too that he regarded the war as "the real turning point of my life."

This turning point is one juncture at which it is perhaps safe to say that the experience which intervened between the 1940 report, when he endorsed Heidegger's concept of *Mitsein,* and *Being and Nothingness*, when he no longer found the concept much "help," was not largely academic. Sartre's experience of being "among others" became concrete in the prisoner of war camp: "I . . . experienced absolute proximity. The boundary of my living space was my skin. Day and night I felt the warmth of a shoulder or of a thigh against my body."[16] The intervening experience was concrete, but philosophy intervenes with a shift in *level* when Sartre adopts the criterion of concreteness, and I'll return in my Conclusion to consider this criterion.

The Affiliate

Since Sartre thought of himself as above all else a writer, the war was also the turning point in how he thought of himself as a writer,[17] and it was in his sequence of novels *Roads of Freedom* that he most obviously "made the transition from individualism and the pure individual to the social, to socialism." In the initial novel the protagonist is still *l'homme seul* (as he was in *Nausea*), and not only is the sequel, *Le sursis*, his first significant effort in social history, but his second significant effort in the theory of the novel set forth in *What is Literature?* The prewar *l'homme seul* put a premium on his own originality as an individual, which seemed briefly threatened when he encountered Husserl. With the "transition from . . . the pure individual to the social," Sartre's emphasis switched to the waiting public, of which he was a member, "among others." Thus he makes a transition in *What is Literature?* from "Why Does One Write?" to "For Whom Does One Write?"

Recall our earlier surprise when Sartre referred to his disgust with a "Husserlian work" and we discovered it to be a novel. I then offered this discovery as indicating that we had to take the shift in *affiliation* into account (as well as the other shifts) in dealing with Sartre's relation to Husserl. But we must also take it into account in dealing with Sartre's relation to Heidegger—that is, to the two Heideggers of the two different periods in Sartre's development (I forbear nicknaming them "Heidegger I" and "Heidegger II"). The experience of history and of the social is consummated in a novel of Sartre's (as previously his experience of contingency had been) before he was able to follow out the philosophical implications of the experience in a fashion which satisfied him. Sartre does not regard himself as elaborating a social philosophy until his quasi-Marxist *Critique of Dialectical Reason* (1960).[18] To this extent, the shift in *subject* to the social takes place in the affiliate before it takes place in Sartre's philosophy. I have already discussed *Le sursis*, the novel in which Sartre at last becomes "a zealous convert to Heidegger" by immersing its characters in history. It is also a distinctively social novel in that these characters, many of whom have never met one another, nonetheless share the experience of waiting upon the outcome of the Munich crisis.

If a lag is to be acknowledged between *Le sursis* (1945) as a social novel and Sartre's achievement of a social philosophy in the *Critique* (1960), a lag should also be acknowledged with respect to his earlier treatment of contingency—only, in this instance, Sartre himself is explicit. He explains that he treated contingency in the scene in the public garden in *Nausea* and that he had treated it in a novel because his conception was "not yet solid enough to make a philosophical work out of it."

There may be more than mere coincidence in the fact that it was in 1931 that Sartre abandoned as unpublishable *La légende de la vérité* in favor of reworking his treatment of contingency.[19] For that was the year in which Sartre read Corbin's translation of *What is Metaphysics?* in the same issue of *Bifur* as a fragment Sartre had salvaged from *La légende*. When Sartre confesses that he did not understand Heidegger in 1931, it could be taken as meaning he did not understand him for philosophical purposes in the way he could in 1939, after the Corbin anthology had been published and he himself was immersed in social history and launched on the writing of *Being and Nothingness* (1943). I argued earlier that we have to account for Sartre's debt to Heidegger for the literary purposes of *Nausea*—the debt which A. De Waelhens was able to recognize even before *Being and Nothingness* was published. I then further argued that an alternative or reinforcing explanation was that the war had become for Sartre so sharp a historical dividing line, in the light of his philosophical understanding of Heidegger's concept of historicity, that he disregarded his earlier literary understanding of Heidegger's concept of contingency.[20]

Development

I warned earlier that in order to focus on the relations between philosophers, I could not linger in this history with the internal development of any philosophy. Yet I have gone to some lengths in examining the dividing line in the internal development of one of our four philosophers. An obvious reason is that this dividing line was a "turning point" which entailed his turning "toward Heidegger against Husserl" and thus illustrated how the internal development of a philosophy can involve changing relations between philosophies.

Another reason is that the problems of dividing lines—of discontinuities and how they are to be measured against continuities—cannot be shirked in any history. Of our four philosophers, Sartre is committed to the "break" that is the sharpest and so the most easily located. It is, he has explained, "between two periods almost completely separated." It seemed worthwhile to exhibit what this break involved, because the problems of discontinuity (or of discontinuities) in Heidegger's development, even if it is of much more philosophical interest than Sartre's, are so difficult to assess that it is not even certain that the term "development" is appropriate to Heidegger.

So far I have taken up only the most accessible problems of Heidegger's "development"—or at least those that are the most canvassed—those having to do with his Nazism. We have heard Aubenque assert that "there is really a rupture . . . between Heidegger's philosophical works before 1933 and his discourses of 1933 having reference to circumstances." Other interpreters were equally confident that there is a definite continuity. Even aside from the issues of Heidegger's Nazism, there are the issues of his long-run development: Is he to be sliced up into "Heidegger I," "Heidegger II," and perhaps Heidegger III, or is one of his favorite citations from Hölderlin applicable—"Where you started out, there you will remain"?[21]

However, I must repeat, it is not even certain that the term "development" is appropriate for Heidegger, especially since he finds himself involved in a "turning" in the "history of being" which is more sweeping in scope than any "development" that could be segregated from it as internal to his philosophy. The only other generality that can be offered now is that the "turning" does not seem to represent the sharp "break" that Sartre's "turning point" does.[22] Yet the "turning" in Heidegger is a "break" inasmuch as with it the end of philosophy is being reached. Indeed, it is because I am concerned in the long run with the concept of "the end of philosophy" that I am concerned to provide illustrations, within the confines of the history of philosophy, of significant "breaks."

Sartre may ostensibly borrow from Heidegger the concept of "historicity" (*Geschichtlichkeit*). But Heidegger protests that "Sartre . . . does not recognize the essentiality of history [*Geschichte*] to being."[23] With the shift in Sartre to "a level where there are only men," Sartre obtains a concept of "history" that approximates what we vulgarly think of as history: I have begun with this concept as more accessible than Heidegger's concept of "historicity" and have accordingly considered the most significant moment in Sartre's history—the "break," or "rupture," that was the "turning point."

This "break" is of some general interest to the historian in that it was promoted by Sartre's sudden immersion in history itself, he having been previously ahistorical, a disciple of Husserl's. But we have seen that Sartre's immersion was not simply immersion in raw history; it was abetted by Heidegger's philosophy of history, which enabled Sartre "to understand my historicity," at the same time that history was enabling him to understand Heidegger—or so Sartre supposed.

Here the originality to which Sartre was committed, his freedom, seems in jeopardy. But now that I have made my comparison with Heidegger, I can claim that the sharpness of the break is a feature not of Heidegger's but of Sartre's own philosophy. If I have not yet pursued this claim, it is because its implications are more readily followed out when it is couched in terms of another comparison—between Sartre's and Merleau-Ponty's philosophies. In these terms, the sharpness of the break is a feature of Sartre's philosophy as a philosophy which Merleau-Ponty found "too exclusively antithetical." [24]

Merleau-Ponty is thinking of the antithetical dialectic of *Being and Nothingness* itself. Thus what I am suggesting is that the history of phenomenology is not a history in which any of our four philosophers hew to the same conception of the history of the development of his own philosophy as would the other three. Husserl can be included in this comparison if we recall how his unremitting efforts to carry out the re-flective turning of consciousness back on its own acts, in order to examine their essential structures, precluded any concern with merely contingent, particular facts—including the facts regarding his previous efforts as having fallen short of grasping essential structures and the facts regarding the succession of those efforts—in short, the facts which would compose the history of the development of his philosophy. [25]

Accordingly, we are up against philosophies which are recalcitrant, each in its own different way to being lined up in a single overall history of phenomenology, within which the development of each could be fitted. An expedient the historian can then adopt is to locate decisive junctures at which the different ways our philosophies are recalcitrant can be discerned. These are the junctures at which the shifts I have sorted out take place. These shifts constitute the "breaks" in the relations between philosophers. And these are the "breaks" on which I would rather focus than on any "breaks" which may punctuate the internal development of each philosophy. This is why I brought to the forefront of my analysis the "lurch" of Heidegger's "break" with Husserl.

I conceded that this "break" might have defeated the undertaking of a history of phenomenology had it not been repaired by Sartre and Merleau-Ponty. We remember how when Sartre turned "toward Heidegger against Husserl," he soon came to entertain "a central idea which will at last allow me . . . to reconcile Heidegger and Husserl."

Accommodation

This reconciliation, which Sartre carried out in *Being and Nothingness,* I would now compare with Merleau-Ponty's reconciliation, in order to provide still another illustration of the point I have already illustrated with regard to the three preceding phenomenologists: none of them hew to the same conception of the development of his philosophy as the others. Thus Merleau-Ponty, unlike Sartre, does not acknowledge a "turning point" in his development after which he can no longer recognize what he had been previously. It is not surprising then that what Sartre emphasizes at the beginning of his memorial essay is how "Merleau told me one day . . . that he had never recovered from an incomparable childhood." The same continuity is displayed in Merleau-Ponty's philosophy; he is not prone to the sharp "breaks" we find in Sartre's. Thus he is an important exception to the general pattern I have discerned of turning "toward Heidegger against Husserl." For when Merleau-Ponty turns "toward Heidegger," he does not turn "against Husserl."

Merleau-Ponty's reconciliation of Heidegger with Husserl is correspondingly easier. From his assessment of *Being and Nothingness* as "too exclusively antithetical" we can infer that he would also find Sartre's handling of the relation between Heidegger and Husserl too exclusively antithetical—if, that is, my claim holds that the relation between philosophies can be as much a feature of the philosophy in which this relation is found relevant as any other seemingly more substantive feature. Thus the fashion in which Merleau-Ponty's philosophy is more accommodating than Sartre's is a feature of Merleau-Ponty's philosophy, rather than of either Husserl's or Heidegger's, just as the fashion in which Husserl and Heidegger become antithetical in *Being and Nothingness* is a feature of Sartre's philosophy, not of either of their own philosophies.[26]

When Merleau-Ponty appraises *Being and Nothingness* as "too *exclusively* antithetical," he betrays his own commitment to accommodation, which precludes his accommodating the commitment to the exclusively antithetical that he discerns in Sartre. Leaving aside the broader question of the relation between being and nothingness in Sartre, it can be said that Sartre's handling in *Being and Nothingness* of the relation between Husserl and Heidegger, though often initially antithetical, is only an occasion for *Being and Nothingness* to supervene as their reconciliation. Thus the more general differences between Sartre's and Merleau-Ponty's philosophies include the differences between the ways each of them handles the differences between Husserl and Heidegger. However, the problem still remains as to how to be more specific about the differences between all four of our phenomenologists.

THREE . METHOD

TEN

Access

Phenomenology is accessible only via *a
phenomenological method.—Merleau-Ponty*

Via

The last of our four phenomenologists, Maurice Merleau-Ponty, begins his major work
with the question, "What is phenomenology?" He adds, "It may seem strange that
this question has still to be asked half a century after the first works of Husserl. The fact
remains that it has by no means been answered."[1] It may seem even stranger that I
am making still another attempt to answer
the question, nearly a century after the first
works of Husserl. But another fact will soon
emerge: Merleau-Ponty's answer does not do
justice to the differences between our four
phenomenologists, including their different
conceptions of the relations between them.
To seek access to the relation in Sartre between Husserl and Heidegger, I have gone
behind the shift in Sartre's allegiance from
the one to the other to reach the shifts in *subject, level,* and *affiliation.* This was a step in
working out in this preliminary volume the
method by which I would analyze the relations between philosophies. Before I go any
further with this method, I come up against
the fact that phenomenology has its own
method. This has to be taken into account,
as I continue to work out my own method.
Thus Merleau-Ponty's answer to the question, "What is phenomenology?" is dictated
by his assumption that "phenomenology is
accessible only *via* a phenomenological
method."[2]

I am retaining the idiom of *via* here for
two reasons. On the one hand, I would mark

my own transition from the *viae,* the access routes, which I have consigned to intellectual history, to what I regard as the sense in which a
method can be an access route that a philosopher followed in arriving at
his philosophy and, so, can become an access route for the expositor to
follow—indeed anyone who would understand this philosophy as a philosophy. On the other hand, the idiom of going along "a way" (*meth-
odos*) was retained by Heidegger even after he repudiates (as we shall
soon see) phenomenological method, and method itself, as Cartesian and
modern.

For the present, I would observe that Merleau-Ponty specifies what
phenomenological method is by expounding the three procedures that
compose it: the phenomenological reduction, the eidetic reduction, and
intentional analysis.

The shifts I have already sorted out are traditional proceedings: by
carrying through these shifts, a philosopher proceeds from a previous
philosophy (or philosophies) to reach his own philosophy. I employ "proceeding" here in a philosophically neutral sense. But how any philosopher carries through these shifts is never neutral, for it is the elaboration
of his own philosophy. It is determined in Merleau-Ponty's case, for example, by his particular version of the three procedures he expounds.
Thus I am attaching terminological weight to the distinction the diction-
ary offers: a "procedure" is "the manner of proceeding"; it is a "proceeding" considered "with reference to its . . . method."

Shifts in Method

The shifts I have distinguished are no longer neutral but have become
specifically adapted to the history of phenomenology. What can be referred to as a "subject," as an "affiliation," or as a "level" (along with
what the specific subject is, as well as the specific affiliated subject, and
the specific level) can vary not only from one philosophical movement to
another but also from one philosophy to another within the same philosophical movement. I am not putting forward a metaphilosophical
schema that can dictate from some higher tribunal to philosophies what
they are undertaking but, rather, merely heuristic expedients designed to
help out in the no-man's-land of the relations between philosophies
where ignorant armies clash by night.

I shall try to analyze the differences in the method relied on by our
different phenomenologists as involving shifts in *method*—that is, as different respects in which each of Husserl's successors departs from the
procedures that compose phenomenological method in Husserl himself.
This is my final contribution to resolving one problem of access route—
of discovering what a philosopher is doing "in his own terms." I am re-

calling a standard demand, likely to be offered in objection to my focus on the relations between philosophies. We have encountered it in Rorty and in Sartre's mild rebuke to himself for having initially "understood Heidegger *via* Husserl much more than in his own terms." [3]

Although I am endorsing Merleau-Ponty's conviction that "phenomenology is accessible only *via* a phenomenological method," I am also recognizing that each of our four phenomenologists relies on a different method—that is, applies different procedures (or seemingly the same procedure but actually differently conceived) as composing this method. Having gone behind such shifts in allegiance as are instanced by Sartre's turning "toward Heidegger against Husserl" to the shifts in *subject*, in *level*, and in *affiliation* which distinguish Sartre's phenomenology, for example, from Husserl's and Heidegger's, we can get to the shifts in *method* that determine how Sartre carries out the other shifts.

I defer further consideration of these other shifts until after some preliminary consideration of the shifts in *method*. I take up Merleau-Ponty first, since he has offered the prospect of access *via* method. When he, in his presentation of a phenomenological method, reaches intentional analysis, he explains why he takes it up last of the three procedures: "We can now consider the notion of intentionality, too often cited as the principal discovery of phenomenology, whereas it is understandable only *via* the reductions." [4] I have not expounded adequately any of the three procedures, but even someone not familiar with them can see the access route Merleau-Ponty is following and the cogency he claims on behalf of it: first, "phenomenology is accessible only *via* a phenomenological method; next, "the notion of intentionality" is "understandable only *via* the reduction." By following this route, Merleau-Ponty is making a transition from "a phenomenological method," such as it might be applied in any phenomenology, to the specific phenomenological method he will himself apply.

Dismemberment

We become even more aware of Merleau-Ponty's access route when he disparages "the notion of intentionality" by complaining that it is "too often cited as the principal discovery of phenomenology." Although Merleau-Ponty could have other expositors of Husserl in mind too, we must not forget "the living dialogue, never interrupted with Sartre." [5] For Merleau-Ponty knows that Sartre's access route to phenomenology was by expounding intentionality as "A Fundamental Idea of Husserl's." Merleau-Ponty knows too (since it was just after the publication of *Being and Nothingness* that he put down on paper this disparaging remark regarding "the principal discovery") that intentionality had there again come to the fore in Sartre as "Husserl's essential discovery." [6] Merleau-Ponty insists that there is "nothing new" about it.

The procedure to which Merleau-Ponty accords priority in answering the question "What is phenomenology?" is the phenomenological reduction. In his later commemorative essay on Husserl, he singles it out as his "theme." I have already shown how elaborate is his preparation for announcing this theme: he sees himself confronted with German students of Husserl's who "initially invested philosophy completely in phenomenology," and he warns them that they "now risk being too severe toward it," whereas certain phenomenological themes . . . , in contrast, retain for the foreign spectator all their prominence." [7] He must have known how particularly severe Husserl's German students had been, almost without exception, toward the phenomenological reduction. Indeed, as soon as Husserl himself had offered them a formulation of it in his lectures, he discovered it was "unhappily, not understood." [8] He reformulated it at great length in *Ideas I* without its securing acceptance. It was the procedure which Husserl felt Heidegger had never understood. [9]

The transition that I make from intellectual history, which is punctuated by shifts in allegiance, to their implications for a history of philosophy now becomes more specific. Heidegger, and Husserl's German students who turned "toward Heidegger against Husserl," were repudiating as philosophers the phenomenological reduction. But Merleau-Ponty, who turned "toward Heidegger" without turning "against Husserl," continues to accord as a philosopher the phenomenological reduction the prominence Husserl accorded it.

The methodological issue between Merleau-Ponty and Sartre is thereby sharpened, for in *L'imaginaire* Sartre neglects the phenomenological reduction and relies on the other two procedures, intentional analysis and eidetic intuition. [10] Even in *Being and Nothingness,* he will not only give precedence to intentionality but will also characterize the work as a whole as "an eidetic analysis of self-deception." [11]

This dismemberment of the method of a philosopher who founded a movement—or, at any rate, the according of priority to one or more of his procedures over others—is a not uncommon trait of the relation between a founder and his successors. It can be regarded as a traditional proceeding, like dismembering his corpus and according one of his works (or the works of one of his periods) preeminence over other works. [12]

Sequence

The sequence whereby one philosopher may give one procedure priority over another as a component of a method may not seem all that crucial.

But sequence itself is not a casual affair. Method itself is conceived by Heidegger as a "succession of steps" (*Schrittfolge*),[13] and this conception is the most obvious trait of his conception of method itself as *meth-odos*.

I acknowledged earlier that differences in the sequence which each philosopher follows, as he proceeds along his "way," pose an obvious difficulty for the expositor who would discover how one philosopher is proceeding in relation to another. The expositor has to follow one of them long enough to determine the direction in which he is proceeding and then switch for a spell to the other philosopher's sequence. This difficulty I discussed earlier, when I first encountered it in my own exposition.[14] The difficulty is a juncture at which the historian of philosophy is obviously at cross-purposes with the philosopher who would maintain his own sequence and would suspect the historian of short-circuiting it.

When I was worrying earlier about the risks of my departing from the sequence followed by the philosopher I am expounding, I was in effect worrying about the damage that might be done thereby to his method. At the same time it is a risk to my own exposition of the philosopher, since the actual succession of steps he takes is itself important evidence as to the method he is following. In Volume 2 the difficulty will be less disconcerting: I shall usually be dealing there with just two philosophers, and I shall be able to follow the sequence in which Sartre proceeds in his analysis of imaginative consciousness. I shall pause only long enough to point out how what he takes over from Husserl belongs to a different sequence, which will be evidence of a different method.

At last I have reached the juncture in my own sequence at which it becomes feasible to explain more fully the difficulty which persuaded me to defer dealing with the relation between Husserl and Heidegger until Volume 3. When Husserl protests that Heidegger does not understand the direction in which he (Husserl) has proceeded, the reason he gives is that Heidegger did not understand the phenomenological reduction. This reduction is a *Zugangsmethode;* it provides "access" to phenomenology by a shift in *level*, which is also a shift in *subject*.[15] It not only thereby determines the direction in which Husserl proceeds, but it also itself has to be followed out in a "succession of steps" (to retain Heidegger's term) which Husserl carefully lays out in *Ideas I*.

This analysis, however, is difficult to translate into Heidegger's terms, as became clear when Husserl envisaged *Being and Time*, in the margin of his copy, as a perverse trans-lation of his own phenomenology which deprived it of its "entire meaning."[16] Now I can be more definite as to the difficulty. If I have taken note first of the different priority assigned the reductions, as over against intentionality, by Merleau-Ponty and Sartre, it is because Heidegger, in contrast with them, does not in *Being and Time* refer to any of the three procedures that, according to Merleau-Ponty, compose phenomenological method.

The Priority of Method

Earlier I commented on another difficulty: references to Husserl and phenomenology disappear from Heidegger's writings in the 1930s and 1940s. We are thus left without the *prima facie* evidence on which I prefer to rely. A longer-run explanation of how Husserl became irrelevant to Heidegger can now be offered, and it bears directly on my own procedure. When the references to Husserl are finally renewed near the end of Heidegger's career, it is with a criticism of Husserl for according "priority" (*Vorrang*) to method itself.[17] There is some prospect of obtaining some understanding of the differences between Sartre's and Merleau-Ponty's phenomenological methods: by considering the priority each accords to different procedures of Husserl's and following this up, of course, with an examination of the differences in their conceptions of the procedures themselves. There is no comparable prospect in Heidegger's case. Instead we are eventually confronted with the larger issue, less manageable for the purposes of a comparison, of his rejection of "the priority of method" itself.

What can we anticipate making out of this rejection? So long as Heidegger himself accorded a measure of priority to method, it was to a method which was phenomenological. In the *Prolegomena* (the lectures of 1925 which I have noted are often regarded as an early draft for *Being and Time*) phenomenology is identified as "originally a pure concept of method,"[18] and this method is expounded as the procedures of intentional analysis, the eidetic reduction, and the phenomenological reduction, as they will later be in Merleau-Ponty. In *Being and Time* itself the longest section of the Introduction is devoted to phenomenological method and culminates in Heidegger's acknowledgment of his debt to Husserl, though the absence now of any references to the three procedures marks so drastic a revision of Husserl's phenomenological method as to complicate any attempt to deal with the differences, as I have conceded.

When in the last essay Heidegger himself published, he rejects "the priority" Husserl accords to method, we can see in a preliminary fashion what is at stake. This rejection marks the end not just of phenomenology but of philosophy itself. In fact, the essay in which the rejection is put forward is that entitled "The End of Philosophy and The Task of Thinking," which I quoted in my Introduction for the retrospect it yielded on the history of philosophy.

The "priority" Husserl accorded to method is viewed by Heidegger as having a decisive consequence:

> The method is not just directed towards the subject of philosophy. It does not just belong to the subject as a key to a lock. Rather it belongs to the subject because it is "the subject itself".[19]

Heidegger is recalling Husserl's principle "to the subject itself." But he regards method in Husserl as no longer simply directed toward this subject; a flip-flop has intervened, and method becomes itself the subject of philosophy. This usurpation dramatically undercuts the prospect of method's continuing to perform its traditional function in philosophy, that of applying to a subject which is recognized to require its application. There is no longer a subject to which method can be applied—except method itself. This flip-flop is a final exacerbation of the subjectivization of the subject of philosophy, which in modern philosophy (as conceived by Heidegger) became with Descartes the "subjectivity of consciousness."

The Destruktion

I have suggested that Heidegger himself in the 1920s was committed to "the priority of method." The longest section of his Introduction to *Being and Time* is the one entitled "The Phenomenological Method of Investigation." This commitment is closely associated with the scientific character he then, like Husserl, still credited to phenomenology. In his lectures of 1929, *The Basic Problems of Phenomenology*, he explains that "phenomenology is the name for the method of scientific philosophy as such," and he makes a final effort to formulate a phenomenological method.[20] The only ingredient procedure of this method to survive in his later writings is the *Destruktion*.

It is tempting to suppose that Heidegger intended the *Destruktion* to be a revision of Husserl's philosophical *épochē*. Husserl uses similarly vigorous terminology; in particular, the term *Umsturz* ("demolition") of his procedure.[21] Though the two procedures are very different, this is a decisive juncture, at which, for my purposes as a historian, Husserl and Heidegger will have to be compared, since the *Destruktion* is Heidegger's fundamental procedure for dealing with the history of philosophy, just as the philosophical *épochē* is Husserl's fundamental procedure for dealing with the history of philosophy.

We have seen that Heidegger had adopted the idiom of "structure" in the first section of *Being and Time*, which includes in its title a reference to the "Structure . . . of the Question of Being." In the ensuing lectures in *Basic Problems of Phenomenology* this idiom becomes associated in effect with the procedure of "phenomenological construction," and thereby with the *Destruktion*. For having warned that "the most radical attempt to start all over again is pervaded by traditional concepts," he concludes that "there necessarily belongs . . . to the reductive construction of being a *Destruktion*—a critical deconstruction of the traditional . . . concepts." [22]

Here the "construction" is still "reductive," as in Husserl; however, in defining the "construction," Heidegger carries over from *Being and Time* a term which is entirely his own and entirely alien to Husserl: "We do not find Being in front of us. . . . It must always be brought to view in a free project (*Entwurf*)." With the intrusion of this term, the procedure of "construction" is no longer philosophically neutral; it has acquired implications that can be tracked down only in terms of Heidegger's own philosophy. That the term "construction" would otherwise remain ambiguous is suggested by the precautions Heidegger takes in using it in *Being and Time*. Its ambiguities are comparable to the familiar ambiguities of Husserl's idiom of "constitution." [23]

They do not require examination here, for I propose to use "construction" in the neutral, ambiguous sense that seems derivable from its association with the term "structure." It is common usage to speak loosely of the "structure" of a philosophy." In my usage, "construction" refers simply to how (that is, the procedure[s] by which) a philosophy obtains its "structure."

However, I shall continue to focus on the relations between philosophies—that is, on the respects in which the "construction" of a philosophy involves, at least implicitly, the "reconstruction" of another philosophy or other philosophies which are found relevant. I take advantage of the familiarity of the term "reconstruction" in order to cover roughly what William James spoke of as "considerable rearrangement"—what I have since explained in terms of the different shifts. [24]

My concern, however, as my analysis of these shifts has already illustrated, is not only with "reconstruction" itself but also with its destructive implications for the other philosophy or philosophies. To this extent my usage is broader than Heidegger's, for whom "the term *Destruktion* should above all not be understood in the negative sense of destruction [*Zerstörung*]." [25] Of course, Heidegger's interpretation of almost any philosophy is notoriously destructive—at least of the implications traditionally credited to it. Yet my concern does approximate his to the extent that "the rubric *Destruktion* is to be taken . . . with the etymological meaning of *de-struere*: to de-construct [*ab-bauen*], to bring out the concealed levels." [26] So far our shared usage is innocuous and not very interesting. Any exposition of a philosophy tries in some fashion to expose its structure (*de-struere*). But I am preparing to undertake a comparison in my Volume 3 between my de-construction and Heidegger's, in order to determine if and how the changes in which he becomes involved in reaching the end of the history of philosophy differ from those which have taken place during this history, whenever a philosophy is the "reconstruction" of a previous philosophy (or philosophies). These changes, I have argued in the present volume, have gone on in different fashions throughout history, but they have been dictated, broadly speaking, by the different procedures which philosophers have followed in constructing their philosophies and which have promoted the shifts I am sorting out with my de-construction. However, I have facilitated the comparison with the *Destruktion* by restricting my attention to the history of phenomenology as a stretch of the history of philosophy which, though remaining traditional in Heidegger's assessment, is yet the stretch from which he himself in some sense emerged in reaching the end of this history.

Here again I encounter the question I have faced before: Why did I not embark directly on an analysis of Heidegger's procedure of *Destruktion*? One answer I could not present fully then was that I could not make my comparison with the *Destruktion*, insofar as it was a procedure involved in reaching the end of philosophy, without having determined how this change differs from the previous changes which have taken place within the confines of the history of philosophy. Another answer I would recall is the warning by one of Heidegger's interpreters that the *Destruktion* cannot be isolated as a procedure, for "Heidegger has applied the *Destruktion* throughout his thinking in all of its guises." [27]

This answer I am now at last able to discuss more specifically. I have been restrained in this volume by the recognition that if I were to maintain my focus on the relations between philosophers, and on the problems of analyzing these relations, I could not also analyze in any detail the internal structure of any of these philosophies, much less the process by which it was constructed. Heidegger's *Destruktion* requires particularly detailed examination. In *Being and Time* it is presented in a separate section preceding the section entitled "The Phenomenological Method of Investigation," which culminates in the acknowledgement of his debt to Husserl. Thus the difficulty here is not only that the *Destruktion* is not yet an attempt to reach the end of philosophy but also that Heidegger does not even make any explicit attempt to integrate the *Destrktion* into his presentation of phenomenological method. In the *Basic Problems of Phenomenology*, reaching the end of philosophy is still not in question, but Heidegger may well be interpreted as making this attempt at integration, with his elaboration of a "phenomenological construction," which is paired with the *Destruktion*.

However, since "even the most radical attempt to start all over again is pervaded by traditional concepts," Heidegger cannot retain Husserl's sharp distinction between the "new construction" of his own philosophy and the preceding "demolition" of the tradition. Instead, Heidegger has to conclude that "phenomenological construction is necessarily *Destruktion*." [28] We are left with the difficulty of determining how "construction" and *Destruktion* go together. The only comment I can offer here is with respect to Heidegger's relation to Husserl: the history of philosophy cannot simply be pushed aside by Heidegger, as proposed by Husserl, with a peremptory "demolition"; moreover, this very peremptoriness may well come to illustrate later to Heidegger how the imposition of method, when it obtains "priority" over the subject to which it applies, is the subjectivization of the subject of philosophy.

Back in the 1920s, however, "starting out" (*Ausgang*) in phenomenology still has to be "secured by the proper method." For the problem has to be faced of gaining "access" (*Zugang*) to the phenomena, which becomes a problem of "making our way through" (*Durchgang*) the philosophical tradition which "obstructs" (*verlegt*) our way. [29] Thus the *Destruktion* is needed to disclose the structure of the tradition as an obstruction. This structure later becomes a matter of the different fashions in which the subject of philosophy has been structured during its history—in the instance of modern philosophy, which concerns us here, as "the subjectivity of consciousness." Thus at the juncture where Husserl pushed the history of philosophy aside, philosophy becomes for Heidegger the history of philosophy.

However, Heidegger's history of philosophy is a history in which Husserl has lost most of his relevance. Once the *Destruktion* becomes uniquely Heidegger's procedure in dealing with the history of philosophy, he favors philosophers who were pivotally involved in structuring or restructuring the philosophical tradition; in this tradition Husserl becomes a derivative philosopher, confined within the modern epoch as it had been structured by Descartes's subjective philosophy. This is why references to Husserl disappear from Heidegger.

The Question of Method

In my Introduction, I offered, with help from Heidegger, an identification of the end of philosophy with its coming to an end as *science*. Later I also alluded to Heidegger's identification of the end of philosophy with philosophy's coming to an end as *metaphysics*. Both these identifications are familiar, and whatever need there is for further specification, they do enjoy a certain plausibility. I am putting forward another possible identification of this end which has by and large been neglected, and I shall argue that its specification might assist the further specification of the two previous senses in which philosophy has been taken as coming to an end. This is Heidegger's identification of philosophy (especially modern philosophy) as committed to *method*. We have seen that one respect in which Husserl does still remain relevant in Heidegger's "End of Philosophy" is as illustrating this commitment.

My sorting out of the shifts in connection with the two familiar identifications of the end has been preliminary to dealing with this question of method. For, I repeat, the distinctively scientific character of phenomenology as a *subject* is assured in Husserl, as well as initially in Heidegger, by a phenomenological method; its philosophical character, as a subject distinguished from the empirical sciences, is assured by phenomenological method, which lifts this subject to eidetic and transcendental levels above these sciences.[30]

Although in this volume I have sorted out other traditional proceedings, perhaps method can be regarded as the traditional proceeding *par excellence*. Earlier I stated the obvious—that the philosopher has traditionally been viewed as engaged in a more sustained proceeding, in an area of greater scope, than is usual with other intellectual activities. It is by applying method that his proceeding is supposed to be sustained with some measure of consistency. If method is then the manner in which he proceeds, how he proceeds, to his philosophy, it is at the same time how he proceeds from a previous philosophy (or philosophies) to get there. I have tried to expose this manner as distinctively philosophical by going behind more shifts in allegiance vis-à-vis previous philosophies to shifts in *subject,* in *affiliation,* and in *level.* All these shifts, we have seen to be the case in Husserl, are promoted by the procedures composing his method. And among twentieth-century philosophers, none has probably been more preoccupied with method than Husserl.

Granted that a method which is phenomenological becomes irrelevant to Heidegger in the 1930s (since the method he would elaborate is to be applicable to the history of philosophy), are we to conclude that method itself becomes discredited for him as soon as he arrives at "The End of Philosophy"? Although he then still continues with the *Destruktion* as a "Task of Thinking," is it still a method? Or is method itself left behind as distinctively philosophical?

There is another difficulty. At the same time that Husserl was responding to Heidegger—by reviewing, in *The Crisis of European Sci-*

ences, the history of modern philosophy and becoming dismayed that the prospect of philosophy's coming to an end might be signaled by what was happening to it, as illustrated (I suspect) by *Being and Time* and its vogue—Heidegger in the same provincial German city was assessing in the *Beiträge zur Philosophie* the "turning" in which he had become involved (or more explicitly involved) since he had written *Being and Time.* What interests me for present purposes in the *Beiträge* is that "method" is not envisaged as philosophical at all, but as a distinctively scientific procedure.[31] The distinction between philosophical thinking and science itself is unqualified, and it should be remembered that this is the time at which Heidegger was completing the shift in *affiliation.*

The question of method will come up again with Derrida, who is in some measure indebted to Heidegger's *Destruktion* in elaborating his "deconstruction," even though he applies it to Heidegger. Deconstruction might seem Derrida's distinctive method or procedure, had he not protested, "Deconstruction is not a method and cannot be transformed into a method. Especially if the procedural or technical sense of the word is emphasized."[32] "Especially" leaves a margin of ambiguity, but the protest suggests that for Derrida the end of philosophy may be in some sense the end of method.

We have already seen that the handling of method is also ambiguous in Heidegger's case. When the end of philosophy is reached, how does the way he proceeds differ from a method in the traditional philosophical sense? The only explicit difference we have observed is that Heidegger rejects "the priority of method" in Husserl. This rejection, as a criticism of modern subjectivism, acknowledges a limitation on the initiative a philosopher can exercise by resorting to a method. To this extent, there may be some continuity between this eventual criticism of "the priority of method" in Husserl and the criticism in the 1920s of Husserl's philosophical *èpochē* as unable to emancipate a philosophy from the influence of traditional concepts. In acknowledging this limitation on method as a proceeding, Heidegger may still be stressing, as he had in *Being and Time,* the predominance of *tra-ditio* as itself a proceeding: "What tradition 'hands down . . .' [*übergibt*] becomes so inaccessible, at the outset and for the most part, that it is rather covered up."[33] To gain access to the structure of this obstruction, the *Destruktion* becomes necessary, as we have seen.

What Heidegger takes method to be when he handles the *Destruktion* separately in *Being and Time* from the phenomenological method on which he relies in that work; what he takes it to be when he integrates the *Destruktion* into phenomenological method in *Basic Problems;* what he takes it to be when he later instead allows the phenomenological method to be displaced in effect by the *Destruktion;* whether or not the *Destruktion* is still a method when he rejects "the priority of method" in "The End of Philosophy": these are questions I cannot pursue until I have exhibited in some detail phenomenological method as Husserl employed it and as Heidegger himself interpreted it in *Being and Time.* Only then will it be feasible to trace the process of reconstruction by which this method is first transformed in Heidegger but then eventually is repudiated as a method.

Starting Point

Here it is only feasible to locate what can be taken as the starting point for this process. I have already indicated that Husserl's first fully phenomenological work, the *Logical Investigations,* starts out in the first chapter with an analysis of the "sign." I have also indicated that this starting point becomes relevant in *Being and Time* only belatedly—in the section on "Reference and Signs"—though it regains a different relevance for Derrida.[34] (In Volume 2 I shall consider what happens to Husserl's analysis of the sign in Sartre, as well as the starting point Sartre finds in *Ideas I* for his own analysis of the imagination.) But neither the first section of the *Logical Investigations* nor Heidegger's section on "Reference and Signs" is explicitly an analysis of method: they do not provide me with an obvious starting point for considering the methodological relation between Husserl and Heidegger.

For the purpose of discovering how Heidegger redefines phenomenology in terms of method, I shall take as my starting point the definition of phenomenology which Heidegger reaches at the start of the section entitled "The Phenomenological Method of Investigation" in *Being and Time:*

> The expression "phenomenology" means primarily a concept of method. It characterizes, not the what of the objects of philosophical research as subject-matter [*das sachhaltige Was der Gegenstände*] but the how of this research. The more genuinely a concept of method is worked out the more comprehensively it determines the fundamental proceeding [*Duktus*] of a science, the more originatively it is rooted in the confrontation with the things [*Sachen*] themselves, and the more remote it is from what we call a technical procedure [*technischen Handgriff*].[35]

On the one hand, Heidegger's definition entails no obvious break with Husserl and seems consistent with Heidegger's statement at the end of the section that "the following investigation would not have been possible if the foundation had not been laid by Edmund Husserl, with whose *Logical Investigations* phenomenology first reached its breakthrough." [36] But, on the other hand, Heidegger's endorsement of phenomenology as he defines it does seem inconsistent with his later rejection, on the basis of the principle "to the subject [*Sache*] itself," of the "priority" accorded to method by Husserl—that is (in Heidegger's earlier terminology), to the "how" over the "what." Furthermore, it seems as if Heidegger's later dropping the distinction between method and "a technical procedure" depends on his reapplying the same principle (granted the change from the plural *Sachen* to the singular *Sache*) which he applies in upholding the distinction in *Being and Time*—"the more originatively [*ursprünglicher*] the concept of method is rooted in the confrontation with the things [*Sachen*] themselves."

Not only is there no obvious break with Husserl when Heidegger adopts this principle, but its very formulation seems indebted to the conclusion of Husserl's *Philosophy as Rigorous Science*. There Husserl makes the move from subject to method that Heidegger repeats in *Being and Time* when he identifies phenomenology with a method but which he will later disavow. This is Husserl's move: "The science that is concerned with what is radical, must also be radical in its method [*Verfahren*]." Before making the move, Husserl explains the "radical" character of his subject by exploiting the etymological reference to "roots" (*radices*): "Philosophy is in its essence a science of true beginnings [*Anfängen*], of origins [*Ursprüngen*], of the 'roots of everything.' " [37]

Such resort to the historical origin of a term, I have already mentioned, is more characteristic of Heidegger than of Husserl,[38] and it is consistent with Heidegger's resort to the history of philosophy, which intervenes as a tra-dition between us and its origins. We have seen that Husserl's "radicalism" entails pushing the history of philosophy aside in order to get directly to "the things themselves," the "origins," the "roots of everything," whereas Heidegger claims that "all philosophical discussion, even the most radical attempt to start all over again is pervaded by traditional concepts," so that phenomenological method requires "a *Destruktion*, a critical process in which the traditional concepts . . . are deconstructed to the sources from which they were drawn."

Direction

The implications for phenomenological method of philosophy becoming what it could not be for Husserl—the history of philosophy—have to be left for Volume 3. But we can take note now of Heidegger's other criterion in *Being and Time* for working out a method—"the more comprehensively it determines the fundamental proceeding [*Duktus*] of a science." This comprehensiveness precludes my exposition of Heidegger's method, short of examining long stretches of *Being and Time*. But Heidegger's use in of the idiom *Duktus* suggests that so long as he would accord method "priority" and keep it distinct from "a technical procedure," he formulated his "concept of method in a fashion which remained close to Husserl's re-ductions. Indeed, we have seen that after writing *Being and Time*, he recast his phenomenological method, to the extent he could, in terms of the reductions.

All that I would attempt now is to do some justice to the very distinction between a philosophical method and a merely "technical procedure," as employed in an empirical science. So far I have myself analyzed method in terms of the shifts that it promotes. What should be reconsidered is the sense of direction which these shifts involve and which I derived earlier from the way Heidegger distinguishes how a scientist proceeds from how a philosopher proceeds:

> To the sciences there is always an immediate transition and access, starting from everyday representation. If one takes everyday representation as the measuring stick of all things, then philosophy is always something out of wack [*Verrücktes*]. This shifting [*Verrückung*] of the attitude of thought can be carried out only with a lurch [*Ruck*]. In contrast scientific lectures can start immediately with the presentation of their subject.
>
> Philosophy, however, entails a continuous shifting of location and level.[39]

The differences involved in this shifting, as I analyzed it, are not differences in the static "structures" of the different philosophies. In carrying out a shift, each philosopher is proceeding in a different "direction" from whatever predecessor he may find relevant, as we first saw when we examined Heidegger's "lurch" in relation to Husserl.[40] Thus a deconstruction, as I conceive it, should not simply expose the static structure of a philosophy but should bring out the shift (or shifts) in "direction" which are fundamental to the elaboration of this philosophy.

Conversions

The issue of "direction" emerged most obviously with the shift in allegiance whereby almost an entire generation of philosophers turned "toward Heidegger against Husserl." That the successive shifts in Sartre's allegiance were conversions to (his versions of) Husserl and Heidegger (and later Marx) was particularly obvious (as compared with their conversions) by virtue of the fashion in which his turnings toward and against were braced by his methodological commitment to the antithetical.

I have already traced the lineaments of a conversion in Sartre's initial turning toward Husserl. He became "almost pale with emotion." It was "the encounter of his life; he will never give it up." As he himself reports, "I read Husserl in Berlin; everything was changed forever." [41] In Volume 2 I shall show how "everything" embraced the "direction" he took in philosophy: in an essay he wrote in Berlin, he found in Husserl a "philosophy of transcendence" that he enabled him to turn against the French "philosophy of immanence."

Earlier I indicated that although such shifts in allegiance could be discounted as merely episodes in intellectual history, they could also have philosophical implications to the extent that more fundamental shifts were involved. [42] What I would now recognize is that Sartre's conversion to Husserl was geared into a conversion that Husserl's philosophy itself entailed. In the instance to which Sartre was initially responsive, Husserl's philosophy entailed, according to its principle, turning "toward the things themselves." We have just seen that this principle is also endorsed by Heidegger when he conceives method as "rooted in the things themselves."

However, the principle acquires different implications in each of our three philosophies. Husserl is applying this principle when he pushed the history of philosophy to one side; he is turning "back to the things themselves." But Heidegger, we have just seen, regards such a conversion as complicated, inasmuch as "the most radical attempt to start all over again is pervaded by traditional concepts."

The Reductions

Here too the issues raised by Heidegger's relation to Husserl are less manageable than those raised by Sartre's relation to Husserl. Although the principle does entail in Husserl himself a turning toward "the things themselves," each of the reductions intervenes to promote further turning in another direction. "The things themselves" are not particular things (such as the "glass" that Aron and Sartre were perceiving) but are, for example, the essential structure of the act of perception itself, to which we are "led back" by the eidetic re-duction. To this turning back Sartre seems to some extent indifferent—the extent is a problem for Volume 2. Nonetheless, we could at least observe in the present volume Sartre's preference for the terminology "eidetic intuition" over "eidetic reduction." Moreover, in Husserl the eidetic reduction has to be reinforced by the phenomenological reduction, which he regarded as explicitly a conversion, since it enforced a "turning around" of consciousness on its own acts—for example, on the act of perception.[43]

Thus the three other procedures, which (along with the philosophical *èpochè*) compose phenomenological method in Husserl, intervene to determine the direction of the turning in accordance with his principle "to the things themselves." Intentional analysis turns in the direction taken by acts of intentional reference to the intentional objects that consciousness is consciousness of. But consciousness becomes "lost" in the performance of these acts (for example, of perception).[44] Thus the eidetic reduction is insufficient to "lead" consciousness "back" from the particular objects it may happen to be conscious of in order to re-flect on and analyze the essential structures of these acts in correlation with their intentional objects. The "naive" or "natural attitude," which is the direction taken by consciousness when it becomes "lost," is at once perpetuated and strengthened by the naturalistic attitude of the natural or empirical sciences, most menacingly by psychology. The natural and the naturalistic attitude (and the accompanying danger of "psychologism") can only be overcome if the eidetic re-duction is supplemented by the phenomenological re-duction, which "leads" consciousness "back" to the transcendental level, where a pure phenomenological analysis of consciousness can be undertaken. It might be observed that Husserl's idioms ("lost," "led back") are also featured by religious conversions and that with reference to phenomenological reduction Husserl cites Augustine's formula for a conversion.[45]

Heidegger may retain some concern with these re-ductions of Husserl's when he employs the term *Duktus* or recasts them in *Basic Problems*. But just as Sartre weakens the force of the eidetic reduction (perhaps we might say "vulgarizes" it) by treating it simply as an "eidetic intuition," so he does not acknowledge in his treatment of the imagination the need for a phenomenological reduction.[46] Thus while Husserl found the phenomenological reduction so difficult that he spent years working over its formulation, Sartre's conversion—since it was largely to "the things themselves"—was an almost instantaneous response to Aron's secondhand account.

When during the war Sartre turned "toward Heidegger against Husserl," he was again being converted to a philosophy which itself entailed a conversion. *Being and Time* has readily been interpreted as a *Konversionsgeschichte,* and it held out to Sartre the prospect of redemption from "inauthenticity."[47]

Konversionsgeschicht

There is one feature of conversion in Sartre to which I would give a more general emphasis: "For years this had been his fervent wish: to speak of things, as he came into contact with them, and that this would be philosophy."[48] Sartre's conversion to Husserl is not simply a conversion to a particular philosophy and to a principle which was specific to it. The "that this would be philosophy" suggests the extent to which Sartre's conversion was to philosophy itself.[49]

Conversion to philosophy has been a traditional philosophical proceeding. It has been a characteristic direction taken ever since Parmenides. Philosophy assumed its traditional guise as a *Konversionsgeschichte* with the "turning around" (*periagogē*) that takes place in Plato's cave, where it is the proceeding by which the prisoner is liberated to arrive eventually at the level of dialectic—that is, at what is in some sense the distinctively philosophical level. But the proceeding of his liberation (the *Konversionsgeschichte*) is also dialectical. I am suggesting, on the one hand, that the detailed attention Heidegger paid to this itinerary followed by the philosopher in Plato had something to do with his own involvement at the time in his "Turning" (*Kehre*), granted that he denies that his "Turning" was a "conversion' (*Bekehrung*).[50] For the "Turning" in Plato is for Heidegger a step taken toward the subjectivization which takes place only in modern philosophy—a subjectivization from which *Being and Time* is not entirely liberated, though it still does not legitimate (according to Heidegger) Sartre's subjectivist interpretation of it. I am suggesting, on the other hand, that to the extent that Heidegger's interpretation of the entire philosophical tradition as fundamentally Platonic can be accepted, the task of deconstruction, as I would conceive it, should include exposing this structure of conversion as a traditional proceeding. Thus I find in our four phenomenologists four different versions of the conversion that philosophy itself is.

In Derrida's "deconstruction" of its history, philosophy has traditionally been "logocentric," "phonocentric," and "phallocentric," but if some perversion has traditionally become in this way a central point of reference for philosophy, it has been by virtue of some turning toward it, away from, or against something else. Even deconstruction's decentering is a turning away from or against, granted that it may not always be entirely clear what it is turning toward and that it may have become peculiarly vagabond with Derrida.[51]

Phenomenology and Dialectic

To try to reconcile the authentic fundamental tendency of phenomenology with dialectic is to try to mix fire with water.—Heidegger

The Versäumnis

That Heidegger's method (if the *Destruktion* remains a method in the later Heidegger) applies to the history of philosophy, unlike Husserl's phenomenological method, constitutes its interest for me, since I am working out a method which I illustrate by applying it to one stretch of this history—the history of phenomenology. Heidegger has not attempted to deal with this stretch himself, despite the pivotal place he acquires there as the allegiance of Husserl's successors shifts toward him.

To explain this *Versäumnis*—his not making the attempt I am making—is a matter I defer to Volume 3. For the explanation would requre exploring the internal development of Heidegger's philosophy. This exploration presumably would show how the distinction in *Being and Time* between "genuine method" and "a technical procedure" later collapses, and method become predominantly the technical procedures employed in the sciences, as envisaged in the *Beiträge*.

All I have been able to anticipate was how Heidegger at the end of philosophy rejects the "priority of method," in favor of the priority of the principle, "to the subject [*Sache*] itself." At this juncture Heidegger links Husserl's ostensible adherence to this principle with Hegel's. Heidegger makes this linkage, even though he has to admit that Husserl's phenomenological method and Husserl's dialectical method are "two methods" which are "as different as they could be." [1] But the differences can be neglected as a matter of relative indifference, since Heidegger is committed to what he regards as more faithful adherence than either of the two philosophers to the principle "to the subject itself."

However, Heidegger was not always indifferent to method, and he was not always indifferent to differences of method. I would revive an argument of the early Heidegger who was committed to phenomenological method: "To try to reconcile the authentic fundamental tendency of phenomenology with dialectic is to try to mix fire with water." [2]

I have been demonstrating how Heidegger is, for my purposes as a historian, the crux, inasmuch as his initial preoccupation with method (and his initial stress on differences between phenomenology and dialectical method) is succeeded by neglect of method (and neglect of these differences). This *Versäumnis* is not restricted to Heidegger. Because indifference to method in philosophy is so pervasive today, it is all the more worthwhile to make a crucial issue with respect to the end of philosophy—or even without reference to the end of philosophy, for those who prefer its history presented without apocalypse or any other kind of melodrama. This indifference is not just restricted to philosophical method but sometimes extends to scientific method—so long a cherished topic of controversy in philosophy. [3]

However, the historian should not bite off more than he can chew. Let me offer one example that is not without relevance to phenomenology. When Gilbert Ryle and other proponents of so-called analytic philosophy, or Oxford Philosophy, exhibited themselves in France before a group of continental philosophers that very briefly included Merleau-Ponty the fiasco was explained by Charles Taylor:

> the continental questioners wished to discuss matters which are rarely discussed in Oxford and usually thought to be a waste of time. . . . For the questioners naturally wanted to bring the discussion to matters of *methodology,* to the philosophical justification of the procedures of the [analytic] school. And this is not a popular subject of discussion at Oxford.

The respondents defended their ad hoc treatment of specific problems by adopting "the stance of the inarticulate gardener with a green thumb being interrogated by the agronomist—'I just plants it and it grows.' " [4]

This fiasco itself is less relevant to phenomenology than an assumption made by certain so-called analytic philosophers who had some sympathy for phenomenology and who have been responsible for many of the more respectable expositions of it in English. They have tended to assume that if anything had been said in the phenomenological idiom that might be worth saying, it could be trans-lated into the analytic idiom in order for it to become clear what was meant. What they have accordingly been reluctant to trans-late was the phenomenological preoccupation with method.

Since I hope this present history of phenomenology may have some general pertinence to the history of philosophy, let me cite one other example. The philosopher who has suffered the most from indifference to method today is the philosopher who is perhaps most obviously committed to method—Spinoza. It is almost a ritual on the part of his interpreters to disregard his geometric method. A scholar presumably without philosophical *parti pris* might be expected to show minimal respect for what a philosopher thought he was up to, but observe what a scholar does to poor Spinoza. Harry Austryn Wolfson argues that "there is no logical connection between the substance of Spinoza's philosophy and the [geometrical] form in which it is written." Wolfson goes further. He takes up the challenge, "As for Spinoza . . . , if we could cut up all the philosophic literature available to him into slips of paper, toss them up into the air, and let them fall back to the ground, then out of these scattered slips of paper we could reconstruct his *Ethics*."[5] Although Wolfson does accord Spinoza some minimal scope in the way of an effort to be critical and consistent, the scholar's confidence in the outcome of his own procedure of cutting a philosopher to pieces remains a good illustration of how the intellectual historian tends to reduce a philosophy to a welter of influences, and thereby an illustration of how the discernment of a method might rescue a philosophy.

The Synthesis

Whatever the case with the history of philosophy more generally, the historian of phenomenology cannot afford to be this indifferent to differences of method, especially not to the differences between phenomenological method and dialectic. After Sartre recognized that there were differences between Husserl and Heidegger to which he had previously been insensitive, he undertakes a reconciliation in *Being and Nothingness:* he characterizes this reconciliation as a "synthesis of Husserl's non-dialectical consciousness . . . with the dialectical project . . . which we find in Heidegger."[6]

What Heidegger doubtless regarded as an unmitigated confusion between himself and Husserl (even though the anecdote told about this confusion is not true) has become in Sartre an antithesis which Sartre overcomes in a synthesis. Sartre's *projet* translates Heidegger's *Entwurf* (the being "thrown forward" of "being-there"). It is sufficient for present purposes to observe that Heidegger never characterized this *Entwurf* (or his analysis of it) as "dialectical." Thus a shift in *method* has taken place with Sartre's attributing to Heidegger a dialectical method (which Heidegger himself never acknowledged employing), as opposed to Husserl's "nondialectical" (that is, phenomenological) method. The antithesis between the two methods is concomitantly an antithesis between two subjects—Heidegger's "project" and Husserl's "consciousness." By embedding the opposed methods in these opposed subjects, Sartre leaves room for the supervening dialectical method by which he himself overcomes the opposition with a reconciling "synthesis," which he regards *Being and Nothingness* as carrying out.[7]

In Chapter 14 I'll examine Sartre's closing of the gap that the shift in *subject* in Heidegger had opened up; now I am concentrating on the differences between the two methods. Here our phenomenologists themselves provide little assistance. Husserl dismissed "dialectic of all kinds" as "unnecessary, superfluous. Hegel may be ignored, and should be."[8] We cannot turn then to Husserl for assistance in discriminating the dialectic with which Sartre reconciles him with Heidegger. Nor can we turn to Heidegger. We have already observed his relative indifference in the 1960s to the differences between the "two methods." This indifference may have been accentuated then by his refusal to accord "priority" to method. But when in the 1920s he did accord a certain "priority" to method, he was almost exclusively interested in phenomenological method. The only alternative method he envisages is the dialectical method, but he does not just discount it as "unphilosophical"; as we have seen he dismisses altogether the attempt "to reconcile the authentic fundamental tendency of phenomenology with dialectic" as a perverse attempt "to mix fire with water."

Dialectical Method

We are seeing that the *prima facie* evidence on which I have relied in this volume is insufficient to extend its analysis to a dialectical method. Even Sartre himself offers little in the way of comment on the kind of dialectical mixture of phenomenology and dialectic that can be found in his *Being and Nothingness*. Indeed, when he does later become preoccupied with the Marxist dialectic, he will deny his philosophy was dialectical at the time he wrote *Being and Nothingness*. What then was the character of the "synthesis" with which he overcame the opposition between Husserl's "nondialectical consciousness" and Heidegger's "dialectical project"? In what sense did Sartre suppose Heidegger's "project" itself was "dialectical"?

Given this lack of assistance from the phenomenologists themselves, as well as the fact that the dialectical method, with its longer history, has taken on more miscellaneous guises than the phenomenological method, it seemed to me that the pressing task with respect to *Being and Nothingness,* which after all is reputed to be Sartre's major work, was to clarify the dialectical character of its method.

In my *Starting Point* I supplied an account of *The Dialectic of Existence.* One version of this dialectic is the "dialectical project" which Sartre attributes to Heidegger. The attribution, as an adaptation of Heidegger's "analysis of existence," is facilitated by Sartre's borrowings from Hegel's dialectic. But since Sartre's version of the dialectic of existence could be presumed to be contaminated by the admixture of phenomenological method which Sartre believes he is taking over from Husserl, I made more extensive use of Kierkegaard's version, which illustrated a more purely dialectical method than Sartre's as well as a more accessible dialectical method than could be extracted directly from Hegel. Moreover, Kierkegaard's dialectic is geared to his opposition to Hegel, and Sartre's own dialectic is also geared to this opposition, as it is to the opposition between Heidegger and Husserl. "Everywhere," Sartre declares in *Being and Nothingness,*" we should oppose to Hegel[,] Kierkegaard." [9]

The adaptation of Heidegger's "analysis of existence," the borrowings from Hegel and Kierkegaard, were clues to the dialectical character of Sartre's method in *Being and Nothingness.* But in the absence of much explicit commentary by Sartre on his method, it was necessary to eke out these clues by tracking down the way in which Sartre actually proceeded in *Being and Nothingness.* I also proposed a rendering of Heidegger's method which would explain how Sartre could suppose it was dialectical.[10] Finally, I anticipated some of Sartre's later revisions of Marxist dialectic. As a discrimination of the characteristics of a dialectical method, *Starting Point* becomes in retrospect a sequel to the preliminary exposition of phenomenological method I am laying out in the present volume.

Phenomenological Method

Starting Point remains incomplete as an analysis of Sartre's method, inasmuch as my argument there abstracts from the hybrid character of this method. What is still needed is a supplementary analysis. All I can show here is how this analysis, which I shall present in Volume 2, has been prepared for in the present volume by the delineation of shifts.

Just as Kierkegaard provided in *Starting Point* a more accessible version of dialectical method than Hegel's, so Sartre provides a more accessible version of phenomenological method than Husserl's. A suitable juncture for conducting this examination is Sartre's prewar writings, when he read Husserl, if not "exclusively" (as Solal-Cohen alleges), at least without being distracted by the differences between Husserl and Heidegger (which will later prompt Sartre to seek their reconciliation dialectically in *Being and Nothingness*).

One respect in which Sartre's phenomenological method is more accessible than Husserl's is by virtue of a shift in *level*, which is comparable (despite the difference in method) with the shift in *level* that takes place in Kierkegaard. When Sartre lays down the requirement that "everywhere we should oppose to Hegel[,] Kierkegaard," he explains that Kierkegaard "represents the claims of the individual as such." The comparable shift in *level* that Sartre makes in relation to Husserl is by repudiating the transcendental ego, to which Husserl's phenomenology is anchored.[11] The claims of the individual as such can then be represented by Sartre's phenomenology, as over against Husserl's claim that phenomenology does not "deal with the experiences of empirical persons" and "knows nothing . . . of my experiences." But Sartre presents his *Transcendence of the Ego* (1937) as merely a "sketch," as he also does his *Theory of the Emotions* (1939), which we have seen him salvage from *Psyché* when he abandoned it in favor of *Being and Nothingness*.

The other essay, besides *The Transcendence of the Ego*, which Sartre wrote in Berlin in 1933–34, is the essay which I mentioned earlier, in which he endorses "intentionality" as "A Fundamental Idea of Husserl's" and, thereby, a conception of phenomenology which, we have seen, differs from Merleau-Ponty's. This endorsement also provides a *prima facie* continuity with Husserl that is disrupted by Sartre's repudiation of the transcendental ego. Intentionality continues to be fundamental in Sartre's major philosophical undertaking before the war—his analysis of imaginative consciousness in *L'imagination* and *L'imaginaire*.

At this juncture we encounter what I have delineated as a shift in *subject*. The imagination is not just a specialized topic for Sartre; it is almost coextensive with the subject of his philosophy, to the extent that it is phenomenological, since the imagination "is consciousness as a whole [*toute entière*] insofar as it is free."[12] Thus the imagination is "the constant preoccupation" of Sartre's, as Christina Howells has pointed out, and Sartre's analysis of it not only "inaugurates" his career in the two works I have mentioned but also "closes" it in the longest of his works—his analysis of Flaubert's imagination, in *The Idiot of the Family* (1971–72).[13]

In *L'imagination* and *L'imaginaire* Sartre sees himself as taking over Husserl's phenomenological method, and applying it to a subject to which he assumes Husserl must have applied it "in his lecture courses and unpublished works." Husserl himself, however, never suggested that the imagination is "consciousness as a whole insofar as it is free." His preferred examples of intentional consciousness are taken from perception. Whether or not we can then attribute to Husserl the same commitment Merleau-Ponty has to "The Priority [*primat*] of Perception" is a question I postpone answering, but I raise it to indicate how the shift in *subject* which takes place when I move from Husserl to Sartre can be further clarified when I eventually take up Merleau-Ponty's relation to both Husserl and Sartre.[14]

What I propose to demonstrate in Volume 2 is that although Sartre by and large presupposes Husserl's analysis of examples from perception, there is nonetheless a considerable shift in *subject* to the imagination. Concomitantly, there is a shift in *method,* which is not simply determined by the shift in *subject,* in the fashion in which we see the shape of a key determined by the lock which it must fit. (If this comparison of Heidegger's held, there would be no occasion to distinguish between the two shifts.) The shift in method is Sartre's tendency to transform Husserl's phenomenological method into a dialectic, although this dialectic is even more rudimentary in *L'imaginaire* than that in *Being and Nothingness;* thus guidance is needed from the clues provided by my analysis in *Starting Point* of the method Sartre employs in the later work.

Eclecticism

There may be a temptation to dismiss in advance the problem of discriminating between a phenomenological method and a dialectical one. The mixture of the two methods in Sartre's prewar writings, and the reshufflings of the mixture in his later writings, may seem merely to deserve the epithet *Quelle salade!* which Sartre himself expected would be de Beauvoir's reaction when he indicated the ingredients which he was putting together in *Being and Nothingness.*[15] That Sartre would have resented this reaction, if seriously entertained, is suggested by the ardor with which he rallies to the defense of a painting he favors of Tintoretto's against the criticism that Tintoretto's "bravado betrays his eclecticism." Sartre disdainfully recalls "the famous formula 'Michelangelo + Titian = Tintoretto.' " I may seem to have been treating *Being and Nothingness* here as if Husserl + Heidegger = Sartre. But Sartre's contempt for eclecticism in painting as "a happy insignificance which mingles traditions and styles agreeably" [16] (as well as his sensitivity to the possibility of the reaction *Quelle salade!*) manifests his concern with the coherence of *Being and Nothingness:* this should be encouragement both to finding out how he could believe he had overcome there the differences between Husserl and Heidegger and to working out (as I tried in *Starting Point*) what his dialectical method was.

Whether or not Sartre was successful in this regard is not at issue in this present volume. Instead, the extent to which Sartre puts together as ingredients of his own philosophy portions of Husserl and Heidegger has brought Sartre's philosophy to the fore for my own purpose of stating some problems of dealing with the relations between philosophies. Metaphilosophy is often an inconsequential undertaking, but Sartre's philosophy is itself by and large a metaphilosophy—a construction which is the reconstruction of other philosophies.

Deconstruction

The temptation to dismiss questions having to do with the mixed salad in Sartre is reinforced today by his now being, in his own *franglais*, a "has been." [17] But the problem survives his eclipse. Derrida, whose disdain for Sartre is impeccable, speaks of "the profound convergence at many points between Hegel's and Husserl's thinking." [18] My reaction: *Quelle salade!* Derrida's appraisal, like Heidegger's comparable appraisal in "The End of Philosophy and the Task of Thought," manifests indifference to differences of method.

Such indifference on their part, I have suggested, may spell the end of philosophy. Even if it be granted that philosophy has traditionally been metaphysical preparation for the sciences that supersede it, that the metaphysics in question has been onto-theological, logocentric, phallocentric, and so forth, method itself cannot be discarded as yet another metaphysical heirloom.

Let me be somewhat more specific. When philosophy reaches its end in Heidegger, he still envisages thinking as responsive to its subject. Are there then to be no further shifts in *subject?* Heidegger's response to Hölderlin in his own thinking implies that thinking will continue affiliated. Are there then to be no further shifts in *affiliation?* Will the thinker not undertake some thinking about how to proceed with the task of thinking—that is, some thinking about thinking? Thus there is still a prospect of a shift in *level* and of considerations of method being raised. Would they not be, minimally, considerations as to the consistency with which the thinker is proceeding in his thinking?

Would Derrida deconstruct the concept of a "subject" for thinking to be about? And would my concept of affiliation have its fate sealed by his deconstruction of the cognate concept of "genre," depriving thinking of familial relations and distinctions? These are questions I leave largely in abeyance. But can problems of method be shirked when the task of thinking is deconstruction, unless we are persuaded with Derrida that "each 'event' that takes place with deconstruction remains unique." [19]

Derrida's conclusion seems to imply that the distinction between particular and general has not been disposed of by deconstruction. Some measure of generality then survives, so that it seems feasible to assess what has taken place with deconstruction by applying some criterion of consistency such as the youthful Heidegger relied on when he repudiated mixing the phenomenology with the dialectical method. If no criterion of consistency can be applied, then certainly the end of philosophy has been reached.

History

There is another respect in which this end may have been reached—as the end of the *history* of philosophy, at least insofar as what then happens is deconstruction. The uniqueness of an event does not render it entirely haphazard. Does history continue in that a history of deconstruction itself might be feasible?

I have in mind Derrida's brilliant refusal to deal with "deconstruction in America." Only certain of his reasons are directly relevant here. One reason is that "deconstructionist discourses have sufficiently challenged . . . the traditional assumptions [*les assurances classiques*] of history, of genealogical narrative, of periodizations of all kinds, so that one could not without naïveté undertake . . . a history of deconstruction." [20] I hope I have not been in this volume completely at the mercy of "traditional assumptions" or even worse (because of the moral dimension of embedded confidence the French adds) of *les assurances classiques*—assumptions can be set aside, but *assurances* are more implicating and incriminating.

There may be an escape clause in the ambiguity of *ingenuité*. If I had translated it (*plus d'une langue* is the only definition of deconstruction Derrida is half-prepared to risk) "ingenuity" instead of "naïveté," then Derrida himself could have undertaken a history of deconstruction.

"The second reason" that Derrida refuses, "is that with respect to an ongoing process and a process which has the structure of a transference [*transfert*], one should not attempt to survey or totalize its significance. One then assigns it limits which are not its own, one weakens it, one ages it, one impedes." Here too there may be an ambiguity: apparently two reasons are blended.

From the first of these we might glean that a history treating any movement, so long as it is youthful and "an ongoing process," is maltreatment. In this regard it may be pertinent that Derrida rebukes "certain partisans of deconstruction" for "a certain puritanical *intégrisme*."[22] They are more orthodox than the pope. Would Derrida then not have had a historian point out, when phenomenology was still youthful and an "ongoing process," that Sartre's phenomenology was not phenomenology if the philosophical integrity of either Husserl or Heidegger was to be respected? Was there any reason for the historian to wait timidly until 1968 when phenomenology was no longer in its heyday and only then to point out, as Derrida did, how "astonishing and highly significant" was the misunderstanding of phenomenology in France? Would astonishment earlier have been an inopportune impediment to French phenomenology as an "ongoing process?" Movements like phenomenology and deconstruction, once they get underway, have a certain momentum. But the chore of the historian is precisely not to surrender to an "ongoing process" and move on with it.

Derrida's supplementary reason for refusing to undertake a history is that "deconstruction in America" is an "ongoing process" which has the structure of a transference [*transfert*].[23] He asks, "is there a proper history for this?" I observed earlier that Heidegger's philosophy is interpreted by Husserl as a "transference" of his own philosophy that is its "perversion."[24] But deconstruction is so committed to transference that its perversion is apparently not a comparable threat. There cannot be any "highly significant" deviations from Derrida which would be comparable to those Husserl discovered in Heidegger, and Derrida in French phenomenology. Thus if "a proper history" of deconstruction is unwarranted, it is because it is not a proper philosophy with its own integrity. Conversely it is because Husserl had a proper philosophy, ostensibly with "limits" of "its own," a philosophy which was not susceptible to "transference," that phenomenology has a history which is punctuated by "highly significant" deviations.

Despite his proclaimed distrust of "periodizations of all kinds," Derrida himself is sensitive to these deviations and demarcates "an epoch" in the history of phenomenology when a mistranslation of Heidegger dominated *via* the authority of Sartre and fostered, or was caught up in, a perverse misunderstanding of Husserl as well as of Heidegger.

Although our confidence has been renewed in the prospect of a history of phenomenology, we have also become aware that the prospect of a history may be contingent upon the character of the philosophy in question. In fact neither Husserl, nor Heidegger, nor Sartre attempt anything that could be considered a history of phenomenology. The nearest approximation is provided by Merleau-Ponty. I shall accordingly take him up next as a precedent for my own attempt.

TWELVE

Style

Phenomenology can be identified . . . as a
manner or style of thinking.—*Merleau-Ponty*

Accommodation

The historian who deals with a philosophical
movement faces questions of chronology and
of influences at work such as those I have already taken up. But whatever sequence he
adopts for his history, wherever he may follow out the flow of influences, there is usually some implication that he is dealing with
an identifiable movement, so that some measure of consistency, of unity, can be ascribed
to the movement. This is the implication of
the question with which Merleau-Ponty
launches his major work—"What is phenomenology?"

Before arriving at the identification implicit in the conclusion I have made my
own—that "phenomenology is accessible
only *via* a phenomenological method"—
Merleau-Ponty gropes as to how his question
is to be answered:

> A commentary on the texts would yield
> nothing as to what phenomenology is.
> We find in texts only what we put
> there. . . . It is in ourselves that we shall
> find the unity of phenomenology and
> its true meaning. It is less a matter of
> counting on citations than of determin-
> ing and expressing that *phenomenol-
> ogy for ourselves* which has given a
> number of our contemporaries the im-
> pression, on reading Husserl or Hei-
> degger, not so much of encountering a
> new philosophy than of recognizing
> what they were waiting for. Phenome-

nology is accessible only *via* a phenomenological method.[1]

Before offering any commentary on this text, perhaps I should pause to admit that I may soon appear to be bestowing excessive attention upon it, especially since the conclusion does not at all clearly follow from what precedes. I am bestowing this attention not merely because I seek access to phenomenology *via* the procedures which, as Merleau-Ponty goes on to explain, compose this method but also because Merleau-Ponty is the only one of our four phenomenologists who takes the other three phenomenologists into account. In both ways he provides a kind of precedent for my handling of phenomenology.

We have seen that when in his exposition of phenomenological method he arrives at intentional analysis, he denies this procedure the priority assigned it by Sartre, because "intentionality . . . is understandable only via the reductions."[2] Yet Merleau-Ponty still accords intentional analysis its place as a component of phenomenological method. He is similarly accommodating with respect to Husserl and Heidegger. Merleau-Ponty assigns the phenomenological reduction priority in his preface, but while Husserl claimed that Heidegger's phenomenology, as an analysis of "being-in-the world," demonstrated that he had never understood the phenomenological reduction, Merleau-Ponty claims that "Heidegger's 'being-the-world' appears only against the background of the phenomenological reduction."[3] Why does Merleau-Ponty bring together his predecessors in so accommodating a fashion? Just as he does not find the sharp break—the antithesis—Sartre finds between Husserl and Heidegger, so Merleau-Ponty does not find a sharp break between his own phenomenology and that of his predecessors.

This kind of accommodation, however, is no more adequate as history than Sartre's arraying Husserl and Heidegger as antithetical to each other. I have argued that Merleau-Ponty's readiness to accommodate and Sartre's antithesis alike derive from their respective philosophies; hence, they do not really take us outside of the confines of these philosophies and enable us to deal with either Husserl or Heidegger in his own terms.

Style of Thinking

There is, however, another clue that can be taken advantage of in Merleau-Ponty's answer to the question, "What is phenomenology?" Just before the passage I have quoted, he indicates that "*phenomenology can be . . . identified as a manner or style of thinking.*" I have previously identified a philosophical method (or any of its ingredient procedures) as "a manner" of proceeding. Now I would take advantage of the analogy to a "style." Husserl himself does refer to the "style" of phenomenology. He also refers to the "style of the world of our experience." He means, roughly, how we experience it—in such fashion that "scientific knowledge of the world is possible."

Furthermore, in explaining how the "theoretical attitude" of the scientist entails a "shift in direction" (*Umstellung*) from "the natural attitude" of ordinary experience (in some sense a conversion) Husserl again uses the idiom "style" to pick out what is at least relatively constant and consistent in our experience: "Attitude [*Einstellung*] in general means a habitually fixed style of willing life, comprising directions of the will or interests that are prescribed by this style, comprising the ultimate ends, the cultural accomplishments whose total style is thereby determined." [4] Despite his extending the scope of the idiom, Husserl never (so far as I am aware) examines his usage or attaches any significance to its derivation not from science but from art and literature.

If the identification of phenomenology with "*a manner or style of thinking*" can acquire the emphasis of italics in Merleau-Ponty, it may be by virtue of his accepting painting as an affiliate for his phenomenology, as I explained in my Introduction. There I was concerned to be less sweepingly vague than Rorty was when he adopted "philosophy-as-literature" as a rubric for the successor subject to "philosophy-as-science." I wanted to do justice to the selection of different affiliates besides "literature" and to different conceptions of the same affiliate.

To maintain the analogy between a method and a style I would exploit the implication of constancy and consistency which Husserl gets out of it. Yet at the same time the analogy is sufficiently flexible to take care of the differences between phenomenologies—the differences which are blurred by Merleau-Ponty's accommodations.

Questions of Style

With Taylor's help I have pointed out that a certain insensitivity toward method is characteristic of Anglo-American philosophy: to discuss a method (or worse a methodology) is to administer a dull thud and be suspected of impotency, or at least of a failure of nerve, when it comes to anything substantive. No similar loss of vigor is suspected if one discusses a style. I would accordingly enhance the prospect of method becoming controversial by suggesting some of the analogous questions which can be raised with reference to style.

I prepared for the present discussion of style by undertaking in my Introduction some comparisons between the history of philosophy and the history of art. Now I would add that questions of style may even be able to survive the end of philosophy. Thus Derrida has written on *Les styles de Nietzsche*.

Can we imagine a work of art that doesn't have in at least a minimal sense a discernible style? Analogously, can we imagine philosophical thinking which is not sustained as a more or less consistent "manner of proceeding"?

Each of a painter's brushstrokes may have been an "event" which was "unique," as a deconstruction is for Derrida.[5] Yet the brushstroke does not remain unique. In identifying the painting, we can refer to a painter's style, and (if he is a convincing artist) we might, ideally, want to show that each brushstroke that is discernible on his finished canvas is contributory evidence as to what his style is.

We would then be referring to the style either of the unique work of art confronting us or of his oeuvre as a whole, which may itself be in some sense unique. But we would also be referring to the style of the movement to which we would assign him in the history of art, even while we are referring to differences between his style and the style of other artists who belong to the same movement. Alternatively, we might be referring to his style as a mixture of styles—either of his own styles, or of the style we discern in this movement and the style of another movement, or of the styles of other individual artists.[6] There is a comparable range of references for the concept of a method, and comparable adjustments are required in the criterion of "consistency" in making the various references.

The multiplication of possible references of "style" indicates that it is a slippery concept. Yet it is a concept we need, and learn to use, when we are trying to pin down changes in art history. There is a broad sense in which we can identify, for example, Mannerism as a single style which is exhibited by various painters, yet we can acknowledge their differences.

The analogy to a style is suggestive of other complications to which we might otherwise be insensitive in dealing with a method. We have seen that when method is a crucial consideration for Heidegger, then it is also crucial for him to distinguish method from "a technical procedure."[7] The distinction becomes all the more crucial in my history when he rejects the "priority" Husserl accorded method and thereby demonstrates (for my purposes) not only that he is no longer committed to phenomenology but that he is reaching as well the end of philosophy. Analogous to these questions of method are certain questions of style. The difficulty of distinguishing between a method and "a technical procedure" is comparable to the difficulty of distinguishing a style from a technical procedure. Is the Gothic style distinguishable from the introduction of the pointed arch, of the ribbed groined vault, and so forth? Is the style of the Master of Flémalle distinguishable from his reliance on oil as a medium which is slow-drying and viscous?

Since I have identified method as a manner or style of proceeding, let me continue to use Mannerism as an example of a style which yields an analogy for the distinction between a method and "a technical procedure." "Mannerism" can be a term for a legitimate style, but it derives from *maniera,* which referred roughly to a "manner" which is "mannered" and betrays merely technical virtuosity, an illegitimate preoccupation with "manner" or style.

Still another question of legitimacy which can be raised with regard to method is analogous to the distinction between a concept of a style which is merely an art-historical artifact, something artificially contrived by art historians, intruded and imposed on works of art (thus the term "Mannerism" or, more frequently, its extension to certain artists, has been contested as an illegitimate procedure on the part of the historian) and a concept of style which actually picks out the artist's own "manner of proceeding." In other words, the concept is legitimate to the extent that the historian sees an artist "in his own terms," though this may entail seeing him in relation to other artists, much as Sartre saw himself (and his methods) in relation to Husserl, Heidegger, and Marx.

There are further analogous questions of legitimacy. Take an example which is analogous to the shift in *level* with which we are familiar as a difference between French existential phenomenology and German phenomenology: art (or a particular style) may lend itself to being seen as expressing what is personal to the artist, or this may be the historian's own preferred way of seeing any work of art. Analogously, Merleau-Ponty may urge, "It is in ourselves that we shall find the unity of phenomenology and its real meaning." But a Heidegger can insist that "in great art . . . the artist remains inconsequential as compared with the work, almost like a passageway that destroys itself in the creative process for the work to emerge." [8] And this insistence of Heidegger's is consistent with his conception of philosophy. Recall how he scorned any personal references to Aristotle when he lectured on Aristotle's philosophy. Recall too how phenomenology for Husserl "knows nothing . . . of my experiences or those of others." [9]

If in dealing with style I have relied on references to the visual arts, it is not merely because (as I explained in my Introduction) such evidence is more vivid than other evidence—or, at any rate, is so today. "Style" is a concept which applies to literature (Sartre's affiliate), poetry (Heidegger's affiliate), as well as to painting (Merleau-Ponty's affiliate), and identifications such as "Mannerism" and "Baroque" are not restricted in their application to style in the visual arts.[10]

Literary Style

The sharp distinction between method and a technical procedure which is drawn in Heidegger's *Being and Time* is not retained by Sartre despite his indebtedness to that work. We have watched Sartre violate the distinction by having *Being and Time* provide "tools for understanding History and my destiny," and we have seen that the idiom implies Sartre's keeping a certain distance from History.[11] Similarly, when Sartre's debts to Heidegger as a Nazi were held against Sartre by French Communists, Sartre seeks his distance from Heidegger by restricting his debts to "techniques and methods," using the two terms as if they were more or less interchangeable: "What does Heidegger matter? . . . If we ask another philosopher for techniques and methods which can provide us access to new problems, does that mean that we are stuck with all his theories?" [12]

An additional complication is Sartre's debt to Heidegger's philosophy not only for philosophical "techniques" but also for techniques of literary style. In the concluding chapter, "The Situation of the Writer in 1947," of Sartre's *What is Literature?* Sartre reaches the question of the "literary style" or "novelistic technique" (*technique romanesque*) to be adopted as appropriate to the [then] contemporary novel. Previously I quoted his statement of the question only in part. Here is his fuller statement: "The problems [of our period] can, strictly speaking, be attacked by philosophical reflection. But we who want to live these problems— that is, support our thinking by those fictional and concrete experiences which are novels, have available at the outset [only] the technique [of the traditional novel]," which Sartre identifies as "the retrospective novel."

In the wartime notebook of 1940, when Sartre immersed himself in history and was freshly converted to Heidegger, we failed to recognize a continuing debt to Husserl. The requirement of immersion now takes the guise of wanting "to live our experiences," and this heightened sense of "live" betrays Husserl's commitment, in accordance with his "principle of principles," to immediately given experience (*Erlebnis*). However, this Husserlian requirement is to be met by relying on a technique which is appropriate to "une littérature de l'historicité," further defined as "novels of *situation*."[13] The terms "historicity" and "situation" are distinctively philosophical in the humdrum sense in which Sartre is taking them over from *Being and Time*.

With these definitions, Sartre is envisaging not a novel which is still to be written but a novel he has already written—*Le sursis*. In fact, he went to work on *What is Literature?* in 1946, having published *L'age de raison* and *Le sursis* in 1945. I have already explained that *Le sursis* was in effect a Heideggerian novel, in contrast with the "disgustingly" "Husserlian" *L'âge de la raison* and that the title itself derives from Heidegger's conception of "being in suspense." [14] The difference is that what was ontological in Heidegger is psychologized by Sartre, to become the experience of *attente,* which prevailed in *Le sursis* because the novel was "situated" during the Munich negotiations while their outcome was impending and still uncertain. Hence it could be said that Sartre's *une littérature de l'historicité* has little to do with the ontological sense of "historicity" that Heidegger would endorse; it is rather a literature of *attente,* as opposed to "the retrospective novel." This identification of the traditional novel as "retrospective" depends on the antithesis Sartre is setting up with his adaptation of the "situation" in Heidegger of "being in suspense." I'll return later to the psychological character of this experience of *attente.* [15]

For the present, my concern is with the problem of "literary technique," which is the problem of showing how this psychological experience of *attente* was shared, as a matter of social history, by individuals who were entirely unaware of each other. The technique of "simultaneity," which Sartre adopts for this purpose, is literary in the humdrum sense that it is borrowed from the novelist John Dos Passos, to whom Sartre awards the title "the greatest writer of our time." [16] But Sartre's account of this technique is complicated philosophically by Sartre's employing a metaphor derived from Heidegger's *Entwurf* (but applied to the Husserlian subject of consciousness) to describe the effect of the literary technique of "simultaneity"—"the reader . . . is to be thrown from one consciousness into another." [17]

In short, we do not just come up against a shift in *level* from abstract "philosophical reflection" to the "fictional and concrete experiences which are novels"—a shift in *level* which is also a shift in *affiliation* and thus raises issues vis-à-vis Husserl with respect to the scientific status of philosophy and issues vis-à-vis Heidegger with respect to the status of literature as compared with poetry. [18] We also come up against other shifts in *level* which Heidegger would detect as a psychologistic and vulgarizing use of his ontological terminology ("historicity," "situation," "thrown") by Sartre when he characterizes his literary style.

THIRTEEN · # Communication

*Each of us understood the other's work as a
startling deviation from his own .—Sartre*

Periodization

The period whose problems, according to
Sartre, require treatment by the literary technique of "simultaneity" coincides with the
period in philosophy that begins with
Sartre's conversion to Heidegger, which
blends with the impending war. But the historian of phenomenology faces a different
problem of periodization from that provided
by Sartre's conversion and "the turning
point" of the war. Granted that phenomenologists themselves do not share a common
conception of the history of phenomenology,
any more than of phenomenology itself, I
have suggested that the historian still needs
to be able to circumscribe this history as ex-
hibiting some measure of consistency, of
unity.

For this purpose he needs, on the one
hand, to be able to locate some juncture as
the starting point of this history. This starting
point I have already located. And Merleau-
Ponty is alluding to it when he admits with
regard to his question "What is phenomenology?" that "it may seem strange that this
question has still to be asked half a century
after the first works of Husserl." [1] My reason
for taking Husserl as a starting point, I indicated in my Introduction, was that the other
phenomenologists with whom I would be
dealing all looked back to him (and no further back) as the starting point of the movement. On the other hand, it is also desirable
to locate an ending for a history. To Merleau-
Ponty, when he answered his question,

165

"What is phenomenology?" it was still a "starting point, a problem, a vow."[2] But we ourselves, half a century after his answer, are aware of phenomenology as having by and large come to an end, as philosophical movements do. At what juncture, then, did phenomenology come to an end, for the purpose of my history?

Earlier we recognized that phenomenology came to an end *ab extra* as a result of the shift in *subject,* and so forth, whereby its analysis of consciousness is superseded by a structuralist or poststructuralist (or some other) philosophy of language. I singled out Derrida as an illustration,[3] and some pertinent features of the shift in his case might be mentioned. Because he is committed to language as a subject, Derrida does not brush aside commentary on texts, as Merleau-Ponty does, in the text I have cited, when he claims that "the unity" and "true meaning" of phenomenology are to be found in "ourselves." This finding is a matter of consciousness returning reflexively upon itself in order "to tie together deliberately the famous phenomenological themes"—in particular, the procedures composing phenomenological method. This deliberate heightening of consciousness is a higher-level undertaking which Merleau-Ponty calls "the phenomenology of phenomenology."[4] He has prepared for this undertaking in the second of two italicized clauses; I have quoted only the first, with its analogy to style. In the second clause, he explains that phenomenology "existed as a movement before arriving at complete awareness of itself as a philosophy." That the philosophy in question is virtually Merleau-Ponty's own is betrayed by his proposing "to tie together [*nouer*] deliberately the famous phenomenological themes."[5] Such tying together is a feature of his own accommodating phenomenology, in contrast not only with his predecessors but also with deconstruction.

Deconstruction does not tie together, nor purport to find the unity and true meaning of anything, least of all in ourselves. Deconstruction, Derrida explains,

> does not return [*ne revient pas*] to a *subject,* whether individual or collective [as is Merleau-Ponty's "ourselves"], which exercises the initiative in carrying out the deconstruction. . . . The deconstruction takes place; it is an event which does not wait upon deliberation, consciousness, or the organization of the subject. . . . *It deconstructs itself.* . . . And the "itself" or "deconstructs itself" is not the reflexivity of a self or of a consciousness.[6]

Ab Intra

Phenomenology (indeed, almost any philosophical movement) can also be viewed as having come to an end *ab intra:* it "deconstructs itself" (if I may stretch this terminology out of shape and benefit from Derrida's re-luctance to inflict "puritanical '*intégrisme*'") by virtue of the differences which emerge internal to the movement, impairing its unity.[7] Or, rather, this unity itself depends on where the individual philosopher finds it. The historian of philosophy may be able to accommodate these differences in a fashion which I have sketched with the analogy to a single style encom-passing the differences between artists who belong to the same movement in art history. But the conditions of unity laid down by an individual phi-losopher are more constraining and determine his assessment of certain differences as fatal to his relation to some other philosophy. Thus it was Husserl's assessment (on rereading Heidegger) of the differences between himself and Heidegger that brought an end to his practice of announcing, "You and I are phenomenology," and contributed to his dismay that "the dream is over."[8]

Heidegger's reassessment of the differences between them is presum-ably implicit in his relinquishing in the 1930s the label "phenomenology" for his own undertaking. At any rate, Heidegger in the "Letter on Hu-manism" (1947) refers to Husserl's phenomenology as if it were a philos-ophy with which he had never anything to do. Heidegger was thereby in effect repudiating the relation which Sartre had assumed between Hei-degger and Husserl. About the same time, Sartre brought phenomenol-ogy to an end from his side when he dismissed in his *Cahiers pour une morale* (notebooks of 1945 and 1947, published posthumously) both Husserl and Heidegger as "minor philosophers," favoring instead Hegel and Marx.[9] He was in effect discounting the phenomenological method in favor of a method which he explicitly avows as dialectical. (This dis-missal could be said to threaten the unity of Sartre's own *oeuvre* as it had been established in *Being and Nothingness* by the "synthesis" he had sought there between Husserl and Heidegger.) Merleau-Ponty continued faithful to Husserl and Heidegger until his death, even though he also reached out to Hegel and Marx. But what can be viewed as the final fatal impairment of the unity of phenomenology was the break between Sartre and Merleau-Ponty, which happens to coincide chronologically with phe-nomenology's coming to an end *ab extra*.

Deboning

At each of these decisive junctures there is an overt breaking off of rela-tions. But the historian is also concerned with how these relations were initially constituted. I have already explained why I have selected the re-lation between the prewar Sartre and Husserl for examination in the Vol-ume 2. What I would now recall, as *prima facie* evidence for the relation between Sartre and Husserl, is Sartre's admitting how, in order to get

Ideas I "completely inside of him," the work had to be "deboned." This is the *Abbau,* the "deconstruction," of a philosophy.

I grant that these are terms which should not be used lightly, since they have been preempted, and given some precision of meaning as well as scope, by Heidegger and Derrida. But there are two other meanings I would distinguish. There is a commonplace meaning, one which was featured when Sartre was ushered as a philosopher into print, in a biographical note which accompanied the publication of a portion of *La légende de la vérité* in 1931. There Sartre is described as someone who is "elaborating a destructive philosophy." [10] Since this biographical note was supplied by Sartre's alter ego, Paul Nizan, who was apparently acquainted with *Being and Time* before Sartre himself was, there may be an echo of Heidegger's *Destruktion* here. But it seems likelier that what is being announced is merely the emergence of an *enfant terrible* who will lay waste traditional philosophy. Even if there is an echo, I would distinguish the commonplace usage inasmuch as Derrida's "deconstruction" has been vulgarized in America by those who are merely echoing him and elaborating a destructive philosophy to which they would probably have been predisposed (as Nizan, or Sartre himself, may have thought Sartre was at the time of the note) had they never heard of Derrida.

Sartre's own idiom of "deboning" I have adopted as bringing out what I regard as more specifically relevant to what happens to the "structure" of a previous philosophy when it is deconstructed in the more or less commonplace sense. Any philosopher who reconstructs another philosophy in constructing his own philosophy is engaged to some extent in the deconstruction of that other philosophy. "Deconstruction" in this destructive sense is a traditional philosophical procedure, to be distinguished from the procedure of *Destruktion,* which (I explained earlier) is designed to expose the structure (*de-struere*) of a philosophy. This is broadly and minimally what Heidegger and Derrida undertake, but it is also what I am undertaking in a different fashion.

This different fashion will be exhibited in my Volume 2. I shall first expose enough more of the structure of Husserl's philosophy (in addition to what has been exposed in this volume in order to illustrate the shifts), as determined by his method, to enable us to see in more detail how Sartre deboned and destroyed this structure in *L'imaginaire.* The different structure which emerges from Sartre's reconstruction will be seen to have been promoted by Sartre's transformation of Husserl's phenomenological method.

When one philosopher gets another philosopher more or less "completely inside of himself," the intervention of the historian is needed: each succeeding philosopher becomes subject to the constraining structure of his own philosophy, as he constructs it, and so is *ex officio* more or less unaware of, or at least often unconcerned with, his deboning of his predecessor. The "complete awareness" of phenomenology "as a philosophy," which Merleau-Ponty would embody in his "phenomenology of phenomenology," is in fact beyond the scope of any of our phenomenologists.

Ourselves

As my last illustration of how the historian's intervention is needed, let me anticipate the final break with which I view phenomenology as having come to an end *ab intra*. My persistent focus on the relations between philosophers has now narrowed to the constraints that are imposed on each phenomenologist's understanding of these relations by where he finds (in Merleau-Ponty's phrasing) "the unity" and "true meaning" of phenomenology. When Merleau-Ponty finds this unity "in ourselves," he is implying that such personal reference is intrinsic to phenomenology, though we have seen that this is not the case with Husserl and Heidegger.

When Merleau-Ponty speaks on behalf of the philosophy that his "contemporaries" as well as himself were "waiting for," he has Sartre primarily in mind. But he does not mention differences between himself and Sartre. We have seen that the experience of "waiting for" was Sartre's too. But one obvious difference between them was that Sartre had already deboned and digested Husserl before 1939 and was waiting for Heidegger, whereas Merleau-Ponty was still assimilating Husserl, as is evident from his trip to Louvain in 1939.[11]

Merleau-Ponty's interest in Heidegger, like that of other French contemporaries, was in considerable measure stimulated by Sartre's *Being and Nothingness* (1943). Indeed, Merleau-Ponty's own reconciliation of Husserl and Heidegger (and, more specifically, of Husserl's phenomenological reduction with Heidegger's "being-in-the-world") seems to have been prompted in part by his having taken exception to Sartre's treating them as antithetical in *Being and Nothingness*. But in the *Phenomenology of Perception* (1945), he cites Heidegger only on temporality and seems to have read this stretch of *Being and Time* only at a late stage of his writing (after having read *Being and Nothingness*) and only for the purpose of his own chapter on "Temporality"; whereas what Sartre had been "waiting for" (we remember) was Heidegger on "historicity." [12]

It is true that history had slowed down since it had overwhelmed Sartre in 1939 or, at any rate, that Merleau-Ponty was slower in catching up with it, because he was slower in digesting Heidegger. But it is also true that just as Husserl is dismembered differently by Sartre and Merleau-Ponty, so also is Heidegger. Sartre and Merleau-Ponty each of them entered into relation to a different Heidegger. But rebuked by Merleau-Ponty's cautioning against "counting on citations," I am smuggling into a footnote my canvassing of Merleau-Ponty's citations from Heidegger.[13]

Personal Reference

By virtue of Sartre's commitment to what we shall see Merleau-Ponty construes as the "exclusively antithetical," the differences between them emerge more definitely from how Sartre understood their relation:

> Each of us undertood the other's work as a startling deviation from his own work—the alien, sometimes hostile, work that the other was carrying out. Husserl became at one and the same time the distance between us and the basis of our friendship.[14]

Here the historian has to intervene, for it is Sartre's understanding alone of their relation, not Merleau-Ponty's, that is put forward here, and it is put forward in terms of Sartre's own philosophy. While both Sartre and Merleau-Ponty accept the philosophical relevance of personal reference, this reference itself is followed out differently by each of them, since it is implemented by a different analysis of the relation between the individual and the other.

Earlier, I drew attention to the clipped way in which Sartre separates himself (at the beginning of the memorial essay on Merleau-Ponty which I am now quoting again) from the friends he has lost: "They were they; I was myself."[15] So abrupt a separation is incompatible with Merleau-Ponty's readiness to accommodate his friends—a collective "ourselves"—when he proposes, "It is in ourselves that we shall find the unity of phenomenology and its real meaning." Even when Sartre's wartime experience was refuting (with the assistance of Heidegger's *Mitsein*) the solipsism of Husserl's first personal *cogito*, Sartre was not proposing to find phenomenology in ourselves. Recall instead his suggestion, "If Corbin has translated *What is Metaphysics?* it is because I am (among others) freely constituted as the public, waiting for this translation, and in this respect I am taking upon myself my . . . epoch."[16] There the "I" comes to the fore, even though it does find itself parenthetically "among others," who also belong to the epoch. It is an "I" which is taking this epoch "upon myself."

Merleau-Ponty reads Sartre as insisting, in his treatment of the relation between the individual and the other, "Between the other or myself one must choose," whereas in Merleau-Ponty's own philosophy, "I borrow myself from the other." Indeed, Merleau-Ponty attributes to Husserl the proposition, "Transcendental subjectivity is intersubjectivity." [17] This proposition might well have Merleau-Ponty's confidence that "we shall find in ourselves . . . the unity and true meaning of phenomenology," and this confidence helps explain why he is prepared to answer the question, "What is phenomenology?" on behalf of Sartre as well as himself. It might also help explain the reticence which inhibits him from singling Sartre out for criticism, so that when Merleau-Ponty entertains the prospect, "Between the other or myself one must choose," he presents us not with a forthright claim that this is something Sartre states but with an evasive "It is stated." [18]

The Distance

Take a look at their relation now from Sartre's side. If Husserl in Merleau-Ponty buttresses his confidence that "it is in ourselves that we shall find the unity of phenomenality and its true meaning" with the proposition "transcendental subjectivity is intersubjectivity," Husserl becomes in Sartre "the distance" separating him from Merleau-Ponty. But just as Husserl never upheld the proposition that Merleau-Ponty attributes to him (hence the historian has to consider it a feature of Merleau-Ponty's own philosophy), so "the distance" Husserl becomes between them in Sartre is a feature of Sartre's philosophy, which is first-personal—the philosophy of a *cogito*—in which he cannot presume to speak for Merleau-Ponty as a phenomenologist in the way Merleau-Ponty speaks on behalf of phenomenology at large. "The distance" between them is something Merleau-Ponty has difficulty acknowledging in his own philosophy, a philosophy in which "I borrow myself from the other." So Merleau-Ponty makes repeated efforts in his own writings to arrive at some understanding with Sartre, even though Sartre made no effort meantime to overcome the distance in his own writings. [19]

When their mutual friend Jean Hyppolite stresses Merleau-Ponty's "living dialogue, never interrupted, with Sartre," he neglects to add that there is little evidence of a dialogue going on from Sartre's side. [20] It is Merleau-Ponty who appeals in his philosophy to the experience of the dialogue when "we are for each other collaborators in a perfect reciprocity." [21] Sartre's memorial essay on Merleau-Ponty is a report not of a dialogue that was reciprocal and never interrupted but of how "the distance" between them became a breakdown in communication and a breaking off of their relation. The break was not satisfactorily repaired before Merleau-Ponty's death rendered it irreparable.

By taking under advisement their different analyses of the individual's relation to others, we are able to recognize that the breakdown of communication between them extends even to how a breakdown in communication is to be analyzed. Merleau-Ponty may make a concession in his analysis to Sartre, but he soon circumvents it:

> With the *cogito* begins that struggle between consciousness, each of which, as Hegel states, seeks the death of the other. For the struggle ever to begin, and for each consciousness to be capable of suspecting the alien presences which it negates, all must *necessarily* have some *common ground*.

Or again:

> The objectification of each by the other's look is felt as unbearable only because it takes the place of possible communication. . . . The refusal to communicate is *still a mode of communication*.[22]

On the one hand, since Merleau-Ponty's claim to speak on behalf of phenomenology itself—and to locate the common ground phenomenologists shared—can be pinned down as a feature of his own phenomenology, he has not provided us with a precedent for a history of phenomenology, though there was initially some hope he might, by virtue of his readiness to accommodate other phenomenologies. His phenomenology encourages him to override differences between phenomenologies, including Sartre's different conception of the relation between their phenomenologies.

On the other hand, I am not suggesting that it would be more appropriate for the historian to model his exposition on the ferocity with which Sartre often proclaims his differences from others, so that even his "How many friends I have lost" is not quite unmitigated regret but betrays a certain philosophical self-satisfaction on the part of his *cogito*.[23]

What I have been suggesting is that the historian can undertake to go behind the relation between philosophies, as conceived in a philosophy, to this philosophy in order to show how the relation is conceived in a fashion consistent with the rest of the philosophy. In the present instance of Sartre and Merleau-Ponty, this undertaking has been facilitated since their analysis of the relation between the individual and the other is explicit.

The Breakdown

By the light of this analysis, the breakdown in communication which took place between Sartre and Merleau-Ponty is more accessible than that between Husserl and Heidegger. Breakdowns in communication are clichés of our time, the stock-in-trade of literature. But they are heightened in Sartre by antitheses, contradictions. In *What Is Literature?* he defines a novel as an effort at communication but admits that communication breaks down in a society riven by class conflict and that he is himself read only by the bourgeoisie, whom he despises.

In his novels themselves we find breakdowns of communication which are fitted to antitheses in rather the same fashion as is the breakdown of communication with Merleau-Ponty. The episode between Annie and Roquentin in *Nausea* is too familiar. So I cite instead the breakdown of communication during a conversation between Daniel and Marcelle. The obvious breakdown is his trying to get her to explain to him what is going through her mind while withholding from her what is going through his mind. But the breakdown undergoes elaboration. His behest to communicate is *"ne vous fermez pas,"* which we could translate as "Open up [to me]" or (to retain the negative) "Do not shut yourself up [against me]." [24] Though the primary application of the metaphor of opening (as opposed to shutting herself up) is to her communicating with him, Daniel assimilates the metaphor of opening up to a physical seduction, which he cannot implement literally, since he is homosexual and impotent with women. Thus what takes its place as literally relevant is rather the prospect of allowing herself to be opened up in order to abort the child she is pregnant with. This displacing of the more obvious literal relevance to opening up for sexual intercourse by the "filthy business" of opening up for an abortion continues the discrediting of the process of communicating by assimilating it to a process of seduction.

The *interplay* between the literal and the metaphorical gets an extra flourish when Daniel characterizes his own relation to Marcelle with a comparison which is literally justified by her condition: "Now there was a new relation between them, a bond that was unclean and flabby [*mou*], like an umbilical cord." [25] Elsewhere Sartre comments on the process of communication as "a continual flabby coming and going between the particular and the general," by which human relations are established in their "promiscuity." Let us consider this "coming and going" and the "promiscuity" as it is illustrated by the present episode. Daniel's assimilation of communication to seduction, to sexual intercourse, and to an abortion violates—and perhaps destroys—its general character, at least as communication is conventionally conceived, for its distinguishability from such performances is indispensable to its being carried on with confidence.

Neither Husserl nor Heidegger have anything of philosophical interest (or of much other interest) to say of the breaking off of their personal relation. But in Sartre and Merleau-Ponty an explicitly worked out analysis of how the individual is related to others at the personal level can be obtained from the philosophical level. By outlining this analysis now I have wanted to demonstrate that my focus on the relations between philosophers is not necessarily an adjustment I am arbitrarily intruding on my own as an impertinent historian wielding a metaphilosophy; it can be a matter of how these relations are brought into focus expressly by the breakdowns of communication between them. The "break" between Husserl and Heidegger was a breakdown in philosophical communication as well as a breaking off of their personal relations, but we do not find in either of them, as we do in Sartre, an explicit analysis of the breakdown in communication between philosophers (himself and Merleau-Ponty) backed up by such concrete literary renderings as the breakdown between Daniel and Marcelle.

Nevertheless, there are two difficulties with pursuing further now Sartre's and Merleau-Ponty's analyses of the relation between the individual and the other. They reach this relation late in the setting forth of their philosophies.[26] Also, when Sartre does finally undertake his analysis of this relation, it is by turning against both Husserl and Heidegger. He discovers that he "cannot escape solipsism, as I formerly believed . . . by refuting Husserl's concept of . . . the transcendental ego."[27] He also discovers that "the relation of *Mitsein* [in Heidegger] cannot help at all to resolve the psychological, concrete problem of our recognition of the other."[28]

Sartre then turns toward Hegel and Kierkegaard. He derives an analysis of the relation between the individual and the other from Hegel's master/slave dialectic, though it is Hegel to whom he opposes Kierkegaard. Thus the terminology which crops up in Sartre's account of the breakdown between himself and Merleau-Ponty—"alien," "hostile"—betrays some debt to Hegel.[29] The debt is concomitant with a shift in *Being and Nothingness* to a dialectical method, which I examined in *Starting Point* and which cannot be taken directly into account here, where I am relying on episodes in the history of phenomenology.

Dialectic

Even though this shift in method seems to have been induced by an awareness of the problem of communication (as a problem which emerged, at least in Sartre's view, from the failure in both Husserl's and Heidegger's phenomenologies "to escape from solipsism"), the shift itself hardly improved communication between Sartre and Merleau-Ponty regarding the character of a dialectical method. On the one hand, Sartre regards Merleau-Ponty as undialectical, or as dialectical only in a quixotic sense: "He jumps from one point of view to another, denying, affirming, changing more to less, and less to more. Everything is contradictory and also true." On the other hand, Merleau-Ponty regards Sartre as undialectical: "In Sartre there can be no dialectic between the being, which is wholly positive, and nothingness, which 'is not.' "[30] Their failures here to understand each other is a warning that the traits of a dialectic require the discrimination that I began in *Starting Point* and shall continue in Volume 2 of the present work.

Neither of their analyses is a dialectic from the other's perspective. From Sartre's perspective, Merleau-Ponty jumps around inconsistently, so there is no reliable relational continuity to his analysis. There is a problem of direction here, which presumably explains why Sartre finds it difficult to get his "bearings" in the *Phenomenology of Perception*.[31] From Merleau-Ponty's perspective, *Being and Nothingness* is so "exclusively antithetical" that Merleau-Ponty finds no reliable continuity in so disjunctive an analysis. There can be little mutual understanding between two philosophers whose criteria for a relation (or for an analysis of a relation) are this different. The relation between Sartre's and Merleau-Ponty's philosophies depends not just, as I have previously shown, on their different analyses of personal relations but ultimately on their respective analyses of a relation itself.

There is here an additional argument (besides those I have advanced already) for why I should consider in Volume 2 Sartre's relation to Husserl first: Husserl was for Sartre "the distance" between him and Merleau-Ponty. The idiom of "distance" itself Sartre could possibly have borrowed from Heidegger, for a favorite quotation of Sartre's from Heidegger is that man is a "being of distances." [32] But Sartre's adoption of the idiom reflects his own analysis in which the individual asserts himself over against the other, instead of borrowing himself from the other, as in Merleau-Ponty. In this instance, what Sartre is assertive about, what constitutes the "distance," is a philosophically different interpretation of Husserl. Thus my reference in the present volume to their different analyses of the individual's relation to the other still needs to be supplemented in Volume 2 by reference to Sartre's and Merleau-Ponty's different interpretations of Husserl, and specifically to the differences between each of their analyses of a relation and Husserl's analysis.

: *Understanding*

> The greatest thinkers fundamentally never
> understand each other.—Heidegger

Failure to Understand

Breakdowns of communication between philosophers are failures of understanding. (Indeed, I have noted that in Heidegger's German *Verständigung* can refer either to
"communication" or "understanding.") Failures of understanding are one of the most
tantalizing of traditional proceedings in philosophy. It sometimes seems almost as if a
philosophy could not have been successfully
elaborated had the philosopher not in the
process significantly failed to understand
predecessors. They can then only receive
their philosophical due from historians, who
make up for this characteristic *Versäumnis*
on the part of the philosopher himself.

Failures of philosophers to understand
each other have dogged this history of phenomenology. We have listened to Husserl's
complaint that Heidegger never understood
him, that Heidegger's philosophy was an interpretation of his [Husserl's] philosophy
which deprived it of its "entire meaning." We
have heard a historian, Souches-Dagues, intervene and dismiss Husserl's interpretation
of Heidegger's interpretation as itself a
"crude misinterpretation." I have taken the
further step of exposing decisive junctures,
where shifts in *subject, level, affiliation,* and
method occur and help explain such misinterpretations and to relieve them of some of
their crudity. In taking this step, I have
sought more ample evidence than Husserl
mustered against Heidegger—the evidence
Heidegger mustered in support of his com-

plaint that Sartre had failed to understand his philosophy. Since after this complaint Heidegger and Sartre went their separate ways philosophically, it was still left to the historian to cope.

Sartre did admit that he had "understood Heidegger much more *via* Husserl than in his own terms." This relation of *via* assumed additional significance, which I took into account, not only because this understanding was embodied in *Being and Nothingness* but also because this was the work *via* which Heidegger came to be understood, not just in France but worldwide.

A necessary remaining step is to recognize that different philosophies can embody different understandings of "understanding" itself. Here is in some sense the nub of philosophers' failures to understand each other. At this juncture the problem of "understanding" can be separated from the problem of communication, which has been more readily treated in terms of the breakdown of communication between Sartre and Merleau-Ponty—more readily because of their mutual preoccupation with the individual's relation to the other.

In considering the problems of understanding "understanding" in the respective contexts of Heidegger's and Sartre's philosophies, it should be remembered that in Heidegger's philosophy personal reference does not have the relevance it has for Sartre. When Heidegger speaks of being misunderstood, it is not a personal affair: "This is not the lament of someone who is misunderstood, but rather indicates the insurmountable difficulty of understanding." [1]

Heidegger is blunt: "The greatest thinkers fundamentally never understand each other." [2] But Heidegger himself fails to push very far the attempt to understand their failure. What I would emphasize is that Heidegger's attitude, while nothing personal, is still based on a prolonged learning experience— "*Durch eine lange Erfahrung belehrt.*"[3]

My present point is that Sartre may well have contributed to this learning experience, for there is no other prolonged effort on Heidegger's part to rescue his philosophy from being misunderstood by another philosopher, granted that Heidegger would not rate Sartre one of "the greatest thinkers" and that he blames in large measure "public obviousness" for Sartre's failure. But the learning experience is still worth considering from the perspective afforded by the eloquent optimism with which Heidegger had greeted in 1937 the prospect of his being translated into French. In the preface he then wrote for the Corbin anthology, Heidegger announced:

> By a translation, the work of thought finds itself transposed into the spirit of another language and thus undergoes an inevitable transformation. But this transformation can become fertile, for the fun-

damental position of the question appears in a new light. It thus furnishes the opportunity to become oneself more clear-sighted and to discern more definitely the limits of one's thinking.

This is why a translation does not merely facilitate communication with the world of another language but is in itself a turning over of the soil [*défrichement*] of the question posed in common. It serves reciprocal understanding in a higher sense.[4]

The idiom may still be rustic in "The Letter on Humanism" (1946), after Heidegger had read Sartre, but the prospect of reciprocal understanding is no longer entertained: "With its saying, thinking lays inapparent [*unscheinbare*] furrows in language. They are still more inapparent than the furrows that the peasant, slow of step, draws through the field."[5] Whatever else is being drawn in this sketch of "thinking", since it comes at the end of a letter which involves a critique of Sartre, some sort of contrast must be hinted between "thinking" and the rapidity and facility of Sartre's public performance in *Existentialism is a Humanism*.

Coming to Understand

At this juncture where Heidegger, in concluding his account of Sartre's failure to understand him, becomes almost inaccessible himself, with his "inapparent furrows," I return to Sartre's admitted initial failure to understand Heidegger, as reported in a 1940 entry in his notebooks—the entry which I have quarried so extensively. I have already anticipated Sartre's admission at the end of his career that he had initially failed to understand Heidegger because he had attempted to understand him *via* Husserl.[6] In the 1930s the way was in fact blocked:

> When I started Heidegger in April [1934] . . . I was saturated with Husserl. My mistake was that I believed one could *come to understand* in succession two philosophers of that importance as one comes to understand in succession the exports of two European countries. Husserl had captured me, I saw everything in terms of the perspectives of his philosophy, which was besides more accessible, by virtue of its apparent Cartesianism. I was "Husserlian" and would remain so for a long time. At the same time the effort I had put out in order to *understand*—that is, to break my personal prejudices and to grasp Husserl's ideas starting from his own principles and not mine—had exhausted me philosophically that year.[7]

The fact that Sartre italicizes "understand" suggests that he may be admitting to using a technical term. In any case, "understanding" is a

technical term for Heidegger, who devoted an entire section to its definition.[8] It is not a technical term in Husserl. Despite Sartre's claim to have
become "saturated with Husserl," when he generalizes how he could not
"*come to understand* in succession two philosophers" as important as
Husserl and Heidegger, he is envisaging a sustained effort at understanding, which Heidegger had in fact defined, not Husserl. In Husserl an essence is immediately grasped in intuition.

Insofar as Sartre's "*come to understand*" seems more than a casual
comment, I have to qualify my previous account in which I argued that a
philosopher's conception of his relation to another philosophy is a feature
of his own philosophy, for when the first philosopher is enmeshed in the
process of coming to understand the other philosophy, his conception of
this process may well be colored by this philosophy to an extent which
should diminish (this is the expositor's working hypothesis) as the first
philosopher more fully digests this philosophy into his own. In coming to
understand Husserl, Sartre reports honoring the requirement of Husserl's
philosophical *époché*, whereby the philosopher should start out by sus-
pending all his prejudices. But we saw earlier that with Heidegger's philosophy Sartre is no longer engaged in "an effort . . . to break my personal prejudices" and to start "from his own principles, not mine." [9]
Rather, it is history (the course of history Sartre is going through in World
War II being comparable to what Heidegger had already gone through)
which finally enables Sartre to come to an understanding of Heidegger,
so that the Heidegger he finally comes to understand is primarily Heidegger on "historicity," who superseded Sartre's earlier Heidegger, whose
conception of an ahistorical "contingency" had influenced Sartre's writing of *Nausea* at a time when he was otherwise "saturated with Husserl." [10]

I have been qualifying my earlier analysis not in order to argue that
Sartre soaks up other philosophers' concepts like blotting paper (though
in a sense he does—*Quelle salade!*) but to allow for how what got in the
way of Sartre's coming to understand Heidegger was not merely, as Sartre
alleges, his saturation by Husserl or the difficulty of coming to understand two such important philosophers at once. I would add that the incommensurability of the two philosophers extends even to the process of
coming to understand them, inasmuch as Sartre succumbs successively to
features of each of their conceptions of this process.

I am not, however, abandoning my contention that a philosopher's
conception of the relation of his philosophy to another philosophy that
he finds relevant can be as much a feature of his philosophy as any other
conception of his. This contention becomes plausible when Sartre eventually recognizes the incommensurability between Husserl and Heidegger

and it becomes the antithesis which Sartre overcomes in the "synthesis" of *Being and Nothingness*. But even if we go back to the 1940 notebook entry, we find that Sartre's conception of coming to understand both Husserl and Heidegger involves roughly the shift in *level* with which we are already acquainted. The "prejudices" which Husserl's philosophical *épochē* requires us impersonally to suspend have become "personal" to Sartre, and he is not seeking philosophical understanding as such but the understanding of a particular philosophy. Similarly in Sartre's account of how he finally came to an understanding of Heidegger, it was a particular war which enabled him to do so, and there is a concomitant shift in *level* from Heidegger's "being-toward-death" to Sartre's own "being-for-war." [11]

Dialectical Understanding

This shift in *level*, which we shall, in Volume 2 of the present work, watch take place in *L'imaginaire*, can be more fully appreciated if we anticipate now how it will also take place in Sartre's relation to Heidegger in *Being and Nothingness*. We then can see that it is a pervasive commitment of Sartre's as a phenomenologist and that it is best examined first at some decisive juncture in his major work, where his understanding of the relation between Husserl and Heidegger becomes intrinsic to his own phenomenology—that is, at the juncture where the relation becomes an "antithetical" relation that is overcome in his own "synthesis." At this juncture Sartre's conception of "understanding" itself changes and becomes more or less dialectical. What this illustrates is that "understanding" is never an entirely uncodified undertaking. In Sartre's case not only is it colored by the historicism which we have watched him derive from Heidegger, but in becoming more or less dialectical it also acquires methodological implications which are not found in Heidegger.

This change in Sartre's conception of understanding I can largely disregard now, since I have already examined Sartre's dialectic in my *Starting Point* and am now concerned with *Being and Nothingness* only as the context in which the shift in *level* is more definitively carried out (with a concomitant shift in *method*) than it is in *L'imaginaire*.

The dialectical "synthesis" in *Being and Nothingness* is the closing of the gap which had opened up in Husserl when Heidegger criticized him for a *Versäumnis*—for failing to treat "the question of Being." [12] In order to avoid, for the present, taking on the full scope of *Being and Nothingness*, I select a particular juncture at which Sartre closes this gap, first by rejecting a position of Husserl's in favor of Heidegger's opposing position, and then by turning around and rejecting a position of Heidegger's in favor of Husserl's position:

> Heidegger, wishing to avoid . . . the antidialectical isolation of essences, starts with the analysis of existence without going through the *cogito*. But since the "being-there" has from the start been deprived of the dimension of consciousness, it can never regain this dimension. Heidegger endows human reality with a self-understanding which he defines as an "ekstatic pro-ject" of its possibilities. . . But how could there be an understanding which would not in itself be the consciousness (of) being understanding?[13]

At this decisive juncture, Husserl's phenomenological analysis of "consciousness" is conflated with Heidegger's ontological analysis of "understanding."

Conflation

A conflation of this sort is not simply a juncture in intellectual history at which two influences flow together. It could not take place in *Being and Nothingness* unless Sartre understood Husserl's and Heidegger's respective positions dialectically—that is, as not *"exclusively* antithetical," in Merleau-Ponty's phrase criticizing Sartre's *Being and Nothingness*.[14] Husserl and Heidegger can, instead, be brought into a relation because Sartre himself is committed to a relational analysis, granted that it is less accommodating than Merleau-Ponty's, as we have already recognized. This commitment of Sartre's is implicit in his initially crediting to Heidegger a complaint (nowhere to be found in Heidegger himself) about the "antidialectical isolation of essences" in Husserl—that is, an isolation that precludes getting a dialectic under way in the fashion I am illustrating by the dialectic that takes the guise of the reconciling "synthesis" Sartre is carrying out.

The conflation is again not simply the flowing together of two influences, because it also involves a shift in *level* which prepares the way for the shift I have characterized as a shift to the particular and personal. This preparatory shift is the shift in *level* for which Heidegger will later rebuke Sartre—the shift from the "level [in Heidegger] where there is "principally Being" to the "level [in Sartre] where there are only men."[15] In the passage I have quoted from *Being and Nothingness,* it is no longer "the question of Being" which was raised by Heidegger as the subject Husserl had failed to treat. The question for Sartre shrinks to the question of "being-there" (the "human reality").

The philosophical implications for Sartre's conflation of Heidegger's ontology with Husserl's phenomenology of consciousness emerge at another decisive juncture in *Being and Nothingness,* when Sartre undertakes to "apply to consciousness the definition which Heidegger reserved for 'being-there,'" so that consciousness becomes in Sartre "a being such that in its being, its being is in question." [16]

The definition may be Heidegger's, but when applied by Sartre, the gap that is closed is in Husserl's analysis of consciousness. In other words, there is in Sartre a shift back to Husserl's subject from Heidegger's subject, though consciousness does not fully regain the status it had as a subject in Husserl; consciousness instead makes its comeback as a "dimension" of Heidegger's "being-there."

Just as a conflation of Husserl's "consciousness" with Heidegger's "understanding" took place in the previous passage I quoted (when Sartre challenged Heidegger, "But how could there be an understanding which would not in itself be the consciousness [of] being understanding?"), so in the present passage there is an conflation of two distinct problems in Heidegger himself. This conflation is at once a misunderstanding of Heidegger, based on a mistranslation, and a philosophical translation (in the sense I brought out in my Introduction) into Sartre's own terms. Heidegger refers to "Being as that which is going on [*geht*] ... with being-there," and certain restricted implications of this reference he works out later in his analysis of "conduct" (*Umgang*)—that is, of how being-there "goes about" the *Umwelt* (the world around us).[17]

With the mistranslation whereby Heidegger's "that which is going on" becomes in Sartre that which is "in question," "the question of Being" in Heidegger can become in Sartre what "being-there" is conscious of, inasmuch as it has become in Sartre the being whose "being is in question." This conflation entails in turn the conflation of two different modes of understanding in Heidegger. On the one hand, "being-there" involves a "mediocre and vague understanding of Being," inasmuch as "Being" is "that which is going on ... with being-there." On the other hand, *Umgang* involves a more circumscribed and articulated *Umsicht*— an understanding of one's conduct, of how to make one's way about the *Umwelt.*

Conflation, whether of problems and terminology in different philosophers, or in different passages of the same philosopher, is a traditional proceeding, but it is less obvious than dismemberment or the sharper undercutting of a precedecessor's distinction, so I have postponed its illustration until now.

Project

One juncture at which Heidegger takes exception to the shift in Sartre from an ontological subject back to Husserl's phenomenological subject of consciousness is implicit in Heidegger's criticism of Sartre's misunderstanding of Heidegger's term "project": "If we understand what *Being and Time* calls 'project' as a representational positing [by consciousness—which is the way Heidegger understands Sartre's understanding of "project"], we take it to be carried out by subjectivity and do not think it in the only way the 'understanding of Being' in the context of the 'existential analysis' of 'being-in-the-world' can be thought." [18]

The nub of a philosopher's attempt to understand another philosophy (and of his failure to do so), I have assumed, is his understanding of what "understanding" itself is in that philosophy. But I am not following out the implications of Heidegger's rebuking Sartre for "understanding what *Being and Time* terms 'project' as a representational positing [by consciousness]." For the rebuke leads Heidegger on to an account of the "Turning," in which he became implicated after *Being and Time* and so raises a problem of his internal development—of the extent to which his own original understanding of *Being and Time,* including the concept there of phenomenological "understanding," is now transformed in the context of the "history of Being," from which his conception of "the subjectivity of consciousness" receives its definition.

Instead I return to what Sartre read into the term when he translates Heidegger's *Entwurf* as *projet* (or sometimes *pro-jet*); for a philosophical translation is involved as well, which is not adequately conveyed by Heidegger's "a representational positing." I requote Sartre: "Heidegger endows human reality with a self-understanding which he defines as an 'ekstatic pro-ject' of its possibilities." Sartre's understanding of this "self-understanding" must be based on such passages in *Being and Time* as the following, where Heidegger asks, "Why does the understanding always press forward toward possibilities?" Heidegger answers, "It is because the understanding has in itself the existential structure that we term 'being thrown forward.'" The *pro* in Sartre adds a voluntaristic implication to the temporal implication in Heidegger himself and thus provides a further illustration of the shift that takes place in Sartre back to Husserl's subject, consciousness. [19]

Possibility

Another term associated here with "project" is the idiom "possibility." We encountered it before when we dealt with the relation between Heidegger's phenomenology and Husserl's. In *Being and Time* Heidegger announced, "the following investigations would not have been possible if the foundations had not been laid by Edmund Husserl."[20] There was an ambiguity in this announcement that Heidegger used to his advantage in order to press forward with his understanding beyond Husserl: "What is essential in phenomenology does not reside in its *actuality* as a philosophical movement. Higher than actuality stands *possibility.*" Heidegger said, "in phenomenology." But whose phenomenology? His phenomenology or Husserl's?

What I proposed earlier was that Heidegger may have italicized "actuality" and "possibility" by way of cautioning that they were terms to be understood in the context, which he was about to elaborate, of *Being and Time*.[21] For his emphasis on the distinction could hardly be understood in the context of Husserl's phenomenology, where (in accordance with Husserl's "principle of principles") understanding is a matter of actually grasping intuitively what is immediately given—for instance, in the experience of perception. In contrast, in *Being and Time* understanding, as I have already observed, has to be sustained, since a temporal dimension intrudes, for which Heidegger has prepared with his assertion, " 'Being-there' understands itself in terms of its existence—in terms of a possibility of itself." And he will follow this up later with the question I have quoted, and which would have been opaque to Husserl, "Why does the understanding always press forward toward possibilities?" [22] This is what Heidegger's understanding is doing in *Being and Time* in relation to Husserl, and one of these possibilities is his working out an understanding of "understanding" that differs from Husserl's.

I have postponed the relation between Husserl and Heidegger in favor of the relation between Husserl and Heidegger in Sartre since there is more *prima facie* evidence available here as to how Sartre conceived this relation than how they did. But I would suggest that although Husserl goes unnamed at the juncture in the "Letter on Humanism" at which Heidegger rebukes Sartre for failing to understand understanding's projective character in *Being and Time,* Heidegger is disassociating himself from Sartre at a decisive juncture at which he had earlier disassociated himself from Husserl, not only in *Being and Time* but even more definitely in the *Basic Problems,* where he reemphasizes the projective character of understanding with his explanation, "We do not find Being in front of us. . . . It must always be brought to view in a free project." [23] If, as I have been assuming, a different understanding of "understanding" can be regarded as at the nub of the differences between philosophers, we can expect that examining the relation between Husserl and Sartre, which I shall present in Volume 2, may in some measure equip us to deal with the relation between Husserl and Heidegger, which I shall explore in Volume 3.

Transition

The present chapter accordingly ends by providing us with some perspective on the sequence of my volumes, as did the last chapter, which was also transitional. There we ended with the different analyses in Sartre and Merleau-Ponty of the relation between the individual and the other. Comparing these analyses rendered more accessible the problems of the relation between each of their respective philosophies and the other's philosophy. The comparison was transitional to my Volume 2, inasmuch as Sartre characterized Husserl as "the distance" between himself and Merleau-Ponty, so that a plausible next step (once we recognized that the distance Sartre found generally between himself and the other was a concomitant of his commitment to the antithetical) is to examine Sartre's interpretation of Husserl with some reference to Merleau-Ponty's different interpretation and to focus the comparison on Sartre's and Merleau-Ponty's different conceptions of a relation or, rather, of how a relation is to be analyzed. In Volume 2 we shall also be able to bring Husserl's conception within the scope of the comparison.

So far I have focused less on Husserl and on his relation to other phenomenologists than on the relation between Sartre and Merleau-Ponty (as the most accessible relation between phenomenologists) and on the relation between Sartre and Heidegger, for Husserl never read any of Sartre's writings, whereas we have in the "Letter on Humanism" Heidegger's appraisal of Sartre's relation to him, as well as the evidence I have already deployed as to how Sartre himself turned "toward Heidegger."

In order to complete the transition to my Volume 2, I would reconsider some of this evidence and bring out the principle that presides over the wartime transition Sartre makes from Heidegger's philosophy to reach his own: for although Sartre did not then avow it explicitly as a principle, it had already in effect presided over the prewar transition he made from Husserl's philosophy. This principle is the ultimate justification which Sartre would find for the shifts that take place during both these transitions, including the procedure of vulgarization. Thus the principle will yield, from Sartre's perspective, a philosophical response to Heidegger's charge that Sartre had succumbed to Öffentlichkeit.

Toward the Concrete

We were disappointed by this "toward."—Sartre

Öffentlichkeit

I do not pretend that the failures of philosophers to understand each other are the only failures of understanding of concern to the historian of philosophy. I have sought to illustrate certain problems of understanding by bringing within the scope of my history appraisals from Cohen-Solal's biography of Sartre and from Boschetti's social and intellectual history, *Sartre et "Les temps modernes."* The biographer and the social historian can, of course, plead the limitations of their respective genres. Although the historian of philosophy must accept some limitations too, he can at least observe (as I have) how the interest of the public in Cohen-Solal's book is assumed, quite accurately, to rise barely above the level of the personal to reach the philosophical, despite the fact that this limitation entails a certain neglect of the man who said of himself that "the only thing I really like to do is to be at my desk and write—preferably philosophy." [1] In Cohen-Solal's failure to give Sartre's own preference its due, the historian of philosophy can suspect a failure of understanding.

The preferences of intellectual fashion fluctuate, and the historian can observe how their fluctuation effects the understanding of Sartre: "To the public figure of the period after the war is now preferred the young Sartre revealed by his letters and the wartime notebooks." [2] The historian of philosophy cannot surrender entirely to the fluctuating preferences of the intellectual public. Whatever the assessment of the public, there is a philosophical issue as to how public assessment is itself to be assessed. This issue we have come across as an issue between philosophies. For according to Heidegger's interpretation of Sartre, Öffentlichkeit ("public accessibility" or "obviousness") explains in considerable measure Sartre's failure to understand him, but Sartre in contrast argues in favor of what he himself called "vulgarization." [3]

I now have to conclude for the present my discussion of this issue, since I am leaving behind the relation between Sartre and Heidegger. In concluding, I would anticipate certain complications in Heidegger which I could not unravel in the present volume without taking into consideration his internal development—something I explained I could hardly manage while maintaining my focus on Heidegger's relations with other philosophers.

When Buchheim construes the Destruktion as a procedure which "Heidegger has applied . . . throughout his thinking in all of its guises," among its tasks are "to open up [öffnen] and clear the way of the obdurate obstructions of current opinion, the usual formulation of problems and traditional prejudices." [4] Heidegger himself employs öffnen and comparable terms in a fashion which seems paradoxically pitted against Öffentlichkeit. The paradoxical complication (put in terms of my clumsy translation) is that a task of the Destruktion is to gain access to what "public accessibility" renders inaccessible.

Tradition

There is a second complication which bears even more directly on Heidegger's interpretation of Sartre in the "Letter on Humanism." There Sartre's philosophy is, on the one hand, condemned as a misguided attempt to render Heidegger's philosophy "publicly accessible," but it is also interpreted, on the other hand, as at the mercy of the philosophical tra-dition, which "takes what has come down to us and hands it over to "obviousness [Selbstverständlichkeit]." My translation "obviousness" does not bring out how we are up against still another mode of understanding that is a misunderstanding, but it does bring out (in addition to the play with the idiom of access via) the overlap between the outcomes of succumbing to tra-dition and Öffentlichkeit, which I have also translated "obviousness."

This overlap too is a complication which cannot be delineated without taking into consideration the internal development of Heidegger's philosophy. On the one hand, in Being and Time Öffentlichkeit is an existential catagory which belongs to the perennial framework of experience. But when Heidegger applies this category in criticism of Sartre's philosophy in the "Letter on Humanism," the framework has become "the history of Being." Indeed, one of Heidegger's efforts in the "Letter" is to draw attention to this change in his own philosophy. What Heidegger fails to make clear is how what had been perennial can survive in this "history," apparently without transformation. There would seem to be a *Versäumnis* here in Heidegger—a failure to deal with the relation between the two ways in which he deals with failures of understanding (including Sartre's failure to understand his philosophy): by resorting, on the one hand, to the perennial existential category of *Öffentlichkeit* and, on the other, to the historical outcome of tra-dition.[6]

Versäumnis

Take as an example of this *Versäumnis* Heidegger's later explanation of the dilemna he faces: "Every effort to bring what has been thought closer to prevailing modes of representation must assimilate what is to be thought to those representations and thereby inevitably deforms the subject [*Sache*]."[7] It is not clear from this explanation how these modes come to prevail—whether by *Öffentlichkeit* or by tra-dition.

Heidegger's dilemma has been restated by Derrida, though without specific reference to the explanation by Heidegger I have just quoted. "Each time," Derrida comments, "Heidegger has to explain something and wishes to be understood, he makes a compromise with the coherence that is logico-systematic, but this type of coherence is articulated with, compromised by, in negotiation with, something it does not exhaust; and it is this very enigmatic opening that one must question." He adds, "I don't believe it possible to submit everything to coherence. In Heidegger's case . . . there is a classical logico-metaphysical coherence, and then the other [type] which is not simply juxtaposed to the first."[8] Derrida's restatement seems to reduce the coherence that is necessary for communication (understandability) in Heidegger to the coherence that prevails from the metaphysical tradition. Derrida does not mention any other type of coherence, though it is arguable that, in *Being and Time*, *Öffentlichkeit* organizes some type of coherence.

I would be less concerned with the *Versäumnis* in Heidegger himself if so indefatigable and incisive an elucidator of Heidegger as Derrida had not seemed insensitive to it. Derrida's Heidegger is preoccupied with the *Destruktion* of the tradition as imbued with the metaphysics of presence. But Derrida finds this metaphysics still implicit in Heidegger's own conception of "authenticity." With Derrida's discrediting of "authenticity," "inauthenticity" inevitably is discredited too and, thus, such existential categories as *Öffentlichkeit* that are in Heidegger involved in the constitution of "inauthenticity." [9]

In short, it is not just Sartre's vulgarized Heidegger whom Derrida disposes of but the Heidegger whom Sartre vulgarized—the Heidegger of the "existential analysis" in *Being and Time*. Thus a complication I am leaving unraveled is whether the *Destruktion* can be restricted in its application to the tradition, as it seems to be by Derrida and his deconstructionist allies,[10] or whether it is in Buchheim's loose formulation a procedure which "Heidegger has applied throughout his thinking in all of its guises."

Vulgarization

Now we can put these complications having to do with Heidegger and the *Destruktion* to one side until Volume 3 and concentrate on the construction of Sartre's philosophy, in order to make the final transition to Volume 2. Earlier I contrasted with the philosophical menace *Öffentlichkeit* constituted in Heidegger (as exhibited by Sartre's lecture *Existentialism Is a Humanism*) the philosophical legitimacy Sartre himself conferred on "vulgarization" in that lecture. If Sartre as a self-acknowledged "has been" has deserved the place I have accorded him, it is not only because his philosophy is a *salade* composed of other philosophies, and thus well suited to expose the problems posed generally by the relations between philosophers, but is also because he is by far the most successful philosophical vulgarizer of philosophy in this century—perhaps since Cicero. The phenomenon of vulgarization itself can hardly be dismissed as a "has been." Presumably it will be with us always, and this prospect renders Sartre's accomplishment still worthy of consideration.

Sartre was a vulgarizer in the first instance of Husserl, in the second instance of Heidegger, and in the third instance—in the lecture—of his own philosophy. To judge by the reprintings of the published version, the lecture was Sartre's most successful philosophical vulgarization of his philosophy. Since Sartre largely repudiated the work himself, its success may be a problem for the social historian or social psychologist concerned with the intellectual delinquency of the *vulgus* itself. I have been concerned instead with what was involved philosophically in Sartre's vulgarization.

What is necessary finally to recognize is that vulgarization is not merely a specific concession on Sartre's part to the public character of politics, as it may seem in the lecture itself; it is also associated with, and can even to some extent be subsumed under, a comprehensive principle which is avowed by Sartre—"toward the concrete." I have kept stressing how pivotal is the issue of the direction in which a philosopher is proceeding, and Sartre's principle is a criterion that determines the direction in which we have been watching Sartre proceed in relation to other philosophers, as indicated by the shifts I have sorted out.

Whereas Heidegger brought his category of "public accessibility" or "obviousness" to bear in explaining Sartre's failure to understand him, Sartre himself explained in his 1940 report that he had failed to understand Heidegger until his historical epoch enabled him to do so, when he became "(among others) . . . the public" which was "waiting for" the translation of Heidegger by Corbin.[11]

This "public" was academic; at any rate, we saw that it was waiting for books. Among these there was one prewar book in French philosophy which Sartre singles out later in his life (1976)—Jean Wahl's *Vers le concret* (1932). This suggests that the principle at stake takes on an even greater and more definitive significance for Sartre when he comes to review his career and recognizes in retrospect that he was not simply a convert to Husserl before the war (as he then thought) or to Heidegger during the war (as he then thought) or to Marxism after the war (as he then thought). The principle dictates the one turning which he had made, as it were, distinctively his own.

Sartre recalls Wahl's book in a report on his original café conversion to Husserl's phenomenology:

> "Here at last—philosophy." We [Sartre is already a spokesman for the "waiting public"] used to think a lot of one thing: the concrete. There was a book by Wahl which was entitled *Toward the Concrete*, which had us all dreaming, because the concrete, which we did not as a matter of fact think was what Wahl said it was (it was rather pluralism in Wahl's case) we did think existed.[12]

With this casual assessment of Wahl's work, Sartre is being unresponsive to the philosophies that Wahl was presenting, which were British (Sartre never was tempted by British philosophy of any variety) and pluralistic (Sartre was committed to the "totalistic"). What Sartre is borrowing is only the principle conveyed by Wahl's title.

That Sartre applies this principle in his works renders most of them more accessible than any work by Husserl or Heidegger, as is evident from his having become, as a matter of intellectual history, the major access route to Husserl and Heidegger. I have accordingly given this route its due in the present volume, and I shall take in Volume 2 Sartre's *L'imaginaire* as a particularly accessible introduction not just to phenomenology but also to the problems of the relations between philosophers. Phenomenology yields a remarkable illustration of these problems, as I argued in my Introduction to the present volume, and in the course of this volume these problems have been defined in terms of the failures of philosophers to understand each other. In the instance of *L'imaginaire* these problems are simplified: we have heard Sartre himself single it out as "an entire work" which was "inspired by Husserl."[13] Thus his relation to Husserl is not yet complicated by his wartime conversion to Heidegger, as we have seen it is in *Being and Nothingness*. Another reason I have myself singled *L'imaginaire* out is that the extent of Husserl's inspiration is more readily assessed, since *L'imaginaire* can be compared with Sartre's treatment of the same subject in his *diplôme* on "L'image," which was written before he had read Husserl.

The Shifts

L'imaginaire will illustrate within the confines of a single work, and in much more detail, the shifts I have sorted out in this volume. I have anticipated the shift in *method* that takes place with Sartre. His analysis, as compared with that by any other of our three phenomenologists, is predominantly an intentional analysis.[14] This can be explained in some measure by the extent to which the direction imposed by Sartre's principle "toward the concrete" reinforces in Sartre the direction imposed by Husserl's principle "to the things themselves."[15] Sartre is thereby encouraged to follow out the direction taken by intentional reference to the intentional object. Thus intentional analysis comes to enjoy in Sartre, as a matter of principle, the priority as a procedure that Merleau-Ponty, in particular, would disallow.

Though this principle "toward the concrete" is not mentioned in Sartre's prewar writings, the movement "toward the concrete," and its conflation with "to the things themselves," also helps explain the shift in *level* whereby Sartre's phenomenology becomes what Husserl disdained as *Bilderbuchphänomenologie*.[16]

The things to which Sartre is directed in his intentional analysis are concrete things themselves (for example, the glass of beer—or was it an apricot cocktail?). When we encountered this controversy over Sartre's café conversion, I commented on how the shift in level betrayed the weakening of the distinction of level presupposed and enforced by Husserl's eidetic reduction. In the Volume 2 we shall see how intentional reference itself can no longer be abstracted as a logical "act," as it is by Husserl's eidetic reduction, from such voluntaristic psychological activities as *attente* and *attention*, which is an ingredient in *attente*.[17] The "act" is put back by Sartre into the concrete context of these activities from which it had been abstracted by Husserl.

The principle "toward the concrete" presides not only over the pre-war transition, which we shall be tracing in Volume 2, from Husserl's phenomenology to Sartre's own phenomenology but also over Sartre's wartime shift in allegiance from Husserl to Heidegger. When Sartre turns in the 1940 notebook entry "toward Heidegger against Husserl," Sartre is turning from Husserl's philosophy as abstract (an "academic synthesis") toward Heidegger's philosophy as concrete ("unscholarly" but "pathetic" and in the grip of historical circumstances).[18] The principle is in effect adduced again in *Being and Nothingness,* when Sartre having derived from Husserl in his introduction a conception of consciousness as intentional, makes a transition to Heidegger at the beginning of part 1: "Consciousness is an abstraction . . . . The concrete is man in the world with that specific union of man to the world which Heidegger, for example, names "being-in-the-world." [19]

I have observed that Sartre does not mention the principle "toward the concrete" in his prewar writings, and it seems possible, since he discounted Wahl's illustration of the principle, that the principle itself only crystalized for Sartre with his conversion to Heidegger. To discover a movement "toward the concrete" in Heidegger, Sartre need not have read any further than the opening paragraph of *Being and Time:* "The concrete working out of the questioning of the meaning of "Being" is the aim of the following treatise." Sartre would have taken "concrete" here to refer to the working out of this question in terms of "being-in-the-world." [20]

However, the intrusion of "man" in the reformulation with which Sartre himself makes the transition is a warning that he is not only making a transition from Husserl's phenomenology to Heidegger's but also from Heidegger's phenomenology to his own phenomenology, in which the question no longer has to do with "Being" in Heidegger's sense, but with man's "being-there"—"in-the-world." This shift to the "level where there are only men" has already been examined as leading Heidegger to accuse Sartre of "anthropologism" and "humanism." I am now merely bringing out how the shift was promoted by the principle "toward the concrete." [21]

When Sartre finally deserts Heidegger in *Being and Nothingness* and shifts his allegiance toward Hegel, the same principle promotes this turn that promoted his turning to Heidegger at the beginning of part 1: "The relation of *Mitsein* [in Heidegger] cannot help at all to resolve the psychological, concrete problem of our recognition of the other." [22] The same principle promotes the shift in *level* with which Sartre makes his transition from philosophy to its affiliate, literature: "Problems can be attacked abstractly by philosophical reflection. But . . . we want to . . . support our thinking by those fictional and concrete experiences which are novels." When Sartre, in dealing with the novel itself, makes the transition from its writer to its public, he is again moving "toward the concrete." I re-quote: "For the work to emerge, a concrete act is necessary, which is reading." [23]

Starting Out

In the present volume I have lingered, as I promised I would in my Intro-duction, with the *prima facie* evidence phenomenologists themselves present with respect to what they are doing and how it relates to what other phenomenologists have done. But in weighing this evidence, we have learned that there are decisive junctures at which it is necessary to go behind it. This I have attempted, in a preliminary fashion, by sorting out shifts in direction and finally concentrating on the principle in Sartre which presides over these shifts.

Sartre's presiding principle, "toward the concrete," tends to exempt him from the attempt at understanding that I am making on his behalf, especially if his exacerbation of this principle is taken into account. When Sartre borrows this principle from Wahl's title, he speaks for his epoch with the protest, "Yet we were disappointed by this 'toward': it is from the concrete as a totality (*le concret total*] which we would *start out from.*"[24]

The philosopher who would start out from the totality of the con-crete is unlikely to pause long enough to tolerate the process of abstrac-tion necessary to discriminate more specifically what he himself is doing. Thus we shall find in Volume 2 that the prewar Sartre does not notice that his predisposition to start out from the totality of the concrete tends to expand the scope of his subject: the imagination becomes "conscious-ness as a whole [*la conscience toute entière*] insofar as it actualizes its freedom."[25] Further indifference to discrimination is illustrated by his treatment of this subject: in *L'imaginaire* he takes over Husserl's proce-dures of intentional and eidetic analysis but fails to notice the shifts in *level* and in *method*, and the shift in *affiliation* from science to literature, to which he is also impelled by his principle.

Philosophers do not just bump against the "limits" of their under-standing when they reach the outer "boundaries" of their philosophies.[26] These "limits" are in the offing as soon as the philosopher starts out, as we have just seen to be the case when Sartre adopts the principle "toward the concrete," which he conflates with Husserl's principle "to the things themselves" and which confers priority on Husserl's procedure of inten-tional analysis while weakening the distinction of level between the eidetic character of this analysis in Husserl and any merely psychological analysis of the imagination.

Has Been

The "has been" that Sartre himself thought he had become before his death is not quite the Sartre that Boschetti presents to us at the end of her book:

> The period of assessment which started at the death of Sartre confirms the incomplete, reduced recognition to which his work from now on can aspire. Even his most zealous partisans are no longer thinking of recovering him in his totality.[27]

But Sartre's own commitment was to "totality," and his philosophy he viewed as "the unity of all I wrote"—including his literary and critical writings as well as his strictly philosophical writings.[28] When his philosophy is no longer this "totality," this "unity," Sartre is suffering dismemberment—as philosophers usually do, sooner or later.

Sartre deserved this "destiny" (to borrow the term he borrowed from Heidegger),[29] since he had himself, in composing his own philosophy, dismembered Husserl and Heidegger with little scruple—as philosophers usually do to their predecessors. But unless a historian belatedly happens along with some zeal to recover Sartre's philosophy in its totality and unity, Sartre remains philosophically the "has been" he has become in Cohen-Solal's biography and in Boschetti's social and intellectual history.

Zeal here need not imply partisanship. For the province of the historian of philosophy should not be limited to the recovery of any particular philosophy. Rather, the recovery should be transitional to uncovering such issues between philosophies as are brought out by the shifts I have sorted out. Failure to understand what is at issue is not a "has been" but a recurrent threat to communication between philosophers.

When there are issues between philosophers such as those between Sartre and Husserl, when there are such overt breakdowns in communication as those between Husserl and Heidegger, between Heidegger and Sartre, and between Sartre and Merleau-Ponty, the historian of philosophy can attempt to understand the failures of the philosophers concerned to understand each other, and he can include in his attempt how the philosophers themselves are by and large precluded by their own philosophies from arriving at this understanding. If there were no prospect that an attempt might be carried out to understand the failures of philosophers to understand each other, this might be one sense in which the history of philosophy could be said to come to an end.

Introduction

1. This is the eleventh of Marx's *Theses on Feuerbach*.

2. Though I have picked on Rorty primarily because of his prominence, he is also more straightforward (or less sophisticated) than some other American philosophers who uphold an end-of-philosophy perspective. But since most of them are prompt to acknowledge their debt to Heidegger and/or Derrida, the appropriate juncture at which to consider them will be later, when I am dealing with Heidegger and Derrida. In general I have assumed that my citing German and French commentaries (most of them untranslated elsewhere) will be more useful for many of my readers.

3. Derrida, *La voix et le phénomène*, p. 83.

4. Levinas, "Tout autrement," p. 33.

5. James, *Essays in Radical Empiricism*, p. 40.

6. Quite aside from the ambiguities of what Heidegger and Derrida mean by "end," which I am entirely overlooking *pro tem*, there is a range of ambiguity, for which my alternatives allow, in the presentation of the end of philosophy. Sometimes this end is taken to be almost a foregone conclusion, as it is by Philippe Lacou-Labarthe: "If philosophy still exists, it is only as tradition, and a tradition which is from now on closed. Where is there to be seen today an intellectual undertaking of whatever sort (that is, with respect to its origin, its own domain, its scope) which can pass as philosophy?" (*La fiction du politique*, p. 14). This conclusion may be intuitively plausible, as may the further implication that there is nothing to be done about it, because it is "the result of a necessity inscribed in the epoch" (ibid.). But then the *Destruktion* would hardly be the indispensable undertaking it is for Heidegger, or de-

construction the indispensable undertaking it is for Derrida, unless it too is the result of a necessity inscribed in the epoch.

7. See p. 140 below.

8. Buchheim, *Destruktion und Übersetzung,* p. v.

9. *Psyché,* p. 390.

10. Heidegger, *Introduction to Metaphysics,* p. 42.

11. Heidegger, *Basic Problems of Phenomenology,* p. 23.

12. Heidegger, *Basic Writings,* p. 375–76. I have retained Joan Stambaugh's translation, "What does it mean . . . ?" But this translation might have disconcerted Heidegger, partly because it does not respect his break with Husserl's phenomenology as an analysis of meaning. A conference on *Heideggers These vom Ende der Philosophie* includes an exposition of the thesis by Gadamer.

13. Husserl, *The Crisis of European Sciences and Transcendental Phenomenology,* p. 389.

14. Heidegger, *Basic Writings,* p. 235.

15. Heidegger, *Introduction to Metaphysics,* p. 26. This lecture course was not published until 1953. Observe that Heidegger is not yet drawing here his later sharp distinction between "philosophy" and "thinking," as the "task" which appropriately supervenes after the end of philosophy itself. I shall not draw the distinction either, since it will not be my concern in this volume to trace Heidegger's internal development. Rorty employs the rubric "philosophy-as-literature" for the successor subject, even though he regards the shift in *subject* as the end of philosophy.

16. Heidegger, *Poetry, Language, Thought,* p. 224. Because of modern philosophy's affiliation with science, the problem of incommensurability has usually come up as a problem in the history and philosophy of science. Whether or not Heidegger is aware of this version of the problem, his transformation of the problem itself helps us to get outside the scientific context and to focus on the problem as a problem of the relation between philosophies.

17. *Existence and Being,* p. 360.

18. Heidegger, *Poetry, Language, Thought,* p. 26.

19. Husserl, quoted in Diemer, *Edmund Husserl,* p. 29. That Husserl here exploits an etymology is a rather unusual procedure on his part, and it may derive from the philosopher he is denouncing. Souche-Dagues, who offers a larger sample of Husserl's marginal comments than does Diemer, turns the idioms from the comment I have quoted back against Husserl: "This text . . . , seen from Heidegger's side must be regarded as a crude misinterpretation. . . . It will preside over Husserl's reading of the work as a whole. . . . It must be said that Husserl carries out the inverse 'transposition' of what he reproaches Heidegger for" ("La lecture husserlienne de *Sein und Zeit,*" p. 10). Although such idioms gain specific implications in the setting of Husserl's philosophy, I am quoting them at this preliminary stage because they are standard for historians making the transition from one philosophy to another. Thus Merker in her *Selbsttäuschung und Selbst-*

erkenntnis: Zu Heideggers Transformation der Phänomenologie Husserls employs (in addition to the idiom of "transformation" in her subtitle) the same idioms as Husserl without any reference to his own marginal comment. She reports that "the divergency in phenomenological methods depends on this inverse specification [*inversen Bestimmung*] of the starting point of phenomenology" (p. 8). Again, Husserl's "eidetic reduction is transformed [by Heidegger] into the "phenomenological construction" (p. 17). Heidegger himself is interpreted as taking over such Christian categories as "the Fall," which he "transposes [*transponiert*] into what is most inward in men" (p. 9). My argument, which I have briefly illustrated by reference to Heidegger, will be that such standard idioms need to have their implications worked out in terms of the philosophy involved.

20. See p. 120 below.

21. Merleau-Ponty, *Le visible et l'invisible,* pp. 236–37.

22. Mill, quoted in my *Human Nature and History,* 1:14–15, 2:339–40. Mill is stressing the shift in method which is (in my terminology) concomitant with the shifts in *subject* and in *affiliation,* but I have not yet distinguished this shift. Even when scientific, the "other studies" or affiliates hardly yield a firm or final anchorage. Mill finds his father's antagonist, Macaulay, "wrong . . . in assimilating the method of philosophizing in politics to the purely experimental method of chemistry," but Bentham, whom Mill links in error with his father, had sought a model for his political philosophy in the analytic method of chemistry (2:234). We have already watched Husserl adopt geometry as the model for his philosophy as an eidetic science, though his philosophy is not deductive.

23. For the preeminent place of Newton in the history of philosophy, see *Human Nature and History,* vol. 2, chap. 13 and pp. 227–28.

24. Merleau-Ponty, *Le primat de la perception,* p. 78.

25. Heidegger, *Existence and Being,* p. 360.

26. The details of the break between Husserl and Heidegger will be taken up in the third volume of this history. For the present, I would only point out that since Heidegger, after he becomes involved in the "Turning" (roughly in the 1930s), no longer refers to Husserl, there has been an inclination to assume that Heidegger has brusquely dismissed Husserl from his thinking. Günter Figal points out that "to characterize Heidegger's philosophy as a whole as '*Phänomenologie*' [as Figal does in his interpretation *Martin Heidegger,* subtitled *Phänomenologie der Freiheit*] seems to overlook the 'Turning' " (p. 27). Figal justifies his book's title by observing that Heidegger still speaks of phenomenology "in a positive sense" in his last work. However, it should also be observed that in this work, "My Way to Phenomenology," Heidegger gives an account of his relation to Husserl which he carries no further than *Being and Time.* My guess is that Heidegger wanted to allow a margin of ambiguity but that the end of philosophy was for him also the end of phenomenology.

27. Rorty, *Philosophy in History,* p. 52.

28. Ibid. I have taken my quotations from Rorty out of their context. Let me supply some of it. A debate was initiated by Jonathan Bennett's claim that "we

understand Kant only in proportion as we can say, clearly and in contemporary terms, what his problems were, which of them are still problems and what contribution Kant made to their solution." Michael Ayers had protested on behalf of the distinction between "understanding a philosopher in his own terms . . . and what we ourselves might want to say." Rorty leans toward Bennett by urging (in part) that "there is indeed a sense in which we can understand what a philosopher says in his own terms before relating his thought to ours, but . . . this minimal sort of understanding is like being able to exchange courtesies in a foreign tongue without being able to translate what one is saying into our native language. . . . Translation is necessary if 'understanding' is to mean something more than engaging in rituals of which we do not see the point. . . . Ayers overdoes the opposition between 'our terms' and 'his terms' when he suggests that one can do historical reconstruction first and leave rational reconstruction for later. The two genres can never be *that* independent, because you will not know much about what the dead meant prior to figuring out how much truth they knew."

29. Rorty, *Philosophy and the Mirror of Nature*, pp. 393, 6, 5. Rorty reports that the three "are in agreement that the notion of knowledge as accurate representation, made possible by special mental processes, and intelligible through a general theory of representation [i.e., the mirror theory], needs to be abandoned." But in the preceding sentence Rorty has also found them in agreement in that "their later work is therapeutic rather than constructive, edifying rather than systematic, designed to make the reader question his own motives for philosophizing rather than to supply him with a new philosophical program." Later he adds that "the common message of Wittgenstein, Dewey, and Heidegger is a historicist one" (p. 9).

30. Husserl, *The Crisis of the European Sciences*, p. 392. I am suggesting a broad distinction between Husserl's indifference to making discriminations, which is conveyed by his metaphor of "a torrent," and the clumsy discriminations practiced by crating and forklifting. Here Jürgen Habermas is a noteworthy offender, especially when he is dealing with something as unmanageable as "modernity," which encourages crating and forklifting.

31. Thus I have indicated that Heidegger no longer refers to Husserl in the 1930s. Similarly, Husserl does not refer to Heidegger in *Crisis*. My point now is that it is worth considering first the relation between their philosophies in the 1920s (as I shall in my third volume), when references to each other are available as prima facie evidence, before trying to determine what happens to this relation in the 1930s.

32. Heidegger, *Being and Time*, p. 38.

33. Husserl, quoted in Cairns, *Conversations with Husserl and Fink*, p. 9.

34. I am not trying to circumvent Heidegger's own statement that "since 1907 Brentano's dissertation *On the Several Meanings of Being in Aristotle* had been the main help and guide of my first awkward attempts to penetrate into philosophy" (*On Time and Being*, p. 74). But in dealing with the history of phenomenology, Heidegger regards the *Logical Investigations* as "having become the fundamental work in phenomenology," the work in which "phenomenological research

arrived at its first breakthrough" (*Gesamtausgabe* 20:30). Neither Sartre nor Merleau-Ponty took Brentano into account, and their indifference may have been partly responsible for the minimal interest in him in France, as compared with the United States.

35. A disclaimer is necessary here. Since I am dealing with the "interpretation" of philosophies, and in later chapters with "understanding" and "communication" (and in a later volume with Heidegger's conception of "tradition"), I might well be expected to devote some attention to Gadamer, Habermas, Apel, etc., as philosophers who have been influential in elaborating these conceptions. But I shall even avoid, as much as possible, the term "interpretation" and above all "hermeneutics." I find it prudent to examine a less diffuse range of usages, by restricting myself to given evidence as to how four prominent phenomenologists themselves have actually interpreted and understood one another. After all, current philosophers who go in for problems of "interpretation," "understanding," and "tradition" are in important respects heirs to phenomenology. But Gadamer's interpretation of Heidegger, in particular, poses special difficulties, by virtue of his effort to make Heidegger more understandable, more communicable—indeed, more traditional. Robert Bernasconi, in "Bridging the Abyss: Heidegger and Gadamer," has shown how misleading is the "bridge," which Habermas has commended Gadamer for building, between Heidegger and the philosophical tradition. As for Habermas, I am disconcerted by his erecting a philosophy of communication with so little concern for the actual problems of communicating with each other that philosophers themselves illustrate. In fact, as Derrida has pointed out, Habermas is an "advocate of communication" who has attacked Derrida at some length without going to the trouble of actually quoting Derrida's own works, preferring instead to pick on his followers (*Mémoires,* pp. 225–26). Habermas apparently assumes that the deconstructionists can be crated together and forklifted, in much the same fashion as he has done with earlier successions of figures in the history of philosophy.

36. Derrida, "The Time of a Thesis: Punctuations," p. 38. For the idiom, see Derrida's "Living On."

37. Freedberg, *Painting in Italy, 1500–1600,* pp. 177, 487.

1. The Subject of Phenomenology

1. Heidegger, *On Time and Being,* p. 62.

2. Heidegger, *Being and Time,* p. 38.

3. Husserl, *Logical Investigations,* 1:43, 45.

4. Heidegger, *Being and Time,* p. 38. Earlier, in his *Prolegomena,* Heidegger had referred to the *Investigations* as the work with which "phenomenological research arrived at its first breakthrough" (p. 30)." This could be taken as suggesting that a second breakthrough was in prospect.

5. Heidegger, *Being and Time,* p. 329.

6. How fertile a resort to possibility can be when it becomes resort to a possible relation to still another philosophy is illustrated by Figal's recalling, at this

juncture in *Being and Time*, Kierkegaard's conception of "possibility." Figal enlists here a possible relation between Heidegger and Kierkegaard to clarify the relation between Husserl and Heidegger. This is how Figal pursues his interpretation: "Heidegger's conception of phenomenology as the upholding of possibility will be better understood if the *relevant context* [my italics] is made clear. It is the determination of the relation between possibility and actuality as Kierkegaard developed it. In his *Concept of Dread* Kierkegaard employs the expression "possibility" as a determination of freedom. Freedom is 'the possibility of possibility' " (*Martin Heidegger*, p. 38). But there is a larger context which is relevant and which provides the warrant for Figal's interpretation. It is Heidegger's own pronouncement, which enjoys the prominence of display on the dust jacket of Figal's book: "A philosophical text . . . is only superficially understood if it is interpreted in terms of its results; it becomes available only when with it one renews the questioning."

I am not quarreling with Figal's procedure as an interpreter, which has interesting results. I would merely observe, first, that Heidegger's pronouncement, which Figal applies to the interpretation of Heidegger, conveys much the same implications as the pronouncement Heidegger applies in interpreting his relation to Husserl when he discounts the actual results (Husserl's phenomenology) in favor of a possible phenomenology. Second, resort to Heidegger's relation to Kierkegaard's conception of " 'possibility' as a determination of freedom" assists Figal in determining that Heidegger's philosophy is a "phenomenology of freedom" (the subtitle of Figal's book) and thus provides a succinct example of what I characterize as a shift in *subject* from Heidegger's explicit subject, "The Question of Being": Figal's interpretation illustrates how this shift can take place not only between successive philosophies (Husserl's and Heidegger's) but also between successive interpretations of the same philosophy (the standard interpretation of *Being and Time* and Figal's). Third, what I take as "the relevant context" (in Figal's phrase) for interpreting Heidegger's relation to Husserl is *Being and Time*, but this does not necessarily deny the relevance of Kierkegaard to the interpretation of the work, since Heidegger himself commends *The Concept of Dread*, though in other, more restricted connections.

7. Heidegger, *On Time and Being*, p. 77.

8. Husserl, *Ideas I*, sec. 24.

9. Husserl, *The Crisis of European Sciences*, p. 155.

10. Heidegger, *Prolegomena*, esp. p. 180.

11. Heidegger, *On Time and Being*, p. 62.

12. Heidegger, *Basic Problems of Phenomenology*, pp. 21–22. This statement applies to the way being is brought into view in *Being and Time* and specifically to its being brought into view as a "possibility." For projection as the projection of possibilities, see p. 184 below.

13. Cairns, *Conversations with Husserl and Fink*, p. 16.

14. Heidegger, *Phänomenologie—lebendig oder tot?*, p. 48.

15. Heidegger, *Being and Time,* p. 329. Cumming, *Starting Point,* pp. 79–80.

16. I'll take up the issue of autonomy, which in Sartre's case is the issue of originality, in Chapter 7.

17. Sartre, *Les carnets de la drôle de guerre,* p. 239.

18. Sartre, *L'imaginaire,* p. 15.

19. *Sartre, un film,* pp. 43, 44. In the next sentence, however, Sartre mentions having written *The Transcendence of the Ego* in Berlin, and in this work he does refer to other works of Husserl's. But there can be no doubt that he concentrated on *Ideas I.*

20. How incongruous this idiom is in the mouth of Sartre, who in the essay on "Intentionality" (the other essay he wrote in Berlin) had hailed Husserl as rescue from the revolting "digestive philosophy" prevailing in France! (See Sartre, *Situations,* 1:38.)

21. For the accommodating character of Merleau-Ponty's phenomenology, see the "Accommodation" section of Chapter 9.

22. Merleau-Ponty, *Phenomenology of Perception,* pp. 243, 274, 265.

23. Derrida, "The Time of a Thesis," p. 38. The French *discipline* (if that was the term—this essay has been published only in an English translation) has much the same ambiguity as the English "discipline." Thus the "rigor" in question could be either that of philosophy as rigorous science, or it could be merely the stringency of the training this philosophy imposes, or it could be both.

24. Derrida, *La voix et le phénomène,* p. 1.

25. Ibid., p. 6; Derrida's italics. Their emphasis seems to betray the shift in *subject,* for from Husserl's perspective to refer to "the essence of language *in general*" is worse than redundant. "Essence" is the relevant and strong term in Husserl; "in general" is a weak term and applies more obviously to what is reached by a process of generalization—e.g., by an empirical induction. An "essence" is not reached in this fashion, as we shall see in Volume 2.

26. Misch, "Lebensphilosophie und Phänomenologie," pp. 1, 2.

27. See p. 8 above.

28. Heidegger, *What is a Thing?,* pp. 1–2. Anyone who is disconcerted by the proposal that a "confusion" might be "helpful" may be reassured slightly by the suggestion Heidegger may be alluding to the confusion induced by Socratic questioning in a Platonic dialogue.

29. Husserl, *Logical Investigations* 1:252; my italics.

30. When I employ the terms "failure" or "neglect" (or the corresponding verbs) in reporting a philosopher's appraisal of a previous philosopher, it will be with these broader implications of *Versäumnis.*

31. Heidegger, *Being and Time,* p. 4.

32. For the predicament, see the quotation from Heidegger, p. 37 above. I shall later develop the idiom of "turning" in Chapters 6 and 10.

33. See p. 31 above.

34. Husserl, quoted in Diemer, *Edmund Husserl,* p. 29.

35. I shall do so in my third volume.

36. Whether or not Derrida is actually committing himself to a subject requires further examination.

37. Husserl, *Logical Investigations* 1:261.

38. Ibid.

39. Husserl, *Briefe,* p. 43.

40. Heidegger's statement welcoming the prospective of collaboration is cited in *Husserliana* 9:600.

41. Husserl, *Briefe,* p. 56.

42. Husserl, *Husserliana,* 5:140 (see also *Crisis,* sec. 43).

43. Heidegger, *Gesamtausgabe,* 20:31. Heidegger is reporting the then-standard criticism that "the second volume [of the *Logical Investigations*] is a falling back [*Rückfall*] into psychology, whose transposition [*Übertragung*] into philosophy Husserl had directly repudiated in the first volume." Heidegger uses the same idiom in "My Way to Phenomenology," but Heidegger is reluctant there to attribute so "gross an error" to Husserl (*On Time and Being,* p. 76).

44. *The Philosophy of Jean-Paul Sartre* (*The Library of Living Philosophy*), p. 44.

2. The Level of Phenomenology

1. See p. 10 above.

2. A "shift to an undertaking of another kind" is my free rendering of the prohibition which Husserl borrows from Aristotle (see, e.g., *Logical Investigations,* 1:55). A *metábasis* is a "change from one place to another" and could be applied to a "revolution" when one political regime "displaced" another. Husserl may have intended *Übertragung* (see p. 9 above) to coincide etymologically with *metábasis,* since both refer to the "transfer" of the subject of phenomenology from the transcendental to the empirical level.

3. See the "Translation" section of my Introduction. Despite the fact that the subject of Husserl's phenomenology is "inner consciousness" (see p. 31 above), he has to step outside into the spatial realm for the metaphors (*metábasis, Übertragung,* etc.) which will do justice to the perversion of phenomenology that takes place with Heidegger's relapse into this realm of "being-in-the-world," where the transcendental ego is "displaced" by "being-there." My own concern with these inescapable metaphors is with their application to the relations between philosophies. On the one hand, Heidegger speaks of their last attempt at collaboration (in 1927, on the article "Phenomenology" for the *Encyclopedia Britannica*) as an "opportunity to indicate the fundamental tendency of *Being and Time* within [*innerhalb*] the transcendental problematic" (see the "Zigzag" section of Chapter 1). On the other hand, Husserl came to the conclusion in 1929 "that I cannot include the work [*Being and Time*] within the framework [*Rahmen*] of my phenomenology." The distinction "inside/outside" remains too stark to deal with the

complications of the "change of place" or "revolution" which is involved in moving from one philosophy into another. Hence there is a need to distinguish the various shifts I am examining.

4. Heidegger, *Being and Time*, p. 38.

5. See p. 37 above.

6. Husserl, *Ideas I*, p. 45.

7. Souche-Dagues, "La lecture husserlienne de *Sein und Zeit*," p. 10.

8. Heidegger, *Nietzsche*, 1:450.

9. Husserl, *Logical Investigations*, 1:45.

10. Cairns, *Conversations with Husserl and Fink*, p. 32.

11. I'll stick with the term "phenomenological reduction," since Husserl's application of this term may suggest how crucial he considered this procedure to be to phenomenology.

12. Cairns, *Conversations*, p. 38.

13. See p. 81 above.

14. Cairns, *Conversations*, p. 14.

15. Husserliana 15, p. xxxv.

16. Cairns, *Conversations*, p. 22.

17. Heidegger, *Frühe Schriften*, pp. 137–38. I'm not suggesting that this is Heidegger's later appraisal.

18. Husserl, *Logical Investigations*, 1:48.

19. Ibid., 2:549.

20. See my *Starting Point*, pp. 114, 158–61, 251–52, 354–55, 516–17; for the dialectical handling of distinctions of level, see pp. 58, 200–202, 236–38. Throughout the present volume it should be kept in mind that my terminology "shift in *level*" can be misleading if it is taken as indicating that a level is simply discarded. For example, the transcendental level survives in Sartre in his refutation of Husserl's transcendental ego, but it doesn't survive unaltered, for it survives as an "impersonal consciousness." And Sartre's analysis becomes an analysis of the *interplay* between this consciousness and personal consciousness or self-consciousness.

21. Sartre, *Philosophy of Jean-Paul Sartre*, pp. 296–304.

22. Heidegger, *Basic Writings*, 213–14.

23. Ibid., p. 103.

24. Sartre, *Being and Nothingness*, pp. 703–4; italics in original.

25. Sartre, *Qu'est-ce que la littérature?*, p. 217.

26. Sartre, *Situations*, 10:94.

27. Heidegger's remark is reported by Michel Haar in an article entitled "La biographie réleguée" (p. 20). See also Heidegger's pronouncement that "the way which opened up" in his thinking "eludes self-presentation [*entzieht sich der Selbstdarstellung*]" (*Frühe Schriften*, p. xi).

28. Sartre, *Situations,* 2:15–16.

29. Kierkegaard, *Concluding Unscientific Postscript,* p. 319. And see my *Starting Point,* pp. 58–61.

30. Heidegger, "Nur noch ein Gott kann uns retten," *Der Spiegel,* 31 May 1976, p. 201.

31. See p. 77 below.

32. Merleau-Ponty, *Signes,* p. 121. Since the particular paper from which I am quoting, "Sur la phénoménologie du langage," was presented at a conference at which Husserl scholars were in attendance, it is surprising that Merleau-Ponty was not deprived of the quotation. The first time he quotes it (in *The Phenomenology of Perception,* p. xii) it is ostensibly from the unpublished manuscript of *The Crisis of European Sciences.* It may have crept into his notes during his wartime visit to the archives at Louvain (see p. 94 below).

33. See p. 53 above.

34. Merleau-Ponty, *Humanism and Terror,* p. 170. It is significant that, for the purposes of this argument, Merleau-Ponty has conjoined two examples: those who leave the Communist party, and a man who leaves a woman. Having offered the examples, he comments (in the sentence preceding the argument) that "there is nothing frivolous about comparing in this fashion political life with personal life." This contention seems prompted by the fact that the "ideas" in question in the political example are Marxist. Merleau-Ponty would imply that Marxism neglects the significance of personal relations. Thus he has already defended his comparison: "The break [*rupture*] with the Party is total, like the break with a person.. . . It does not leave intact the memory of what preceded it. . . . If they [the ex-Communists] had an inadequate understanding of Marxism during their Communist period, they cannot be asked to return to it and face today questions regarding it, given that they have rejected it as a friendship or a love affair is rejected—*en bloc.* Perhaps they even cling to the image of it as the impoverished doctrine which they have made out of it, because it justifies the break." An image, and the relativity of knowledge, are also features of the example from personal life: "A man who has left the woman with whom he had lived remains incredulous if she becomes precious to someone else: he knew her better than anyone, by virtue of their daily life together, and this image which is so different that another now has of her, can only be an illusion. He knows; the others are deceiving themselves" (pp. 160–61).

I cite Merleau-Ponty's argument, and the examples he offers in its support, as an implicit critique of Marxism, first of all, because historicism (whether Marxist, or Foucaultian, or whatever) is these days a more fashionable form of what Husserl regarded as relativism than is personal relevance. Second, the relativism of the previous lover's and the later lover's respective "knowledge" of the woman helps bring out the difference between Merleau-Ponty's stress on personal relations and the stress in Sartre on first-person relevance. When Sartre criticizes Marxism, it is on behalf of the individual. Sartre quotes Engels: "That such a man, and specifically this man, arises at a determined period and in a given country is naturally pure chance. But, lacking Napoleon, another man would have filled his place." Thus the Marxist, Sartre explains, "ends up getting rid of the particular by defining it as the simple effect of chance." Sartre's contemporary counterexample is the following: "Valéry is a petit bourgeois intellectual, without doubt; but not every petit bourgeois intellectual is Valéry."

Neither Merleau-Ponty's nor Sartre's criticism entails leaving historical circumstances out of account. Comparable to Merleau-Ponty's refusal to maintain a fixed distinction of level between the philosophical and the personal, such as we find in Husserl and Heidegger, is his refusal at the very beginning of *Signes* to maintain a fixed distinction of level between the philosophical and the circumstantial: "Between the philosophical essays and the discussion of circumstances, almost all political, which compose this volume, how great a difference at first sight, how great a disparity!" But this disparity diminishes on further consideration. In Sartre, circumstances acquire specificity as the individual person's appraisal of the circumstances enters into their restructuring as "situations" (see Sartre, *Philosophy of Sartre*, p. 268).

A third reason for my citing this political example is that it has to do with a "break" at once philosophical and personal, and Merleau-Ponty's commentary illustrates how the delineation of such a "break" as those in the relations between philosophers on which I am focusing (the relations between Husserl and Heidegger, between Sartre and Merleau-Ponty, between Heidegger and Sartre) can be as dependent on the philosophy of the delineator as on the other differences at issue between philosophies. See the "Personal Reference" section of Chapter 12.

35. Hyppolite, "Existence et dialectique dans la philosophie de Merleau-Ponty," p. 230.

36. See Sartre, *Philosophy of Sartre*, pp. 185–208.

37. Merleau-Ponty, *Phenomenology of Perception*, p. 360.

38. Sartre, *Situations*, 4:189. Sartre is presumably echoing the classic explanation of a friendship, Montaigne's "Because it was he; because it was me" (*Essays*, p. 226). In Sartre, the explanation no longer applies to a friendship which survives death but to the friends whom "I have lost who are still alive"—to the breaking off of the relation. If Merleau-Ponty had still been alive, he would have retorted that Sartre's having had to twist Montagne's explanation out of shape is evidence that a "common ground" is still a norm for determining what friendship is (see *Phenomenology of Perception*, p. 355; see also the "Distance" section of Chapter 12 below.

39. Merleau-Ponty, *Signes*, p. 201.

40. Merleau-Ponty, *Phenomenology of Perception*, p. 354.

41. Note that in this and in the preceding quotation, the "other[s]" precede "myself," indicating how borrowed I am.

42. Merleau-Ponty, *Signes*, pp. 202–3. Observe how Merleau-Ponty, having distinguished between the two levels at which communication takes place (at the level of "communication with a work" and at the level of "communication with an author"), goes on to trace the *interplay* between these levels.

43. *Husserliana*, 9:253.

44. See p. 19 above.

45. See p. 52 above.

46. Heidegger, *Basic Writings,* pp. 104, 112; for the shift in *level,* see esp. pp. 105, 109, 111.

3. The Terrain of Vulgarization

1. Sartre, *Carnets,* p. 227.

2. Merleau-Ponty, *Phenomenology of Perception,* p. viii.

3. In particular, I am overlooking the role of Jewish refugees who arrived in France (as in the United States) before the war. Sartre's first phenomenological work to be published appeared in 1936 in *Recherches philosophiques,* which was edited by Alexandre Koyré, a student of Husserl's. Sartre's major prewar phenomenological work, *L'imaginaire,* was read in manuscript by Bernard Groethuysen, who had arrived in France before World War I and was prominent in literary and publishing circles. Sartre considered that he had come to Husserl "*via* Levinas" (see p. 89 below), but late in life he confused Levinas's dissertation on Husserl with another refugee's work, Georges Gürwitch's *Tendences actuelles de la philosophie allemande,* which was published the same year, 1930 (*Sartre, un film,* p. 42).

4. Habermas, *Philosophisch-Politische Profile,* p. 78.

5. See p. 65 below.

6. Heidegger, *Basic Writings,* p. 220.

7. See p. 31 above.

8. Granel, "Remarques," p. 351.

9. *L'Express,* 20–26 October 1969, p. 85.

10. Beaufret, *Introduction aux philosophies de l'existence,* p. 6.

11. Ibid., p. 5.

12. Ibid., p. 19; Beaufret, *Entretiens,* pp. 6–7.

13. See Richardson, *Heidegger,* preface.

14. Beaufret, *Philosophies de l'existence,* p. 5. I am abstracting here from the internal development of Heidegger's philosophy: Beaufret was originally unaware of it. His allegiance having shifted to Heidegger *via* Sartre in *Being and Nothingness,* he became so excited over beginning to understand *Being and Time* that he didn't manage to display the enthusiasm he should have when he was interrupted by the news of the Allied landing in Normandy. When the war ended, he looked forward to meeting the author of *Being and Time.* But when he did visit Heidegger in September 1946, he frankly admits, "I didn't know the author of *Being and Time.* When I first met Heidegger . . . in 1946, I discovered it was extremely difficult to take Heidegger back to that 1927 book." Beaufret never explains how this difficulty was overcome. Was it simply due to pressure from Beaufret and other French readers that Heidegger did allow himself to be taken

back to *Being and Time,* in order to rescue it in his "Letter" from Sartre's interpretation? One can conjecture that he may have been initially reluctant to discuss
Being and Time because Beaufret was so imbued with Sartre's misinterpretation.
Yet when *Existentialism is a Humanism* appeared—or when Beaufret formulated
explicit questions, based on Sartre's misinterpretation—Heidegger may have decided a confrontation was appropriate. It is curious that Beaufret's interchange of
letters with Heidegger has never been published. Were they too much of an em-
barrassment to Beaufret once he understood Heidegger? Did the questions he
asked undergo some reformulation, so that their correspondence could be said to
have involved prearrangement? In any case, Beaufret's climactic question is,
"What I have been trying to do for a long time now is to determine precisely the
relation of ontology to a possible ethics" (reported by Heidegger, "Letter on Humanism," p. 231). This question is clearly inspired by Sartre. On the one hand,
Sartre had repudiated Heidegger's distinction between ontology and ethics by
protesting that his "expressions 'authentic' and 'inauthentic' . . . are insincere
because of their implicit moral content" (*Being and Nothingness,* p. 680). On the
other hand, Sartre had promised to follow up the ontology of this work with an
ethics, and since Heidegger's preoccupation was with "humanism" (his "Letter"
was first published in Bern along with "Plato's Doctrine of Truth," in which he
also deals with humanism), he could hardly have overlooked the fact that the title
of Sartre's ethics was to have been *Man.* Beaufret probably then could be counted
as a member of Sartre's "public" (of which Heidegger is so much aware, having
been deprived of the right to publish), which was waiting for Sartre's ethics. That
year (1947) prior to the autumn (the date of the "Letter," according to Heidegger
[*Wegmarken,* p. 397]), Sartre's own theory of the waiting public (see p. 119 below) was appearing in *Les temps modernes.* There is plenty of irony to go around
here. While Heidegger is explaining in the "Letter" why he will not write an
ethics, Sartre was in fact writing an ethics, which he found himself unable to complete and publish. Yet he got far enough along with it to decide that Heidegger would be no help, and he dismisses Heidegger as a minor philosopher (see
p. 167 below).

15. Of course, the access sought may be to a substantive problem. But this
problem, or its formulation, may belong to the successor's philosophy. Thus in
the final seminar Beaufret organized for Heidegger on Husserl, the announced
problem was the one that Heidegger had complained Husserl neglected (see p. 38
above): "An access route [*un accès*] to the *question of being . . .*will be attempted,
starting out from Husserl" [the italics are Beaufret's, presumably to emphasize
that the question was Heidegger's]. Thus the first difficulty to be faced is, "To
what extent is the question of being not to be found in Husserl?" (*Questions,*
4:309). To this extent, raising the question points up (in my terminology) a *Versäumnis* in Husserl. There is an exposition of Heidegger's handling of the problem in Jacques Taminiaux, "Heidegger and Husserl's *Logical Investigations.*"

16. James, *The Art of Criticism,* pp. 376–78.

17. Sartre, *Carnets,* p. 225.

18. Sartre, quoted in de Beauvoir's *Entretiens, avec Jean-Paul Sartre*, p. 223.

19. Heidegger, *Der Spiegel* 31 May 1976, p. 199, reprinted in *Antwort*, where the criticism is mentioned on p. 89.

20. See p. 19 above.

21. See chap. 4, note 8.

22. Heidegger, *Basic Writings*, p. 195. For an account of other issues raised by the confrontation between Heidegger and Sartre, see Fell, *Heidegger and Sartre*, chap. 6.

23. Heidegger, *Being and Time*, pp. 167–69. See below, Chapter 8, note 39.

24. See my *Starting Point*, pp. 331–34.

25. In *Human Nature* I argue, for example, that Cicero's political philosophy in his *Republic* and his *Laws* is a vulgarization of Plato's philosophy in his *Republic* and his *Laws* and that Cicero's vulgarizations had more influence generally on modern political philosophy up until the nineteenth century than did the original Platonic works, much as Roman and Hellenistic statues which were copies or derivative were more influential in the development of modern art than the classical Greek originals that were available. See the analogies I draw to Renaissance and neoclassical art as *ars post artem* (1:129, 133–34).

26. Sartre, *L'existentialism est un humanisme*," p. 102–3. I should point out that my use elsewhere with respect to philosophers, of the term "commitment," which has frequently caught the reader's attention, is not identical with Sartre's use of *engagement*. It is instead an adaptation of Heidegger's terminology. Richardson translates Heidegger's *Schicksal* as "com-mitment" (*Heidegger*, pp. 20–21). I could not survive as a writer of English if I went along with Richardson's translation of the cognate *Geschick* as "mittence." Perhaps it is a hopeless assignment to try to translate what is, with Greek, "the most spiritual of all languages" (Heidegger, *Introduction to Metaphysics*, p. 57). But I am attempting (as I explained on p. 37 above) to work out a terminology that can be laid alongside that of Heidegger's *Geschichte* of philosophy, in order to be able to deal later with the issues posed by the differences between his and my conception of the history of philosophy. These issues have been sharpened by Derrida's deconstruction of Heidegger's terminology; accordingly, Derrida's own conception will also come into question, and with it his and Heidegger's respective conceptions of the end of philosophy.

27. Ibid., p. 101. The shift in *level* that takes place with "vulgarization" can also entail actualization and, thus, provides a contrast (though other factors are present) with Heidegger's upholding of phenomenology as a "possibility" over against what it actually is (see p. 29 above). The theme of vulgarization/actualization is developed by Sartre later in his career, when, in "Socialism in One Country," he explains how a doctrine may "exercise an influence" (*ait une action*): Marxism "became vulgarized, as it made them [Russian peasants] more sophisticated . . . It was fossilized, as they . . . recreated it in each systematic deciphering of their experience. When it became incarnated, its fundamental character as the 'actualization of philosophy' helped to give it a new preponderance . . . , as the

constantly renewed, lived actuality of the Soviet masses" (p. 153). Alongside this claim on behalf of Russian Marxism (as opposed, presumably, to more sophisticated Western versions) can be set Cicero's claim on behalf of the actual Roman Republic (as opposed to Plato's more sophisticated version of an ideal state in his *Republic*): "What argument of philosophers is so well formulated as to be compared with a state with a legal system and traditions?" (cited in my *Human Nature*, 1:290).

28. See p. 34 above. "Without them" might suggest direct access, without anyone else intervening. But another party has in the meantime intruded since the heyday of Sartre and Merleau-Ponty in the 1940s and 1950s. Since I am largely abstracting from the internal development of Heidegger's philosophy (if it is a development—see p. 124 below), I am not allowing for the fact that Heidegger's corpus has changed by the time Derrida becomes an authority. Heidegger's *Nietzsche* was published in German in 1961, and the conjunction between Nietzsche and Heidegger tended to displace the conjunction between Heidegger and Husserl which had been restored after their break by Sartre and Merleau-Ponty. Furthermore, Derrida himself tended to become an access route to Heidegger in the United States from the late 1960s on, especially since Americans were less likely to read German. I am observing how often philosophers turn up in odd pairs (even if the partners keep changing), though (I would demure) without due philosophical attention being paid to the general problems posed by the shifting relations between philosophies.

29. See p. 35 above.

30. See p. 62 above. When Derrida enters the controversy over Heidegger's Nazism, he again zeroes in on a particular word—"spirit" (*Geist*). He makes a transition from *Being and Time* where Heidegger "had decided to 'avoid' this word, and then surrounded it with quotation marks." But six years later, "starting with his 'Address as Rector' (1933), . . . Heidegger raises a hymn to spirit" (*De l'esprit*, p. 457). Here again Derrida is administering a rebuke for "not-reading"—"Why has no one ever noticed?" In my next chapter, on Heidegger's Nazism, I shall not pursue Derrida as he makes his interesting discovery that what I have characterized as Heidegger's vulgarizing his own philosophy took the guise of his spiritualizing it. This pursuit would have required sifting the relevant texts more carefully than is necessary to expound the assessments I have considered. But I would note that in the case of *la réalité humaine* it is not merely a word that Derrida is focusing on but the translation of a word. Derrida's philosophy (if it is a philosophy) is rather more a philosophy of translation than of language, though for the purpose of the present volume I have tried to get away with the shorthand formulation "philosophy of language."

31. Derrida, "The Ends of Man," p. 115. In wrapping up the epoch, Derrida shows that the "anthropologistic" or "humanistic" interpretation of Heidegger also extended to Husserl and Hegel.

32. Derrida, *Les fins de l'homme*, p. 88.

33. Derrida complains about the distortion that deconstruction has suffered

"in certain academic or cultural quarters, . . . particularly in the United States" (*Psyché*, p. 390).

4. Nazism

1. Cited by Janicaud in *L'ombre de cette pensée*, which lays out in a more satisfactory fashion than any other appraisal the wide array of philosophical issues raised by Heidegger's statements and conduct.

2. Heidegger, *Basic Writings*, p. 197.

3. Minder, cited in Husserl, "Letter to Robert Minder," p. 159.

4. Beaufret, *Douze questions*, p. 37. Beaufret cites Heidegger's plea without seeming to be aware that it illustrates one of the counts against Heidegger—his refusal to admit that he had said or done anything that could be counted seriously against him. As I have admitted, it is not my effort here to reach a verdict in this *cause célèbre*. But there are certain counts against Heidegger that are perhaps insufficiently appreciated in America. Heidegger never forgave the University of Freiburg for the part that members of its faculty played in discrediting him. One thing they understood, which he apparently did not want to understand, was that his established reputation as a philosopher was such that at the time he joined the Nazi party it was an inducement to students to follow him. When his enthusiasm dampened, his established reputation protected him; if theirs dampened too, they did not enjoy the same protection. Another cause of local resentment, to be taken in conjunction with the first, was his ingratiating himself with the French when they were the occupying authorities. Finally, some suspicion attached to Heidegger's nationalism, even among his conservative allies, since he had succeeded in getting his military service deferred during World War I (for health reasons) and never served in actual combat.

5. See, for example, Derrida, "Heideggers Schweigen."

6. Aubenque, "Encore Heidegger et le Nazisme," p. 119. This distinction of level I have not examined. See chap. 2, note 34 for Merleau-Ponty's rejection of any attempt to introduce this sort of discrepancy between philosophy and circumstances. Consistent with his distinction, Aubenque further insists that Heidegger's "initial joining of the Nazi movement is not a philosophical act. It's just like thousands of other cases" (p. 119). But it is a philosophical act and not like thousands of other cases. Aubenque's argument, as Janicaud points out, "would be more convincing if Heidegger had not provided any philosophical justification for his joining." And this justification is found, Janicaud adds, "in texts which Heidegger has never repudiated" (*L'ombre de cette pensée*, p. 65), with one exception. In Aubenque's appraisal, the situation changes once Heidegger's period of activism is over: "If Nazism is absent from Heidegger's philosophical work before 1933 and if, conversely, the philosophy which is strictly Heidegger's is absent from the Nazi commitment of the rector in 1933–34, there is clearly visible, from 1935 on, the lineaments of a philosophical reflection on Nazism" ("Encore Heidegger," p. 121). With the qualifications that I have already acknowledged would be necessary, a comparison with Sartre might be undertaken—

Sartre emerged from a period of close collaboration with the Communists (from 1952 to 1956) to engage in philosophical reflection that was to have culminated in the second volume of the *Critique,* with its analysis of "Socialism in One Country" from which I quoted above (see note 27 of Chapter 3).

7. Heidegger, *Martin Heidegger/Erhart Kästner Briefwechsel,* p. 10.

8. One possible philosophical explanation can be reached by resorting to the category of *Öffentlichkeit* and recognizing that it may cut both ways. The banale, philosophically uninteresting excuses Heidegger found for his public conduct (a "human failing" [p. 55 above], "the biggest stupidity," and so forth) may suggest that public opinion is being fobbed off by receiving what Heidegger regards as its due. One trouble with this explanation is that Heidegger does not himself always respect the distinction, even when it could be reinforced by his distinction between the philosophical and the personal. For he justifies his having turned his back on his mentor, Husserl, by referring to Husserl's public criticism of Heidegger's work ("Was Husserl bewogen hat, sich in solcher Öffentlichkeit gegen mein Denken abzusetzen, konnte ich nie erfahren" ["Das Spiegel-Interview," p. 199; *Antwort,* p. 89]) as if such public criticism were not only a personal affront but also a resort to *Öffentlichkeit,* especially since the criticism was publicized by a journalist, who presumably mentioned Heidegger by name—as Husserl had not. Of course, it is impossible to tell if *Öffentlichkeit* retains here its technical philosophical sense. After all, Heidegger himself is being interviewed in a journal. The reprint in *Antwort* provides information on the text of the interview as well as on some of the circumstances of its taking place.

9. Petzet, *Auf einen Stern zugehen,* p. 10. Having likewise drawn a distinction between the philosophical and the personal, Aubenque finds room for personal motives: "Heidegger's particular case is that of a German provincial petit bourgeois, for a long while humiliated or mocked for his background—Frau Cassirer [the wife of a Jewish neo-Kantian philosopher] made a nasty comparison at the time of the Davos debate [with her husband over the interpretation of Kant] of Heidegger with a peasant's son whom one would throw out of the gate of a castle" ("Encore Heidegger et le Nazisme," p. 119). Unfortunately, I cannot linger over the class distinction that this anecdote implies (not to mention the rather nasty light it casts on a "Jewish cosmopolitan" as compared with a "provincial petit bourgeois"). But I do not wish to leave the impression that the only issue raised by Heidegger's case is whether it betrays a merely "personal error" or has some bearing as well on the interpretation of his philosophy. Unlike myself, Habermas does offer a sociohistorical assessment, in which he criticizes Heidegger's philosophy for its "abstraction of historicity . . . from actual historical processes" ("Work and Weltanschauung," p. 437). But Habermas does not quite recognize that undertaking such a sociohistorical assessment (in the guise he offers of a brusque social history of Germany since World War I) is of itself a criticism of Heidegger's philosophy, since it yields no such social history and, consequently, raises philosophical issues between himself and Heidegger regarding "historicity"—a concept of Heidegger's which, from Heidegger's perspective, Habermas is vulgarizing. (Later we shall watch Sartre vulgarize it by a similar movement

from what is "abstract" in Heidegger "toward the concrete.") At the same time, Habermas fails to recognize that his social history tends to blur the issue of Heidegger's not having taken responsibility in the postwar period for his past conduct. Thus Habermas argues that "Heidegger remained bound by his generation and his time, the milieu of the Adenauer era of repression and silence" and that he acted no differently from others, was one of many (p. 454). My misgiving about Habermas's blurring is that, although *Being and Time* clearly does not provide a recognizable social history of Germany, it perhaps does provide a doctrine of responsibility in which acting no differently from others, being one of many, would seem hardly warranted. It is at this juncture that Heidegger's persistent refusal to take significant responsibility ("the biggest stupidity") for his past conduct demands some attention, especially since responsibility gains some of its significance in *Being and Time* from an analysis of the relations between past and future and since his saddling himself with responsibilities as a Nazi may have received some impetus from this analysis.

10. Valéry, cited in Heidegger, *Heidegger/Kästner*, p. 83. Habermas too insists on the distinction between the philosophical and the personal: "Heidegger's work has long since detached itself from his person" ("Work and Weltanschauung," p. 434). But, characteristically, Habermas does not bring out Heidegger's responsibility for this detachment. In this regard, consider how Heidegger "resolutely resisted any suggestion to publish the [*Spiegel*] interview before his death," explaining, "It is neither pride nor stubborness [that is, traits of personal character], but rather care for my work." This responsibility, it might be argued, took precedence over any other responsibility to such an extent that it is not clear what other responsibilities still mattered, besides those that found their scope in the work—e.g., to language. Of course, the distinction between Heidegger's philosophy and his personal political activities as a Nazi can be repudiated, as it is by Adorno when he disposes of Heidegger's philosophy as "fascist to the core" (*Musikalische Schriften*, 6:637). I am not pretending to reach an assessment of Heidegger's Nazism in this volume. The disgraceful facts that are available (and it is also disgraceful that more are not) are dispassionately set down by Hugo Ott, along with the special pleadings and the falsifications in which Heidegger indulged in retrospect. I am only illustrating how the varying assessments can be caught up in the traditional proceedings of drawing or removing distinctions of level. The distinction between the personal level and the philosophical level was first drawn in the original French debate after the war. It was propounded by De Waelhens: "I don't intend in any way to reach a judgment on the *personal* attitude of Martin Heidegger toward National Socialism. All that concerns me is to know if Heidegger's philosophy is intrinsically linked to National Socialism or if it leads there logically, abstracting from the personal reactions . . . of [Heidegger as] a private person" ("La philosophie de Heidegger et le nazisme," p. 115; italics in original). Given that the concern of most of those who would draw the distinction is to salvage Heidegger's philosophy from the imputation of being Nazi, it is striking (1) that they fail to observe that Heidegger himself drew the distinction (e.g., with the quotation from Valéry), (2) that a distinction between the personal

and the philosophical is itself a philosophical distinction, and (3) that its applicability is questionable in the philosophical analysis of responsibility found in *Being and Time*. How can Aubenque, like Habermas, overlook all this when he urges that Heidegger's initial joining the Nazi party "is not a philosophical act. It's just like thousands of other cases" (Encore Heidegger et le Nazisme," p. 119). Habermas further finds the main themes of German conservatism "unreflectingly perpetuated by Heidegger" ("Work and Weltanschauung," p. 438). Unreflecting perpetuation is unphilosophical. How much then is left within the compass of Heidegger's reflection for Habermas to admire as Heidegger's philosophy, which Habermas does profess to admire?

11. Kästner's and Janicaud's comments are all from Janicaud, *L'ombre de cette pensée*, p. 10.

12. Fédier, *Anatomie d'un scandale*, pp. 236–37. I cite him because he is a disciple of Beaufret's *and* would salvage Heidegger's philosophy while repudiating the distinction between the philosophical and the personal, the very distinction which is usually relied on for this salvaging purpose.

13. Ibid., p. 122.

14. Ibid.

15. Ibid. In addition to the shifts in *level* that take place as one moves from one assessment to another, the shift in *affiliation* also impinges. Lacoue-Labarthe points out that "when Heidegger was frustrated in his project [for reforming the university as a Nazi rector] . . . , and thereby Germany itself, science, which underpinned this entire project, yields to art—that is . . . to 'poetic thought'" (*La fiction du politique*, pp. 86–87).

5. Discipleship

1. The story is reported in the first edition of Spiegelberg (*The Phenomenological Movement*, (2:463) and retracted in the second edition.

2. Sartre, *Carnets*, p. 345.

3. See de Beauvoir, *La force de l'âge*, pp. 190–91.

4. Since I have considered some of the issues raised for the historian of philosophy by Heidegger's Nazism, I should now mention that Sartre's not having made an effort to attend Heidegger's lectures is not to be explained by Heidegger's having become a member of the Nazi party (a well-publicized event) the year Sartre was in Berlin, for he was almost entirely immune to the menace of Hitler. Even as late as 1977, Sartre justified his relative indifference in 1933 to Nazism: "I was aware of Nazism but also was aware that we had at home a quasi-dictatorship, for it was the period of Doumergue" (*Sartre, un film*, p. 44).

5. I have sketched a brief explanation of why Heidegger was not dealing with his relation to Husserl (see p. 14), but I will return to the problem in my Volume 3.

6. See p. 39 above.

7. See p. 177 below.

8. Sartre, *Carnets*, p. 228.

9. Cohen-Solal, *Sartre*, p. 139.

10. Sartre, *Carnets*, p. 225.

11. Sartre, *Entretiens*, p. 231.

12. Cohen-Solal, *Sartre*, p. 141; italics in original.

13. Sartre, *Carnets*, p. 226; *Situations*, 10:176. The miscellaneous of Sartre's readings of his literary contemporaries can also be contrasted with his general indifference toward most contemporary philosophy. Anna Boschetti points out, "Husserl and Heidegger are the only living authors whom Sartre confronts openly and systematically as the only competitors he recognizes. The other names [in philosophy] are those of the great dead" (*Sartre et "Les temps modernes,"* p. 108).

14. Sartre, *Carnets*, p. 226.

15. De Beauvoir, *La force de l'âge*, p. 141. Stephen Light has challenged de Beauvoir's report, even though it "has always been taken as a definitive account of Sartre's early philosophical development, recounting as it does that Sartre's interest in phenomenology was first sparked in 1932 by Raymond Aron, who . . . had spoken in a café . . . in 1932 to Sartre about *Husserl* and phenomenology" (*Shūzō Kuki and Jean-Paul Sartre*, p. 3; my italics). When Light later presents the actual challenge, he has altered the issue: "It was Kuki's distinct role to have turned Sartre's attention to *Heidegger* and phenomenology, to have given Sartre an agenda, no matter that it could not be immediately attended" (p. 23; my italics). Then Light anticipates the objection: "But what of the role given Raymond Aron in Simone de Beauvoir's *La force de l'âge*? Clearly, Aron could not have introduced Sartre to phenomenology." However, neither the facts nor the probabilities are in much doubt: (1) Kuki was an admirer of Heidegger, and may well have attempted to draw Sartre's attention to Heidegger in 1928, when Sartre, needing the money, was tutoring Kuki on French philosophy; (2) Sartre later in life remembered the attempt (or at least allowed himself to be reminded of it); (3) but he seems not to have been responsive at the time, when his interest focused on the French and German philosophers and psychologists whom he discusses in his *diplôme*, *L'image*, where Heidegger is not mentioned and Husserl is referred to only as a logician (logic was never Sartre's predilection), so that it seems likely Sartre's reference was based not on the reading of Husserl but on another source; (4) the next year after tutoring Kuki, Sartre did not bother attending Husserl's lectures at the Sorbonne (1929), but the invitation to give lectures in German would not have been issued unless Husserl were well known; (5) during the year preceding Sartre's tutoring Kuki, *Being and Time* had "struck like lightening" in Germany, and by 1929 French philosophers were not unaware of Heidegger, so that it is likely that Sartre had already heard of him before he met Kuki; (6) Sartre's roommate, Paul Nizan, may have arranged for the publication of Corbin's translation in 1931 of Heidegger's *What is Metaphysics?* as he did of Sartre's *La légende de la vérité* in the same issue of *Bifur*—but whatever interest Nizan may have had in Heidegger, he seems not to have imparted to Sartre; (7) after the

café conversation with Aron, Sartre did not seek further information on Heidegger but on Husserl, by reading Levinas; (8) Levinas does refer to Heidegger, but as a disciple of Husserl's; (9) Sartre himself will argue in 1940 that "serious studies must begin with Husserl, the master, and later reach Heidegger," though now at last he recognizes that the latter is a "dissident disciple" (*Carnets*, p. 228). Thus I would conclude that de Beauvoir's account remains plausible, at least as compared with Light's.

16. Sartre, *Situations,* 4:192.

17. Levinas, *The Theory of Intuition in Husserl's Phenomenology*, pp. xxxiii–xxxiv.

18. Husserl, *Briefe an Roman Ingarden*, pp. 41–42.

19. Spiegelberg, "The Way into Phenomenology for Americans," p. 178. The issue of what I label "vulgarization" is an issue of level for Husserl too. He believed that until further work had been done at its fundamental level, phenomenology could not embark on matters as complicated as those of the philosophy of religion.

20. Thus in the essay "Intentionality," which was written in Berlin, Sartre treats Heidegger's conception of "being-in-the-world" as if it were equivalent to Husserl's conception of intentional reference.

21. Sartre, *Lettres,* 1:386.

22. De Beauvoir, *Entretiens,* p. 223.

6. *Turning*

1. Derrida, *Writing and Difference,* p. 87. As evidence, Derrida cites, for example, that "everything which goes beyond [*déborde*] commentary and the 'letter' of Husserl's text is oriented toward 'ontology.' But while there is such evidence to suggest that Husserl is turning "toward Heidegger" there is no evidence that Levinas is thinking of himself as turning "against Husserl." Apparently, Derrida finds it difficult to believe that anyone for whom he has as much respect as he has for Levinas could overlook how fundamental is the divergence between Husserl and Heidegger.

2. The story of Merleau-Ponty's visit to Louvain is told by H. L. van Breda in "Maurice Merleau-Ponty et les archives-Husserl à Louvain." In applying for a grant in April 1934, Merleau-Ponty did list *Ideas I* (see "La nature de la perception," in *Le primat de la perception,* pp. 21–22), but he was only superficially acquainted with the work and relied considerably on Fink's presentation, which had come out in 1933 and which Sartre was making use of during 1933–34 in Berlin. Probably Merleau-Ponty's attention had been drawn by Sartre to *Ideas I* and to the Fink article, though Merleau-Ponty may also have come across references to Husserl in the Gestalt psychologists who were at the focus of his application.

3. Cairns, *Conversations with Husserl and Fink,* p. 106

4. See p. 56 above.

5. Levinas, "La ruine de la représentation," p. 75.

6. See p. 69 above.

7. Derrida, *Margins of Philosophy*, p. 116. This is one of Derrida's summations: "It is astonishing and highly significant that when Husserl's thought was introduced and established in postwar France, even becoming a kind of philosophical fashion, his critique of anthropologism remained entirely unnoticed, or in any case without effect. One of the most paradoxical routes of this motivated misunderstanding passes through a reductive reading of Heidegger. Because the analysis of 'being-there' has been interpreted in narrowly anthropological terms, sometimes Husserl is delimited or criticized starting out from Heidegger. . . . This route is most paradoxical because it follows along the way of a reading of Heidegger that was also Husserl's" (pp. 118). It would seem that all this is astonishing and highly significant because it is at once so complete a misunderstanding of Husserl and Heidegger and so common a misunderstanding. But the motivation of so astonishing and significant a misunderstanding itself would seem to deserve some explanation, at least in the case of Sartre, as the dominant authority behind this reductive interpretation of 'being-there'. In the present volume (especially in my conclusion), I shall try to furnish some explanation of his motivation at certain junctures. At present I would only observe that Sartre's misunderstanding of Husserl did not originally pass through a reductive anthropologistic reading of Heidegger. A reductive psychologistic reading of Husserl was already well established in Sartre's prewar writings, as we shall see in Volume 2. In *La voix et le phénomène* Derrida himself is skeptical of the distinction in *level* that upholds Husserl's transcendental psychology (see pp. 10–11).

7. Originality

1. See p. 87 above.

2. De Beauvoir, *La cérémonie des adieux*, p. 205.

3. De Beauvoir, *La force de l'âge*, p. 220. She explains she does not have Sartre's "inventiveness" herself (p. 228).

4. Husserl, in Fink, "Die phänomenologische Philosophie Edmund Husserls in der gegenwärtigen Kritik," p. 319.

5. Sartre, *Carnets*, p. 226.

6. De Beauvoir, *La force de l'âge*, p. 216.

7. Sartre, *Carnets*, p. 224.

8. De Beauvoir, *La force de l'âge*, p. 142.

9. Cohen-Solal, *Sartre*, p. 139.

10. De Beauvoir, *La force de l'âge*, p. 142. According to Gerassi, de Beauvoir underlined all the errors in Cohen-Solal's biography (see *Jean-Paul Sartre: Hated Conscience of His Time*, p. 49).

11. Levinas, *The Theory of Intuition in Husserl's Phenomenology*, p. 23. Sartre could not have known it at the time, but this crude equation of contingency with negation is a good illustration of the intrusion of Heidegger's influence on

Levinas's exposition of Husserl. It's an equation which Sartre works out in *Being and Nothingness,* so it might also illustrate how Sartre came to Husserl *via* Levinas. But even though Sartre was looking for references to contingency, too much weight cannot be put on this single reference.

12. Cohen-Solal, *Sartre,* p. 139.

13. Husserl, *Ideas I,* sec. 27.

14. Sartre, *L'imaginaire,* p. 15.

15. This put-down is recalled, for example, by Jean Héring in "La phénoménologie d'Edmund Husserl il y a trente ans," p. 370.

16. See p. 89 above.

17. I could have said in *all* of Sartre's prewar works, for the only one of the four in which Heidegger is not referred to, *L'imagination,* was originally the historical preamble to what was later published separately as *L'imaginaire.*

18. De Waelens, *La philosophie de Martin Heidegger,* p. 367.

19. Sartre, *Being and Nothingness,* p. 444.

20. Heidegger, *Being and Time,* p. 134.

21. Sartre, *Situations,* 10:164.

8. Immersion

1. Sartre, *Les mots,* p. 90.

2. Sartre, *Lettres,* 1:350.

3. Sartre, *Situations,* 4:122–23.

4. Sartre, *Sartre, un film,* p. 130.

5. Sartre, *Carnets,* pp. 227–29; italics in original.

6. Ibid., p. 226

7. See my *Starting Point,* p. 98–99.

8. Sartre, *Lettres,* 1:356; italics in original.

9. See p. 52 above.

10. Heidegger, *Being and Time,* p. 142.

11. Sartre, *Carnets,* p. 22.

12. Sartre, *Being and Nothingness,* pp. 682–700, 709.

13. Sartre, *Carnets,* p. 224.

14. Ibid., p. 226. I offer an illustration of the casuistic extreme to which the vulgarization of Heidegger's conception of *Übernahm* went. Having told Sartre (in a letter written 8 January 1940) how much she loves him for his "bold thoughts," de Beauvoir expresses some doubts as to whether or not "one must take upon oneself being French," agrees nonetheless that "it certainly seems to me that to write *Nausea* is in some fashion to take upon oneself being French," and recalls their having discussed this question before (*Lettres à Sartre,* 2:25). Observe that in applying Heidegger's conception, Sartre singles out his having written a novel.

15. Lejeune, *Le pacte autobiographique*, pp. 197–98, 204, 206.

16. Husserl, *The Crisis of European Sciences*, p. 391.

17. A good illustration of Husserl's demoralization is a 1933 letter to Dietrich Mahnke, which is included in Bernd Martin's *Kompendium* of documents, pp. 148–49.

18. Merleau-Ponty, *Signes*, p. 8.

19. See pp. 69, 72 above.

20. Sartre, *Carnets*, p. 225.

21. This work by Sartre was *La légende de la vérité*. Sartre has the date wrong for the issue of *Bifur*; it was 1931. I reemphasize that this translation of Heidegger's inaugural lecture, *Was ist Metaphysik?*, must not be confused with Corbin's anthology bearing the same title in French, which was not published until 1938 and included the selection from *Being and Time* which, I am about to argue, provided Sartre's title *Le sursis* with philosophicl implications.

22. Contat, in Sartre, *Oeuvres romanesques*, p. 1868. *L'âge de la raison* had been announced for publication in 1940, but Sartre held it up until the sequel, *Le sursis*, could be published along with it in 1945, "in order to enable the reader to see more clearly the direction of the work as a whole" (*Oeuvres romanesques*, p. 1864). Since Sartre recognizes that his disgust is inspired by his conversion to Heidegger, it could be said that "the direction" exhibited by *Le sursis* is in some measure his turning "toward Heidegger against Husserl."

23. Heidegger, *Being and Time*, p. 236; Sartre, *Being and Nothingness*, pp. 134–146.

24. Heidegger, *Qu'est-ce que la métaphysique?*, trans. Corbin, p. 126. The concept of "being in suspense" is further elaborated in *Being and Nothingness* and is salvaged when he refutes Heidegger's "being-toward-death" (e.g., p. 694).

25. Sartre, *Carnets*, p. 227.

9. Turning Point

1. Sartre, *Situations*, 10:180. I do not intend any difference of meaning between "period" and "epoch." I have taken over whichever term was used by the philosopher I am expounding.

2. Ibid., p. 175. The fact is that Sartre did recognize himself very well in the still earlier period of his childhood and adolescence, at least as this period is treated in his autobiographical *Les mots*. In my *Human Nature* (vol. 2, pt. 4) I have dealt with the period in Mill's life when he obtained from the social history of the Saint-Simonians a feeling for periodization, which he then transferred to his history as an individual, thus producing the period I was dealing with. This feeling for periodization, I argued, may have been a factor in encouraging him to undertake an autobiography. At any rate, it did encourage him to break up his life in his *Autobiography* into three periods, or "stages," and to delimit the period called "A Crisis in My Mental History" more sharply than the facts warranted.

Sartre's feeling for periodization may similarly have encouraged him to make a sharp distinction between the two periods in his mature life.

3. Sartre, *Situations,* 10:154.

4. Boschetti, *Sartre et "Les temps modernes,"* p. 314.

5. Sartre, *Carnets,* p. 228; italics in original.

6. See p. 75 above.

7. Sartre, *Qu'est-ce que la littérature?,* p. 53.

8. Ibid., pp. 96, 191. I overlook the sexism of Sartre's definition (see also p. 138). Sartre recognizes that to speak of "an entire society" is to abstract from class conflicts.

9. See p. 70 above.

10. Heidegger, *What is Called Thinking,* p. 134. Analysis cannot halt with the shift in *affiliation,* since literature and poetry are each differently identified by Sartre and Heidegger (see p. 11 above).

11. Sartre, *Carnets,* pp. 228–29.

12. Ibid., 227.

13. See p. 110 above.

14. Sartre, *Being and Nothingness,* p. 334. The shift in *level* is a shift from the abstract to the concrete (see the "Shifts" section of my Conclusion).

15. Sartre, *Situations,* 10:180.

16. Ibid., 4:348.

17. Sartre's conception of himself as a writer, and the relation between his philosophy and his literary writings, will be taken up in Volume 2.

18. Having referred to the war as "the real turning point in my life," Sartre admits that it was only "slowly" that he arrived at the *Critique* (*Situations,* 10:180).

19. Sartre also abandoned the belief (which had inspired *La légende*) that philosophy could be "expressed in a literary work" (*Sartre, un film,* pp. 41–42). With this "complete change" he drew a sharp distinction between philosophy and literature. Only when this distinction is drawn does the shift in the *affiliation* of philosophy take on the significance I am ascribing to it. For Heidegger's distinction between thinking and poetry, see p. 13 above.

20. The only documentary evidence (earlier than the 1936 manuscript) for the revisions of *Nausea* is a notebook which Sartre's editors are inclined to date "before the stay in Berlin, probably 1932" (*Oeuvres romanesques,* p. 1684). In the notes that bear directly on the experience of contingency, ennui is closely identified with this experience instead of nausea, of which there is no mention. Thus it would seem that in the eventual novel, nausea may have largely displaced ennui in the rendering of the experience of contingency, just as nausea in *Being and Nothingness* is in turn largely displaced by anxiety or, at least, loses much of its scope to anxiety. If ennui played this earlier role, it would also seem not a mere coincidence that in *What is Metaphysics?* The word *Langeweile,* which is translated as "ennui" by Corbin, plays a role, as well as anxiety. What Sartre got out

of reading Heidegger's lecture may help explain why ennui became for him something more than the usual stereotype of romantic fiction. Another possible date when Sartre could have read some Heidegger which could have influenced *Nausea* is 1936, when Sartre was working on the surviving draft: For de Beauvoir recalls how Sartre had her translate for him "large fragments" (*Entretiens*, p. 232).

21. Heidegger, *On the Way to Language*, p. 7.

22. One reason Aubenque may find it plausible to claim that "there is really a rupture . . . between Heidegger's philosophical works before 1933 and his discourses of 1933 having reference to circumstances" is that Heidegger's "turning" (in contrast with Sartre's more concrete periodization) has, in Heidegger's own conception of it, no reference to circumstances, however unable to overlook the circumstances of his involvement with Nazism many of Heidegger's commentators are. A comparison could also be made with the case of Paul de Man, although in most ways it is not as comparable with Heidegger's as many commentators have suggested. De Man's case is of interest here because he himself "often criticized, or at least considered as fictions, all 'periodizations'" (Derrida, *Mémoires pour Paul de Man*, p. 121). Nevertheless, when Derrida (having learned that de Man had written journalistic articles under the occupation which were pro-German and on occasion anti-Semitic) rallies to de Man, it is in part by attacking the "continuism" of certain hostile commentators, "as if there were no difference in level, no displacement, *a fortiori* no fundamental break (*rupture*). . . . When one would, at any cost, reconstruct artificially continuities . . . , discontinuity must be interpreted as a ruse, conscious or unconscious" (p. 226). Although Derrida elaborates his conception of this break with his usual subtlety, it is not clear if he is admitting that the discontinuity he would respect is merely fictional, as de Man's own conception of periodization would presumably require.

23. Heidegger, *Basic Writings*, p. 220. I would add that when Sartre reports, in the entry I have dissected, the history of his succumbing to the influence of Heidegger's concept of "historicity," his report belongs to what in Heidegger is distinguished from *Geschichte* as *Historie* ("history"—in roughly the ordinary sense). Sartre is tracing a development. But the "way" that Heidegger follows after *Being and Time* is not a "personal development" (*Beiträge zur Philosophie*, p. 85). It is an "undertaking" which is "intended to be completely unbiographical," whereas Sartre's report is obviously intended to be autobiographical. Moreover, the "turning" is not a "development" in some broader sense. It is, for instance, not a "relation between earlier and later" (ibid.).

24. Merleau-Ponty, *Sense and Non-Sense*, p. 72.

25. See the "Developmental History" section of Chapter 2.

26. I could not detail in my text the fashion in which Merleau-Ponty's philosophy is more accommodating. But I can try to bring out how I would assess this feature of his philosophy by criticizing another expositor who does interpret Merleau-Ponty's handling the relation between Husserl and Heidegger. In "Par-delà Husserl et Heidegger" Ricoeur begins his exposition as follows: "In order to

embrace the originality of Merleau-Ponty, in the *Phenomenology of Perception* at least, interpreters have often allowed themselves to be fascinated by the most obvious antinomy which this phenomenology undertakes to overcome, between . . . Neo-Kantian intellectualism . . . , o.1 the one hand, and behavioristic empiricism, on the other. This approach is not to be disregarded, to the extent that it shows how Merleau-Ponty carries out a movement of thought which carries him beyond the two alternative poles. [p. 17]." Ricoeur is recognizing (as I would put it) that the accommodation Merleau-Ponty would achieve is a feature not of the alternative philosophies in question but a movement of his own thought.

This recognition enables Ricoeur, in turn, to argue that it is with a comparable movement that Merleau-Ponty overcomes the opposition between Husserl and Heidegger. Ricoeur locates junctures at which it seems that Merleau-Ponty's analysis "evades any allegiance to Husserl and seems to swing . . . to the side of Heidegger." Ricoeur then has to face the question, "Does Merleau-Ponty hesitate and oscillate between Husserl and Heidegger?" Ricoeur's own claim is that Merleau-Ponty "seems rather to have brought to light *the profound relation between successive philosophical undertakings, at a certain period of indecision on the part of each of them.*" He accordingly concludes his exposition, "It is by revealing their convergence in depth that Merleau-Ponty transcends Husserl and Heidegger" [pp. 19, 21]. This is why the title of Ricoeur's exposition is "Beyond Husserl and Heidegger."

However, I am skeptical about the prospect of locating some "depth" where Husserl and Heidegger converge, even during some "period of indecision" for each of them. When exactly these periods were is not clear. I propose the following summary arguments: (1) Although Merleau-Ponty did conceive himself as moving "beyond Husserl and Heidegger," so also did Sartre. (2) The different guise of this movement beyond in Sartre should be taken into account, inasmuch Merleau-Ponty's conception of the relation between Husserl and Heidegger is prompted more by the opposition Sartre sets up between them in *Being and Nothingness* (published three years before, when Merleau-Ponty was working on the *Phenomenology of Perception*) than it is by any direct evidence as to how they themselves conceived the relation. (With regard to Merleau-Ponty's persistent responsiveness to Sartre, see Jean Hyppolite's assessment, which I cite in "The Distance" section of Chapter 12.) (3) "Indecision" on the part of a philosopher is likely to reflect the way in which he proceeds in his philosophy, but some philosophers tend to be philosophically indecisive, whereas some others tend to be decisive. (4) Merleau-Ponty tends to be indecisive (with his notorious tolerance for ambiguities), whereas Sartre tends to be decisive, with his decisiveness braced by his regular resort to antitheses. (5) But neither of these extreme tendencies is so readily discernible in either Husserl or Heidegger. (6) Like Merleau-Ponty Ricoeur is committed to accommodation as a philosophical procedure. His thinking is characteristically an irenic movement "beyond" seeming antitheses between philosophers toward a possible "convergence in depth." (7) He accordingly finds Merleau-Ponty's philosophical predisposition to accommodate congenial.

10. Access

1. Merleau-Ponty, *Phenomenology of Perception,* p. vii.

2. Ibid., p. viii. Here it is no longer *à travers de* or *par* that I am translating by *via*, but the *à* of Merleau-Ponty's *accessible à.* Although I shall now elaborate the same idiom that Heidegger employs—and to this extent am placing the "way" I am following alongside his "way," as I promised initially I would (see p. 37 above)—the distinction I am drawing between intellectual history and the history of philosophy is not the same distinction as he draws between *Historie* and *Geschichte,* and we shall come in Volume 3 to a parting of our ways.

3. See p. 91 above.

4. Merleau-Ponty, *Phenomenology of Perception,* p. xvii.

5. See p. 56 above.

6. Sartre, *Being and Nothingness,* p. 23.

7. Merleau-Ponty, *Signes,* p. 203; see p. 57 above for fuller citation.

8. *Husserliana,* 2:xi.

9. This accusation is frequently made by Husserl. See Cairns, *Conversations with Husserl and Fink,* p. 43, where the accusation is extended from Heidegger to two of Husserl's former students whom he regarded as defectors to Heidegger.

10. Sartre does not actually criticize the phenomenological reduction here, but he indicates that it is not applied in phenomenological psychology, which is what he is undertaking in his analysis of imaginative consciousness (*L'imagination,* p. 140).

11. Sartre, *Situations,* 4:196.

12. See Chapter 1.

13. Heidegger, *The Basic Problems of Phenomenology,* p. 328.

14. See p. 41 above.

15. *Husserliana,* 5:142.

16. See p. 9 above.

17. Heidegger, *On Time and Being,* p. 63.

18. Heidegger, *Prolegomena zur Geschichte des Zeitbegriffs,* p. 185; see also p. 103.

19. Heidegger, *On Time and Being,* p. 63.

20. Heidegger, *Basic Problems of Phenomenology,* p. 3.

21. Husserl, *Cartesian Meditations,* p. 44. Husserl's usage is presumably Cartesian. The philosophical *èpochè* is not to be confused with the phenomenological *èpochè,* which is a phase of the phenomenological reduction (see *Ideas I,* sec. 34), though both entail a lurching change in direction. The philosophical *èpochè* is the "lurch" with which Husserl repudiated the "back to Kant" of the Neo-Kantians (or any return to a previous philosopher), in favor of turning "back to the things themselves." Merleau-Ponty does not include the philosophical *èpochè* in his list of the procedures composing phenomenological method.

Just as there is accommodation during the development of his philosophy rather than the break that is characteristic of most of his French contemporaries, who turn "against Husserl" when they turn "toward Heidegger" (and thus no break between Husserl and Heidegger themselves in Merleau-Ponty's interpretation of them), so phenomenology itself from his perspective does not represent a break with previous thought. Hence his answer to the question, "What is phenomenology?" concludes, "It merges into the effort of modern thought" (*Phenomenology of Perception*, p. xxi). Observe that he is referring to "modern thought," not distinctively to modern philosophy, for there is also no break for him between philosophy and the kind of thinking that is represented by the moderns he has just mentioned—"Balzac, Proust, Valéry or Cézanne."

22. Heidegger, *Basic Problems of Phenomenology*, p. 22.

23. Heidegger, *Being and Time*, pp. 16, 50n. x, 260, 302, 435.

24. See p. 4 above. In *Heidegger et l'essence de l'homme*, Michel Haar states that "to deconstruct means in fact to reconstruct" (p. 123), but R. Spaemann states that what is at stake "for Heidegger is not reconstruction but the destruction of reconstructions" ("Philosophiegeschichte nach Martin Heidegger," p. 5). Each of the two terms is afflicted with its own ambiguities, and it should be kept in mind that I have retained the German term as a warning that what is at stake cannot be determined until I have dealt, in Volume 3, with Heidegger's concept of tradition. Some of the competing interpretations are briefly indicated in *Destruktion und Übersetzung*, ed. Buchheim, pp. 88–89.

25. Heidegger, *An Introduction to Metaphysics*, p. 17.

26. I am citing von Herrmann's paraphrase, *Hermeneutische Phänomenologie des Daseins*, p. 200.

27. See p. 5 above.

28. Heidegger, *Basic Problems of Phenomenology*, p. 22–23.

29. Heidegger, *Being and Time*, pp. 36–37.

30. See p. 48 above. Distinctions in level (*Niveau*) are drawn in *Being and Time*, but later they seem to disappear (e.g., when Heidegger renders *le plan* in Sartre as "Being" (see Heidegger, *Basic Writings*, p. 241). Perhaps they disappear concomitantly with Heidegger's downgrading of method itself. At any rate, there is a brief critique of the conception of levels (*Stufen*) in Plato (presumably the divided line is in question) and of "Neoplatonic *Stufung* in the *Beiträge*" (pp. 273–74), and a denial that the sequence followed in this work itself is an "ascent from the lower to the higher" (p. 6).

31. Heidegger, *Beiträge zur Philosophie*, pp. 146–47.

32. Derrida, *Psyché*, pp. 390–91.

33. Heidegger, *Being and Time*, p. 21.

34. See "Exposition" section of my Chapter 1.

35. Heidegger, *Being and Time*, p. 27.

36. See p. 28 above.

37. Husserl, *Philosophy as Rigorous Science*, p. 146.

38. See note 19 of my Introduction.

39. See p. 45 above.

40. See the "Direction" section of Chapter 1.

41. See the "Encounter" section of Chapter 5.

42. See p. 84 above.

43. Husserl, *Logical Investigations,* 1:254.

44. Ibid.

45. Husserl, *Cartesian Meditations,* p. 183.

46. Sartre, *L'imagination,* p. 140.

47. Sartre, *Being and Nothingness,* p. 116

48. De Beauvoir, *La force de l'âge,* p. 141.

49. Since conversion is largely a dialectical performance in Sartre, I have commented on it in *Starting Point,* pp. 364–365. Conversion took on greater significance as a topic as soon as his method became admittedly dialectical (see chap. 11, note 6). See Sartre, *Cahiers pour une morale* (written in 1947–48), pp. 488–531, and *Vérité et existence* (written in 1948), which begins with the problem of conversion and, though written as a reaction to the "Essence of Truth," marks a break with Heidegger, like the *Cahiers.*

50. Heidegger, Prefatory letter to Richardson, in Richardson, *Heidegger.* Heidegger's interpretation of Plato's cave (*Republic* 514a–517a) was first given as part of a winter semester lecture course in 1931–32 (*Gesamtausgabe* 34). Sartre has also attempted an interpretation of Plato's cave (reported in de Beauvoir's *Entretiens,* p. 203).

51. I suspect that some of Derrida's embroidery on Plato's description in the *Phaedrus* of the vagabondage of the disreputable "written word" parodies Derrida's own procedure—for example, "erring, he rolls here and there like someone who does not know where he is going, having lost the direct road, the right direction" (*Dissemination,* p. 143).

11. Phenomenology and Dialectic

1. Heidegger, *On Time and Being,* p. 64.

2. Heidegger, *Ontologie,* p. 42.

3. I have alluded to this controversy at p. 11 above, where it is clear that issues of scientific and philosophical method have often been inseparable. One of the appropriate characteristics of Feyerabend's *Against Method* in science is how philosophically unmethodical and random his attack is.

4. Charles Taylor, review of *La philosophie analytique,* pp. 133–34.

5. Wolfson, *The Philosophy of Spinoza,* 1:55, 59, 3.

6. Sartre, "Conscience de soi et connaissance de soi," p. 76.

7. Sartre was presented in an interview with my interpretation of what the interviewer called his "nascent dialectic." Sartre demurred that while "the *Cri-*

tique is a truly dialectical work," it is always possible to show "that I was previously a dialectician without knowing it; one can show that Bergson was Bergsonian at age six when he ate jam and toast" (*The Philosophy of Jean-Paul Sartre*, p. 18). My interpretation was of an article of Sartre's dating from 1945, when he was forty and had already worked out his method in *Being and Nothingness* (1943). Since Sartre was half-blind at the time of the interview, he had not read my interpretation. But his demurral puts me in an interesting position: I am accused of doing to Sartre what he had done to Heidegger—foisting on him a dialectical method which he didn't have. But there are differences between the two cases. Heidegger never acknowledges, at any time in his career, that his method is dialectical; Sartre later vigorously asserts the dialectical character of his method in the *Critique*. Of course, Sartre's foisting a dialectical method on Heidegger does not necessarily render Sartre's own method dialectical at that time. But, in fact, at the very end of his career he does acknowledge that in his *Cahiers pour une morale* (1947–48) "the dialectic slipped into what I wrote" (Sartre, quoted in de Beauvoir, *La cérémonie des adieux*, p. 224). I am not concerned to close the two-year gap between the article on which I was commenting on and Sartre's "slipping." Rather, my argument in Volume 2 will be that a method which is not phenomenological (if we allow this label to be reserved for the method employed by Husserl as the founder of phenomenology) slipped even into Sartre's prewar ostensibly phenomenological writings unbeknownst to him. Sartre himself would reserve the term "dialectical" for Hegel and Marx. But just as his own later method in the *Critique* is not purely dialectical in the Marxist sense but retains (as I have argued in the interpretation the interviewer was citing, as well as in chapter 5 of *Starting Point*) a phenomenological component, so Sartre's prewar phenomenological method was not purely phenomenological in Husserl's sense. There is sufficient continuity in the development of Sartre's philosophy to consider the method that is blended with the phenomenology in *Being and Nothingness* a rudimentary dialectic, as I try to demonstrate in *Starting Point*. I leave the argument as to the character of Sartre's prewar method to Volume 2 of the present work.

8. Boyce-Gibson, "From Husserl to Heidegger," p. 166.

9. Sartre, *Being and Nothingness*, p. 324.

10. At the same time, I displayed a certain caution, sometimes overlooked by reviewers. Just as Husserl repudiated "psychologism" long before he affixed this label to *Being and Time* (see p. 45 above), so Heidegger repudiated the label "philosophy of existence" in 1937 and explained that "the question I am concerned with is not the question of man" (see *Starting Point*, p. 23) long before Sartre affixed the label "existentialism" to Heidegger's philosophy and announced it was a "humanism." I went on to add that my concern in analyzing the *Dialectic of Existence* was "not to do justice to Heidegger's own philosophy in its own terms but to accord him the place his 'existential analysis' [in *Being and Time*] has earned in the development of existentialism, whether Heidegger liked it or not" (p. 24). Thus I left to a future investigation Heidegger's relation to Sartre from Heidegger's own perspective. Similarly, in pursuing my analysis of the

Dialectic of Existence, I recognized that the only time Heidegger "comes close . . . to suggesting that his own method is dialectical, if only in that it is so fluid as to elude exposition" is in his *Hegel's Concept of Experience* (pp. 185, 117). That the characteristics of so fluid a method remain badly in need of further examination will become evident when we find that Sartre, on the one hand, regards Merleau-Ponty as undialectical, while Merleau-Ponty, on the other hand, regards Sartre as undialectical. See pp. 174–175 below.

11. See p. 51 above for this shift in *level.*

12. Sartre, *L'imaginaire,* p. 236.

13. Howells, Sartre, pp. 9–10.

14. *Le primat de la perception* was a lecture in which Merleau-Ponty summarized his argument in his major work, *The Phenomenology of Perception.* When I use the term "priority" (whether applied to "method" as such by Heidegger, or to a procedure that is a component of a method, or to the subject of perception by Merleau-Ponty), I recognize that "priority" is a coarse distinction. Needless to say (but Husserl did say it), "making coarse distinctions and refining upon them" is a procedure of "general applicability" (Cairns, *Conversations with Husserl and Fink,* p. 42). In the ensuing volumes of the present work, I shall be refining upon the coarse distinctions I have made in this preliminary volume.

15. Sartre, *Lettres,* 2:56.

16. Sartre, "Saint Marc et son double," p. 172.

17. Sartre, *Situations,* 10:154.

18. Derrida, Introduction to *L'origine de la géométrie,* by Husserl, p. 58.

19. Derrida, *Psyché,* p. 391.

20. Derrida, *Mémoires pour Paul de Man,* p. 38.

21. Ibid, p. 40.

22. Ibid, p. 39.

23. See p. 155 above.

24. See p. 9 above.

12. Style

1. Merleau-Ponty, *Phenomenology of Perception,* p. viii; italics in original.

2. See p. 131 above.

3. Merleau-Ponty, *Phenomenology of Perception,* p. xiv.

4. Husserl, *Crisis of European Sciences,* pp. 344, 280.

5. See p. 155 above. I am, of course, well aware that the criterion of "consistency," as well as of "unity," may be slated for deconstruction (see Derrida's comments on "coherence," cited in the "History" section of Chapter 11). I have avoided the term "coherence" because of its close associations in Anglo-America with the coherence theory of truth. The point also has to be made with respect to "consistency" or "unity" that these criteria are not univocal but acquire different

implications in different philosophies. The differences can to some extent be determined by taking into account the shifts I am sorting out. To take the obvious example: "consistency" and "unity" do not impose the same requirements when a method is dialectical as they do when the method is a phenomenological analysis of essential structures.

6. If Sartre sought a "synthesis" of Husserl's phenomenological method with the "dialectical project" Sartre attributed to Heidegger (see p. 149 above), Degas sought a "synthesis" of styles, because "the mere existence of several diverging styles 'constituted the great problem'" (Valéry, cited by Reff, *Degas*, p. 87). It may then be a legitimate question as to whether or not he achieves this "synthesis" with a style of his own. Presumably he is considered to, or he would not enjoy his present standing as an artist. Or it may be that "the mere existence of diverging styles" did not in fact constitute Degas's "great problem" in his own terms but is artificially intruded by the art historian. This is an issue I shall reach shortly. But here Sartre's case would no longer be analogous, for he did explicitly set out to achieve a "synthesis," so that it is a legitimate question as to whether or not he did achieve it, or only concocted a *salade*. However, that Nietzsche exhibits different "styles" is no condemnation on Derrida's part.

7. See p. 141 above.

8. Heidegger, *Poetry, Language, Thought*, p. 40.

9. See p. 51 above.

10. In my Introduction I did not carry the relation of affiliation beyond the primary affiliate, except in the case of Sartre's philosophy, where Tintoretto is a privileged painter. But it should be observed that Sartre regards Tintoretto's space as "not the space of a painter but of a sculptor ("Saint Marc et son double," p. 15). Statues are prominent both in Sartre's philosophical works and in his literary works. For the way in which Sartre's phenomenology underpins their prominence, see my *Starting Point*, pp. 525–26. I have taken up the matter of additional affiliates there, inasmuch as Kierkegaard's adjustment of the relations between the arts still depends on Hegel's comprehensive "system of the arts." See the chapter entitled "Finish" (*Ausmalung*) in *Starting Point*.

11. See the "Understanding" section of Chapter 8.

12. Sartre "A propos de l'existentialism," in *Les écrits de Sartre*, p. 654.

13. Sartre, *Qu'est-ce que la littérature?*, pp. 269–270, 260, 271; italics in original.

14. See p. 116 above.

15. See p. 191 below.

16. Sartre, *Situations*, 1:31. It may be an interesting coincidence, with respect to the relation between philosophy and literature in Sartre, that Sartre's article on Dos Passos's *1919* was first published in August 1938, the same year in which Corbin's anthology was published. Having had *Nausea* published that same year, Sartre conceived "suddenly," according to a letter he wrote to de Beauvoir in July, a sequence of novels (*Oeuvres romanesques*, p. 1860) which would later become

his *Chemins de la liberté,* the first volume of which, *L'âge de la raison,* also begins with events in 1938. Some of Sartre's enthusiasm for Dos Passos may have been elicited by the encouragement his trilogy *U.S.A.* (of which *1919* is the second volume) gave to Sartre to "take" his epoch "on" himself in literature as well as in philosophy. Aside from his procedural debt to Dos Passos (Sartre also admits a debt to Virginia Woolf), there is the broad similarity that Sartre, like Dos Passos, begins his sequence before a world war, then immerses his characters in that war. Contat and Rybalka point out that the article on Dos Passos is "one of the most enthusiastic Sartre ever wrote," though they hasten to add that he retracted his verdict that Dos Passos was "the greatest writer of our time" (*Les écrits de Sartre,* p. 67).

17. Sartre, *Qu'est-ce que la littérature?,* p. 261.

18. See pp. 46, 120 above.

13. Communication

1. Merleau-Ponty, *Phenomenology of Perception,* p. vii.

2. Ibid., p. viii. The English translation conceals the shifts my translation would bring out. *Voeu* is translated "a hope to be realized," and this translation cuts the link with the ensuing shifts in *level* and in *subject* from the science of empirical psychology. Merleau-Ponty goes on to claim that phenomenology "is from the start a disavowal [*désaveu*] of science. I am not the outcome or the meeting point of numerous causal agencies which determine my bodily or psychological make up. . . . I cannot shut myself up within the realm of science" (*Phenomenology of Perception,* p. viii).

3. See p. 35 above.

4. Merleau-Ponty, *Phenomenology of Perception,* p. 365.

5. Ibid., p. viii. Such deliberate tying together is not deliberate (from Merleau-Ponty's perspective) in the sense that the relational analysis is an arbitrary intervention by the phenomenologist himself; instead, Merleau-Ponty regards it as conforming to our experience. The concluding sentence of his *Phenomenology of Perception* is a citation from Saint-Exupéry, "Man is but a network (*noeud*) of relations, and these alone matter to him." Other favored metaphors are "fabric" for experience (e.g., p. 166, where the "fabric" is "closely woven") and "net" (*filet*—e.g., pp. xv, 12).

6. Derrida, *Psyché,* p. 391.

7. For Derrida's rebuffing of "puritanical '*intégrisme*'" see Chapter 11, note 19.

8. See p. 19 above.

9. Sartre, *Cahiers pour une morale,* p. 67.

10. See *Les écrits de Sartre,* p. 12.

11. See p. 94 above.

12. See p. 117 above.

13. The preface of which I have made such extensive use (including the discounting of intentional analysis as well as the reconciliation of Husserl and Heidegger ["Heidegger's 'being-in-the-world' appears only against the background of the phenomenological reduction"]) was reportedly added to Merleau-Ponty's dissertation, which was the form that *Phenomenology of Perception* originally took, on the advice of Merleau-Ponty's examiners. I have accordingly been able to use it, confident that it was written after *Being and Nothingness* was published and Merleau-Ponty was familiar with this work. Specific citations from Heidegger are confined to Merleau-Ponty's chapter on "Temporality," which I take to be late, since it is the next-to-the-last chapter, just as the important references to *Being and Nothingness* are in Merleau-Ponty's last chapter, which is entitled "Freedom." It may be that even the topics of these two chapters were more or less dictated by Merleau-Ponty's desire to accommodate what was crucial to the two most important successors to Husserl.

14. Sartre, *Situations,* 4:194.

15. See p. 56 above.

16. See p. 110 above.

17. See p. 56 above. I am of course not suggesting that Sartre is incapable of thinking in terms of a relation between himself and someone else, only that if the relation is significant, he tends to think of it as initially an "antithetical" relation, as we have seen he thinks of the relation between being and nothingness and of the relation between Husserl and Heidegger. Thus his memorial essay on Merleau-Ponty is constructed around a succession of antitheses between them, such as (to put matters too baldly): he was an officer in the war / I was a private; he clung to traditions and his childhood / I rejected both; "he found security in the multiplicity of perspectives" / "I still find the Truth is one," etc. (*Situations,* 4:190, 191, 194). The contrast between Sartre's emphasis on the *cogito* as first-person and Merleau-Ponty's emphasis on the individual's inextricable involvement in relations is illustrated by Merleau-Ponty's most extended personal commentary on Sartre. Merleau-Ponty does not deal with Sartre separately but, instead, in terms of the relation between him and Nizan (see *Signes,* pp. 32–47).

18. Merleau-Ponty, *Phenomenology of Perception,* p. 360. Merleau-Ponty continues, "The other person transforms me into an object and denies me. I transform him into an object and deny him, it is asserted." This is even more obviously a reference to Sartre's analysis of the individual's relation to the other, but Sartre is not named. Similarly, Merleau-Ponty does not refer to Sartre by name when in the preface to *Phenomenology* he mentions those who cite intentionality "as the principal discovery of phenomenology" (see p. 131 above). With the breakdown of communication between them, Merleau-Ponty's criticism (in *Les aventures de la dialectique*) is no longer muted.

19. See n. 32 below.

20. Boschetti does not notice the contrast with Sartre when she lines up writings of Merleau-Ponty's in which "Sartre is the interlocutor whom he is addressing (*Sartre et "Les Temps modernes,"* p. 269). Sartre evades entering into a dia-

logue and responding to Merleau-Ponty by turning the chore of replying to Merleau-Ponty's criticism over to de Beauvoir (see "Merleau-Ponty et le pseudo-sartrism").

21. Merleau-Ponty, *Phenomenology of Perception*, p. 354.

22. Ibid., pp. 355, 361; my italics.

23. See p. 56 above.

24. Sartre, *L'âge de raison*, p. 203. Sutton's English translation dismantles the open/shut rhythm of the relation by translating *ne vous fermez pas* as "Don't be so aloof." For a detailed analysis of the dialectical mechanics of the passage, see my *Starting Point*, pp. 349–55.

25. Sartre, *L'idiot de la famille*, 2:1181.

26. The other is reached only in part 3 of *Being and Nothingness*. Similarly, in Merleau-Ponty's *Phenomenology of Perception*, the other turns up late in the sequence of the analysis.

27. Sartre, *Being and Nothingness*, p. 318.

28. Ibid., p. 334.

29. For the menace of the other and his alienation of my possibilities, see *Being and Nothingness*, pp. 341–44, 354.

30. Sartre, *Situations*, 4:268; Merleau-Ponty, *Themes from the Lectures*, p. 59.

31. See p. 41 above.

32. Heidegger, quoted in Sartre, *Being and Nothingness*, p. 52; see also p. 634. Sartre points out that this is one of Heidegger's "positive terms which hide implicit negations," and Sartre takes "distance" as his primary illustration of a negative relation (pp. 54–55) long before he reaches the problem of the negative relation between the individual and the other. Thus when I claim in the text that "the distance" between Sartre and Merleau-Ponty is a feature of Sartre's philosophy, I am alluding to "distance" as a phenomenon which is more broadly a feature of Sartre's philosophy than the problem of the individual's relation to the other, just as the different handling of relations in Sartre and Merleau-Ponty is a broader difference between them than their specific handling of the relation between the individual and the other.

14. Understanding

1. Richardson, *Heidegger*, preface.

2. Heidegger, *Schelling's Treatise on the Essence of Human Freedom*, p. 13. Heidegger is generalizing with respect to Hegel's "limited understanding" of Schelling. Heidegger's cryptic explanation of these limits is that the greatest thinkers "want *the same thing* in the form of their unique greatness" (italics in original). But I would probe further these limits to understanding.

3. The reference to a learning experience was introduced by Richardson's first question in his preface to *Heidegger*. "How are we properly to understand your

first experience of the question of Being in Brentano?" It may be that Heidegger found this question provided a pretext for him to move on to the question he may have considered more pressing (since Richardson was engaged in an exposition of Heidegger's development)—the question of his experience of being misunderstood, perhaps especially whenever he tried to answer questions regarding his learning experiences.

4. Heidegger, preface to *Qu'est-ce que la metaphysique?*, trans. Corbin, p. 8. So far as I know the German original of this preface has disappeared. But *défrichement* does not translate back readily into any German term I am aware of Heidegger using. Presumably he later learned from experience that translation is "fertile" in misunderstandings?

5. Heidegger, *Basic Writings*, p. 242.

6. See pp. 108, 120 above.

7. Sartre, *Carnets*, p. 225; italics in original.

8. See section 31 of *Being and Time*, "Being-There as Understanding." I don't think it too misleading to characterize Heidegger as using "technical" terms in *Being and Time* since some misgiving must be implicit in his later discarding most of these terms, and this misgiving may well tie in with his discounting method as indistinguishable from a technical procedure.

9. See p. 97 above.

10. See the "Nausea" section of Chapter 7.

11. See the "Interplay" section of Chapter 8.

12. See p. 38 above.

13. Sartre, *Being and Nothingness*, pp. 119–20. Sartre places parentheses around the "of" to indicate that there is no objectification but, instead, immediacy of understanding. He thereby in effect denies that there is involved what we shall shortly see Heidegger describing as "representational positing," but there remains a certain awkwardness in his conception insofar as it is a conflation of Husserlian immediacy with Heidegger's temporally extended "project."

14. See p. 125; my italics now added.

15. See p. 52 above.

16. Sartre, *Being and Nothingness*, p. 24.

17. Ibid., p. 67; and see my *Starting Point*, p. 99.

18. Heidegger, *Basic Writings*, p. 207.

19. For another example of Sartre's voluntaristic interpretation of Heidegger's ontology, see p. 109 above.

20. See p. 19 above.

21. See p. 29 above.

22. Heidegger, *Being and Time*, p. 145.

23. See p. 30 above.

Conclusion

1. See pp. 104–5 above.

2. Boschetti, *Sartre et "Les temps modernes,"* p. 314.

3. Initially, my translation of *Öffentlichkeit* as "obviousness" was designed to tie in with the issue I was raising of the access route to a philosophy, of its viability. Because I shall be dealing at last in this Conclusion with the subject of *Being and Nothingness*, I can now explain the reason I avoided the terser "publicness" (the Macquarrie/Robinson translation of *Öffentlichkeit*). Heidegger criticizes Sartre's commitment to "the subjectivity of consciousness" as the subject of modern Cartesian philosophy, and consistent with this criticism he undercuts the distinction between public and private (*Basic Writings*, p. 197). In the long run, the confrontation between Sartre and Heidegger should involve pitting Heidegger's *Öffentlichkeit* against Sartre's "bad faith" as the concept which in Sartre explains significant failure to understand (including Heidegger's; see *Being and Nothingness*, p. 336), especially since *Being and Nothingness*, which Sartre characterizes as an "eidetic analysis of bad faith," was written in emulation of *Being and Time* and since in *Being and Nothingness*, when Sartre criticizes Heidegger, he often rebukes him for "bad faith" (see Fell, *Heidegger and Sartre*, chap. 6, n. 57). It is curious that Sartre does not make this rebuke when up against Heidegger's Nazism but is satisfied with more vulgar accusations, such as "opportunism," "conformism," and "cowardice" (*Les écrits de Sartre*, p. 654).

4. Buchheim, *Destruktion und Übersetzung*, p. v.

5. Heidegger, *Being and Time*, p. 21. Another concept in the cluster which I mentioned in the last chapter is hard to disentangle from *Selbstverständlichkeit—durchschnittliche und vage Seinsverständnis* ("mediocre and vague understanding of Being"; p. 5).

6. There are two other particularly interesting instances of failure to understand that would merit attention if Heidegger had been as specific about them as he is about Sartre's failure. Heidegger seems to have been taken aback by the failure of the Nazi leadership to understand his philosophy as what was needed for the German people. He also has been taken aback by "the trouble I have in recognizing my thought in certain American interpretations" (Interview in the *Express*, p. 82). Heidegger's reference to America and Americanism suggest that there might even be something distinctively American about our failures. Consider the following pronouncement: "We know today that the Anglo-saxon world of Americanism is resolved to annihilate Europe, and that means the homeland [*die Heimat*], and that means the beginning [*Anfang*] of the West. Beginningness [*Anfängliches*] is indestructable. The entry of America in this planetary war is not entry into history [*Geschichte*] but is, rather, already the final American act of American lacking in historicity [*Geschichtlosigkeit*] and of the laying waste of itself [*Selbstverwüsting*]" (*Hölderlins Hymne "Der Ister,"* p. 68; I am indebted to Joseph P. Fell for locating this quotation and other references to Americanism in this lecture course—see also pp. 80, 86, 112, 179, 191 n.). Except for "Anglo-saxon" (which I resent both as a purebred Scot and as a firm believer in the melt-

ing pot) the terminology here is part and parcel of Heidegger's philosophy, and its implications there could be spelled out. But the questions remain—Is technology, is *Öffentlichkeit*, relevant to the constitution of Americanism? Tra-dition can hardly be, since we are beyond the pale of history.

7. Preface by Heidegger to Richardson, *Heidegger*.

8. Derrida, *Les fins de l'homme*, p. 52.

9. My summary is too brusque, but Derrida's summary makes clear that more than the single concept of "autheticity" (*eigentlichkeit*) is at stake. Commenting on how "the originary, the authentic is determined as ownness [*le propre*] and "in terms of proximity to presence to oneself," Derrida generalizes, "It would be possible to show how this value of proximity and of presence to oneself intervenes at the beginning of *Being and Time* and elsewhere in the decision to pose the question of the meaning of being by starting out with an existential analysis of 'being-there'. It would be possible to show the weight of metaphysics in this decision, and in the confidence accorded to the value of presence to oneself. This question can spread its movement to all the concepts implying the value of 'ownness' (*Eigen, eigens, ereignen, Ereignis, eigentümlich, Eignen* etc.)"—that is, to concepts not found in *Being and Time* but elaborated later by Heidegger. I am quoting "Ousia et grammē" in *Margins*, p. 67.

10. Derrida (as transcribed by David Krell) sketches "four areas of hesitation and disquiet in my current reading of Heidegger" ("On Reading Heidegger," p. 171). He is quiet about *Öffentlichkeit* and the array of concepts with which it is associated and which imply "the value of ownness." Let Derrida get away with the continued dominance of the metaphysical tradition ["the weight of metaphysics"], not only as an all inclusive explanation of why Sartre failed to understand Heidegger when he (Sartre) accepted the "monstrous" Corbin translation of *Dasein* as *la realité humaine* (see p. 72 above), but also of why Heidegger elaborated all these concepts. But when Derrida later reasserts his dismissal of Sartre and his epoch, he explains what he means by "monstrous": the translation "imposed on Heidegger's thought . . . a violence which is inadmissible, because it flattened and normalized monstrously the novelty of his thought." Even if Derrida would himself appeal again to the metaphysical tradition to explain the violence of this flattening and normalization, is he not doing violence to Heidegger's own explanation of Sartre's failure to understand him insofar as this explanation is couched in terms of *Öffentlichkeit*? In fact, Heidegger's explanation culminates in a generalization which allows sweeping scope to *Öffentlichkeit*: "Language succumbs to the dictatorship of *Öffentlichkeit*, which decides in advance what is *verständlich* or discarded as *unverständlich*" (*Basic Writings*, p. 197).

11. See p. 119 above.

12. *Sartre, un film*, p. 39. There is a passing reference to Wahl's book in the 1940 entry in the wartime notebooks that I have exploited: "This élan of curiosity in which I was responsibly implicated and which produced first of all books like Wahl's *Toward the Concrete*, had its origin in an aging of French philosophy and a need, in order to rejuvenate it, for experiencing everything" (p. 228). Since in the preceding and the following sentences Sartre refers to Corbin's translations

from the German, it sounds as if the curiosity was directed towards what was going in philosophy in England as well as in Germany. But this is certainly not Sartre's later perspective.

13. See p. 88 above.

14. See p. 132 above.

15. See p. 37 above.

16. See p. 102 above.

17. Husserl admits that that psychologically consciousness "is often or always accompanied by conation" but he insists that "in talking of 'acts'[of consciousness] all thought of activity must be rigidly excluded." (The procedure of exclusion is the eidetic reduction.) Thus "no allusion to selective attention or noticing is involved in our 'intention,'" (*Logical Investigations*, 2:558, 563; italics in original).

18. See above, p. 108.

19. Sartre, *Being and Nothingness*, p. 34.

20. I am not suggesting that Sartre's principle (or any other philosophical principle) promotes in a merely arbitrary fashion the turning in a different direction from a predecessor. Rather, the movement promoted is built into the philosophy being constructed itself, as we are watching happen in *Being and Nothingness*. Similarly in its vulgarized version—the lecture, *Existentialism Is a Humanism*. The movement behind it (and I deliberately take another interpreter's different exegisis) intimately involves the whole context of Sartre's philosophy: Sartre is coming "to terms . . . with . . . his chief problem: how, specifically, to return to the world from analytic-reflective withdrawal. That the for-itself [consciousness] must always return to the world is guaranteed by the ekstatic intentionality of consciousness" (Joseph Fell, *Heidegger and Sartre*, p. 152). The irony in Sartre's relation to Heidegger at this juncture is that while the "analytic-reflective withdrawal" is what survives in Sartre from Husserl's reductions, the antithetical movement "toward the concrete" by which Sartre would (in Fell's exegesis) "return to the world" is impelled by Heidegger, but this is the juncture at which Heidegger attacks Sartre for "humanism" or "anthropologism"—that is, for construing "being-in-the world as "man in the world." Yet even this movement is an amalgam, as is brought out by Fell's phrasing "ekstatic [Heidegger's term] intentionality [Husserl's term]."

21. Since Heidegger had accused Sartre of "humanism" in the "Letter on Humanism," Sartre preferred the antithetical retort against Heidegger of "mysticism" (*Écrits de Sartre*, p. 200). Nevertheless, it is feasible to watch Heidegger refuse to make the movement "toward the concrete," as Sartre himself conceives it in the lecture, as an engagement in political action. Thus the "Letter on Humanism," which is a critique of Sartre's lecture, begins: "We are still far from thinking of the essence of action decisively enough. We view action only as causing an effect. . . . Thinking does not become action only because some effect issues from it. . . . Thinking acts insofar as it thinks." The transition here from the question of action to the question of thinking is subtler than partial quotation brings out. But how could Heidegger not have known that this first paragraph in his first

postwar publication could not but be read without the vulgar presuming some allusion to the confidence which he himself had once displayed in the effectiveness of action? But it is not even determinable whether or not any allusion to his Nazi period is being offered here. This is an example of what I have considered Heidegger's disavowal of personal reference (and of personal responsibility), but it is also more broadly an example of his refusal to move "toward the concrete" or, rather, an example of what would have been his refusal if he had been able philosophically to visualize the prospect of doing so.

22. See p. 121 above. Heidegger cannot help because his analysis is conducted at the ontological level—which Sartre misinterprets as abstract—as compared with the ontic level. Thus Sartre argues that "the existence of an ontological and hence *a priori* 'being-with' renders impossible all ontic connection with a concrete human reality. . . . The 'being-with,' conceived as a structure of my being, isolates me as surely as the arguments for solipsism" (*Being and Nothingness*, pp. 335–36). I would not leave the impression that in *Being and Nothingness* Sartre only adduces the principle "toward the concrete" in proceeding from previous philosophers. The entire movement of his analysis is "toward the concrete." Thus the discussion of the individual's relation to the other in chapter 1 of part 3, from which I have been quoting, becomes more concrete when "The Body" is introduced in the second chapter and Sartre is able in the third chapter to deal with "Concrete Relations with Others."

23. See p. 119 above. Conflation in Sartre (and the resulting *Quelle salade!*) is not restricted to Husserl and Heidegger and is most obvious when he amalgamates as equivalent terminology obtained from widely different sources. Since the issue here is the individual's relation to the other, I cite his treatment of "the objectivity" of the other: "that which is . . . objective [is] what I shall call *signification*, after the fashion of French and English psychologists; *intention*, according to the phenomenologists; *transcendence* with Heidegger; or *form* with the Gestalt school" (*Being and Nothingness*, p. 391). What I would have recognized is that the principle "toward the concrete" in effect presides over this sort of amalgamation of terminology, for Sartre is presuming that the differences between such approaches are abstract and do not matter at the level of his concrete descriptions.

24. Sartre, in *Questions de méthode*, p. 23.

25. Sartre, *L'imaginaire*, p. 236.

26. In discussing Hegel's limited understanding of Schelling (see n. 2 of Chapter 13 above), Heidegger refers to "*die Grenze des Hegelschen Verstehens gegenüber Schelling.*"

27. Boschetti, *Sartre et "Les temps modernes,"* pp. 314–15.

28. Sartre, in *Sartre, un film,* p. 42.

29. See p. 111 above.

Adorno, Theodor. *Musikalische Schriften.* Frankfort: Suhrkamp, 1976.

Aubenque, Pierre. "Encore Heidegger et le Nazisme." *Le débat* 48 (January–February 1988).

Beaufret, Jean. *Douze questions posées à Jean Beaufret à propos de Martin Heidegger.* Edited by Dominique Le Buhan and Eryck de Rubercy. Paris: Editions Aubier Montaigne, 1983.

———. *Entretiens avec Fréderic de Towarnicki.* Paris: Presses Univeritaires, 1984.

———. *Introduction aux philosophies de l'existence.* Paris: Editions Denoël, 1971.

Beauvoir, Simone de. *La cérémonie des adieux, suivi de entretiens avec Jean-Paul Sartre.* Paris: Gallimard, 1981.

———. *La force de l'âge.* Paris: Gallimard, 1960.

———. *Lettres à Sartre.* 2 vols. Paris: Gallimard, 1990.

———. "Merleau-Ponty et le pseudo-sartrisme." In *Privilèges.* Paris: Gallimard, 1955.

Bernasconi, Robert. "Bridging the Abyss: Heidegger and Gadamer." *Research in Phenomenology* 16 (1986).

Boschetti, Anna. *Sartre et "Les temps modernes."* Paris: Les éditions de minuit, 1985.

Boyce-Gibson, W. R. "From Husserl to Heidegger: Excerpts from a 1928 Freiburg Diary." Edited by Herbert Speigelberg. *Journal of the British Society for Phenomenology* 2 (Jan. 1971).

Buchheim, Thomas. Vorwort in *Destruktion und Übersetzung: Zu den Aufgaben von Philosophiegeschichte nach Martin Heidegger.* Weinheim: VCH, Acta Humaniora, 1989.

Cairns, Dorion. *Conversations with Husserl and Fink*. The Hague: Martinus Nijhoff, 1976.

Cohen- Solal, Annie. *Sartre, 1905–1980*. Paris: Gallimard, 1985.

Cumming, Robert D. *Human Nature and History: A Study of the Development of Liberal Political Thought*. 2 vols. Chicago: University of Chicago Press, 1969.

———. *Starting Point: An Introduction to the Dialectic of Existence*. Chicago: University of Chicago Press, 1979.

Derrida, Jacques. *De l'esprit*. Paris: Galilée, 1987.

———. *Dissemination*. Translated by Barbara Johnson. Chicago: University of Chicago Press, 1982.

———. "The Ends of Man." In *Margins of Philosophy*, translated by Alan Bass, 109–36. Chicago: University of Chicago Press, 1982.

. *Eperons: Les styles de Nietzsche*. Translated by Barbara Harlow. Chicago: University of Chicago Press, 1979.

———. *Les fins de l'homme à partir du travail de Jacques Derrida*. Paris: Galilée, 1981.

———. "Heideggers Schweigen." In *Antwort: Martin Heidegger im Gespräch*. Pfullingen: Günther Neske, 1988.

———. "Living On." Translated by In *Deconstruction and Criticism*, edited by Harold Bloom, 75–176. New York: Continuum, 1979.

———. *Margins of Philosophy*. Translated by Alan Bass. Chicago: University of Chicago Press, 1982.

———. *Mémoires pour Paul de Man*. Paris: Galilée, 1988.

———. *Psyché*. Paris: Galilee, 1988.

———. "On Reading Heidegger." Translated by David Krell. *Research in Phenomenology* 17 (1987).

———. "The Time of a Thesis: Punctuations." In *Philosophy in France Today*, edited by Alan Montefiore. Paris: Cambridge University Press, 1983.

———. *La voix et le phénomène*. Paris: Presses universitaires de France, 1967.

———. *Writing and Difference*. Translated by Alan Bass. Chicago: University of Chicago Press, 1978.

De Waelhens, A. *La philosophie de Martin Heidegger*. Louvain: Edition de l'Institut supérieur de philosophie, 1942.

———. "La philosophie de Heidegger et le nazisme." *Les temps modernes* 3 (1947–48).

Diemer, Alwin. *Edmund Husserl*. Meisenheim am Glan: Hain, 1956.

Fédier, François. *Anatomie d'un scandale*. Paris: Laffont, 1988.

Fell, Joseph P. *Heidegger and Sartre: An Essay on Being and Place*. New York: Columbia University Press, 1979.

Ferry, Luc and Alain Renaut. *Heidegger et les modernes*. Paris: Bernard Grasset, 1988.

Feyerabend, Paul K. *Against Method: Outline of an Anarchistic Theory of Knowledge*. London: Verso, 1978.

Fink, Eugen. "Die phänomenologische Philosophie Edmund Husserls in der gegenwärtigen Kritik." Mit einem vorwort von Edmund Hosser] *Kant Studien* 38 (1933):319–383.

Figal, Günter. *Martin Heidegger, Phänomenologie der Freiheit*. Frankfort: Athenaum, 1988.

Freedberg, S. J. *Painting in Italy, 1500–1600*. Pelican History of Art. New York: Penguin Books, 1971.

Gadamer, Hans-Georg. "Anfang und Ende der Philosophie." In *Heideggers These vom Ende der Philosophie*. Bonn: Bouvier, 1989.

Geraets, Theodore F. *Vers une nouvelle philosophie transcendantale. Phaenomenologica*, vol. 39. The Hague: Martinus Nijhoff, 1971.

Gerassi, John. *Jean-Paul Sartre: Hated Conscience of His Time*. Chicago: University of Chicago Press, 1989.

Granel, Gérard. "Remarques sur le rapport de *Sein und Zeit* et de la phénoménologie husserlienne." In *Durchblicke: Martin Heidegger zum 80. Geburtstab*. Frankfort: Vittorio Kostermann, 1970.

Gürwitch, George. *Tendances actuelles de la philosophie allemande*. Paris: Vrin, 1930.

Haar, Michel. "La biographie reléguée." In *Martin Heidegger*. Edited by M. Haar. Paris: L'éditions de l'Herne, 1983.

———. *Heidegger et l'essence de l'homme*. Grenoble: Millon, 1990.

Habermas, Jürgen. *Philosophisch-Politische Profile*. Frankfort: Suhrkamp, 1971.

———. "Work and Weltanschauung: The Heidegger Controversy from a German Perspective." Translated by John McCumber. *Critical Inquiry* 15 (Winter 1989):431–56.

Heidegger, Martin. *The Basic Problems of Phenomenology*. Translated by Albert Hofstadter. Bloomington: Indiana University Press, 1982.

———. *Basic Writings*. Edited by David Farrell Krell. New York: Harper and Row, 1977.

———. *Being and Time*. Translated by John Macquarrie and Edward Robinson. New York: Harper and Row, 1962.

———. *Beiträge zur Philosophie*. Gesamtausgabe 65. Frankfort: Vittorio Klostermann, 1989.

———. "Das Spiegel-Interview." In *Antwort: Martin Heidegger im Gespräch*. Pfullingen: Günther Neske, 1988.

———. *The End of Philosophy*. Translated by Joan Stambaugh. New York: Harper and Row, 1973.

———. *Frühe Schriften*. Gesamtausgabe 1. Frankfort: Vittorio Klostermann, 1978.

————. *Hegel's Concept of Experience*. Translated by Kenley Dove. New York: Harper and Row, 1970.

————. *Hölderlins Hymne "Der Ister."* Gesamtausgabe 34. Frankfurt: Vittorio Klostermann, 1988.

————. "Interview." *Express*, 20–26 October 1969.

————. *An Introduction to Metaphysics*. Translated by Ralph Manheim. New Haven, Conn.: Yale University Press, 1959.

————. *Martin Heidegger/Erhart Kästner Briefwechsel*. Frankfort: Insel, 1986.

————. *Nietzsche*. 2 vols. Pfullingen: Günther Neske, 1961.

————. "Nur Noch ein Gott kann uns retten." Translated by Peter D. Hertz. New York: Harper and Row, 1971.

————. *On the Way to Language*. Translated by Peter D. Hertz. New York: Harper and Row, 1972.

————. *On Time and Being*. Translated by Joan Stambaugh. New York: Harper and Row, 1972.

————. *Ontologie*. Gesamtausgabe 63. Frankfort: Vittorio Klostermann, 1988.

————. *Phänomenologie—lebendig oder tot?* Karlsruhe: Badenia Verlag, 1970.

————. *Poetry, Language, Thought*. Translated by Albert Hofstadter. New York: Harper and Row, 1971.

————. Postscript to "What Is Metaphysics?" in *Existence and Being*. Edited by Werner Brock. Translated by R. Hull and Alan Crick. Chicago: Henry Regnery, 1968.

————. *Prolegomena zur Geschichte des Zeitbegriffs*. Gesamtausgabe 20. Frankfort, 1979.

————. *Qu'est-ce que la metaphysique*. Translated by Henry Corbin. Paris: Gallimard, 1938.

————. *Questions IV*. Paris: Gallimard, 1976.

————. *Schelling's Treatise on the Essence of Human Freedom*. Translated by Joan Stambaugh. Athens, Ohio: Ohio University Press, 1985.

————. *Vom Wesen der Wahrheit: Zu Platons Höhlengleichnis und Theätet*. Gesamtausgabe 34. Frankfort: Vittorio Klostermann, 1988.

————. *What is a Thing?* Translated by W. B. Barton, Jr., and Vera Deutsch. Chicago: Henry Regnery, 1967.

————. *What is Called Thinking?* Translated by Fred D. Wieck and J. Glenn Gray. New York: Harper and Row, 1968.

Héring, Jean. "La phénoménologie d'Edmund Husserl il y a trente ans." *Revue internationale de philosophie* 2 (January 1939).

Howells, Christina. *Sartre: The Necessity of Freedom*. Cambridge: Cambridge University Press, 1988.

Husserl, Edmund. *Briefe an Roman Ingarden*. Edited by Roman Ingarden. The Hague: Martinus Nijhoff, 1968.

———. *Cartesian Meditations: An Introduction to Phenomenology.* Translated by Dorion Cairns. The Hague: Martinus Nijhoff, 1977.

———. *The Crisis of European Sciences and Transcendental Phenomenology.* Translated by David Carr. Evanston, Ill.: Northwestern University Press, 1970.

———. *Die Idee der Phänomenologie.* Husserliana 2. Edited by Walter Biemel. The Hague: Martinus Nijhoff, 1973.

———. *Ideas Pertaining to a Pure Phenomenology and to a Phenomenological Philosophy,* volume 1. Translated by F. Kersten. The Hague: Martinus Nijhoff, 1983.

———. *Ideen 3.* Husserliana 5. Edited by Marly Biemal. The Hague: Martinus Nijhoff, 1952.

———. Letter to Robert Minder. In *Martin Heidegger und das 'Dritte Reich.'* Edited by Martin Bernd. Darmstadt: Wissenschaftliche Buchgesellschaft, 1989.

———. *Logical Investigations.* Translated by J. N. Findlay. 2 vols. New York: Humanities Press, 1970.

———. *L'origine de la géométrie.* Translation and introduction by Jacques Derrida. Paris: Presses universitaires de France, 1974.

———. *Phänomenologische Psychologie.* Husserliana 9. Edited by Walter Biemel. The Hague: Martinus Nijhoff, 1968.

———. *Philosophy as Rigorous Science.* In *Phenomenology and the Crisis of Philosophy,* translated by Quentin Lauer. New York: Harper and Row, 1965.

———. *Zur Phänomenologie der Intersubjektivität.* Husserliana 15. Edited by Iso Kern. The Hague: Martinus Nijhoff, 1973.

Hyppolite, Jean. "Existence et dialectique dans la philosophie de Merleau-Ponty." *Les temps modernes* 184–85 (October 1961).

James, Henry. *The Art of Criticism.* Chicago: University of Chicago Press, 1986.

James, William. *Essays in Radical Empiricism.* Gloucester, Mass.: Peter Smith, 1967.

Janicaud, Dominique. *L'ombre de cette pensée: Heidegger et la question politique.* Grenoble: Millon, 1990.

Kierkegaard, Søren. *Concluding Unscientific Postscript.* Translated by David F. Swenson and Walter Lowrie. Princeton, N.J.: Princeton University Press, 1941.

Lacoue-Labarthe, Philippe. *La fiction du politique.* Paris: Christian Bourgois, 1987.

Lejeune, Philippe. *Le pacte autobiographique.* Paris: Seuil, 1975.

Levinas, Emmanuel. "La ruine de la représentation." *Phaenomenologica* 4. The Hague: Martinus Nijhoff, 1959.

———. *L'Arc.* 54 (1973).

———. *The Theory of Intuition in Husserl's Phenomenology.* Translated by André Orianne. Evanston, Ill.: Northwestern University Press, 1973.

———. "Tout autrement." In *Jacques Derrida,* edited by L'Arc. Paris: Duponchelle, 1990.

Light, Stephen. *Shūzō Kuki and Jean-Paul Sartre: Influence and Counter-Influence in the Early History of Existential Phenomenology.* Journal of the History of Philosophy Monographs. Carbondale, Ill.: Southern Illinois University Press, 1987.

Merker, Barbara. *Selbsttäuschung und Selbsterkenntnis: Zu Heideggers Transformation der Phänomenologie Husserls.* Frankfort: Suhrkamp, 1988.

Merleau-Ponty, Maurice. *Humanism and Terror.* Translated by John O'Neill. Boston: Beacon Press, 1969.

———. *The Phenomenology of Perception.* Translated by Colin Smith. New York: Humanities Press, 1962.

———. *Le primat de la perception.* Grenoble: Cynara, 1989.

———. *Sense and Non-Sense.* Translated by Herbert L. Dreyfus and Patricia Allen Dreyfus. Evanston, Ill.: Northwestern University Press, 1973.

———. *Signes.* Paris: Gallimard, 1960.

———. *Themes from the Lectures at the* Collège de France, *1952–1960.* Translated by John O'Neil. Evanston, Ill.: Northwestern University Press, 1970.

———. *Le visible et l'invisible.* Paris: Gallimard, 1964.

Misch, Georg. "Lebensphilosophie und Phänomenologie." *Philosophischer Anzeiger* 3 (1928–29).

Montaigne, Michel de. *Essays.* Translated by Charles Cotton. London: Reeve and Turner, 1902.

Ott, Hugo. *Martin Heidegger: Unterwegs zu Seiner Biographie.* Frankfort: Campus, 1988.

Pöggeler, Otto. "Heidegger Heute." In *Heidegger,* edited by Otto Pöggeler. Cologne: Kiepenheur & Witsch, 1970.

Petzet, Heinrich Wiegand. *Auf einen Stern zugehen. Begegnungen und Gespräche mit Martin Heidegger.* Frankfort: Societäts-Verlag, 1983.

Reff, Theodore. *Degas: The Artist's Mind.* New York: Metropolitan Museum of Art, 1976.

Richardson, William J. *Heidegger: Through Phenomenology to Thought.* Phaenomenologica, vol. 13. The Hague: Martinus Nijhoff, 1963.

Ricoeur, Paul. "Par-delà Husserl et Heidegger." *Les cahiers de philosophie* 7 (1989).

Rorty, Richard. "The Historiography of Philosophy: Four Genres." In *Philosophy in History,* edited by Richard Rorty, J. B. Schneewind, and Quentin Skinner. Cambridge: Cambridge University Press, 1984.

———. *Philosophy and the Mirror of Nature.* Princeton, N.J.: Princeton University Press, 1979.

Sartre, Jean-Paul. *L'âge de raison.* Paris: Gallimard, 1945.

———. *Being and Nothingness.* Translated by Hazel Barnes. New York: Philosophical Library, 1956.

———. *Cahiers pour une morale.* Paris: Gallimard, 1983.

———. *Les carnets de la drôle de guerre.* Paris: Gallimard, 1983.

———. "Conscience de soi et connaissance de soi." *Bulletin de la société française de philosophie* 42 (April–June 1948).

———. *Critique de la raison dialectique, précédé de Questions de méthode.* Paris: Gallimard, 1960.

———. *Les écrits de Sartre.* Edited by Michel Contat and Michel Rybalka. Paris: Gallimard, 1970.

———. *Esquisse d'une théorie des émotions.* Paris: Hermann, 1939.

———. *L'existentialisme est un humanisme.* Paris: Nagel, 1946.

———. "Une idée fondamentale de la phénoménologie de Husserl: Intentionalité." In *Situations*, vol. 1: Paris: Gallimard, 1947.

———. *L'idiot de la famille.* 3 vols. Paris: Gallimard, 1971–72.

———. *L'imaginaire.* Paris: Gallimard, 1940.

———. *L'imagination.* Paris: Alcan, 1936.

———. "An Interview with Sartre." In *The Philosophy of Jean-Paul Sartre,* edited by Paul Arthur Schilpp. La Salle, Ill.: Open Court Press, 1981.

———. *Les mots.* Paris: Gallimard, 1963.

———. *Lettres au Castor et à quelques autres.* 2 vols. Paris: Gallimard, 1983.

———. *La nausée.* Paris: Gallimard, 1938.

———. *Oeuvres romanesques.* Paris: Pleiade, 1981.

———. "Penser l'art." In *Sartre et les arts. Obliques* 24–25 (1981).

———. *The Philosophy of Jean-Paul Sartre.* Edited and translated by Robert Denoon Cumming. New York: Vintage, 1972.

———. *Qu'est-ce que la littérature?* Paris: Gallimard, 1948.

———. "Saint Marc et son double." In *Sartre et les arts. Obliques* 24–25 (1981).

———. *Sartre, un film réalisé par Alexandre Astruc et Michel Contat.* Paris: Gallimard, 1977.

———. *Situations.* 10 vols. Paris: Gallimard, 1947–76.

———. "Socialism in One Country." *New Left Review* 100 (1976–77).

———. *Le sursis.* Paris: Gallimard, 1945.

———. *La transcendance de l'ego.* Paris: Vrin, 1965.

———. *Vérité et existence.* Paris: Gallimard, 1989.

Souche-Dagues, D. "La lecture husserlienne de *Sein und Zeit.*" *Philosophie* 21 (1989).

Spaemann, R. "Philosophiegeschichte nach Martin Heidegger," In *Destruktion und Übersetzung: Zu den Aufgaben von Philosophiesgeschichte nach Martin Heidegger.* Weinheim: VCH Acta Humaniora, 1989.

Spiegelberg, Herbert. *The Phenomenological Movement.* 2 vols. The Hague: Martinus Nijhoff, 1960.

———. *The Phenomenological Movement.* 3d revised and enlarged ed. The Hague: Martinus Nijhoff, 1982.

———. "The Way into Phenomenology for Americans." in *Phenomenology: Continuation and Criticism,* edited by F. Kersten and R. Zaner. The Hague: Martinus Nijhoff, 1973.

Taminiaux, Jacques. "Heidegger and Husserl's *Logical Investigations.*" In *Dialectic and Difference,* translated by Robert Crease and James T. Decker. Atlantic Highlands, N.J.: Humanities Press, 1985.

———. "D'une idée de la phénoménologie à une autre." In *Lectures de l'ontologie fondamentale.* Grenoble: Millon, 1989.

Taylor, Charles. *Review of La philosophie analytique. Philosophie Review* 73 (1964).

van Breda, H. L. "Maurice Merleau-Ponty et les archives-Husserl à Louvain." *Revue de métaphysique et de morale* 4 (1962).

von Hermann, F-W. *Hermeneutische Phänomenologie des Daseins: Eine Erläuterung vom 'Sein und Zeit,' vol. 1.* Frankfurt: Vittorio Klostermann, 1987.

Wahl, Jean. *Vers le concret.* Paris: Vrin, 1932.

Wolfson, Harry Austryn. *The Philosophy of Spinoza.* 2 vols. Cambridge, Mass.: Harvard University Press, 1934.